Economic and Social Commission for Western Asia

Survey of Economic and Social Developments in the Arab Region

2015-2016

UNITED NATIONS
Beirut

Requests to reproduce excerpts or to photocopy should be addressed to the United Nations Economic and Social Commission for Western Asia (ESCWA), United Nations House, Riad El Solh Square, P.O. Box: 11-8575, Beirut, Lebanon.

All other queries on rights and licenses, including subsidiary rights, should also be addressed to ESCWA.

E-mail: publications-escwa@un.org; website: www.escwa.un.org

United Nations publication issued by ESCWA.

The designations employed and the presentation of the material in this publication do not imply the expression of any opinion whatsoever on the part of the Secretariat of the United Nations concerning the legal status of any country, territory, city or area or of its authorities, or concerning the delimitation of its frontiers or boundaries.

Mention of commercial names and products does not imply the endorsement of the United Nations.

References have, wherever possible, been verified.

Symbols of the United Nations documents are composed of capital letters combined with figures. Mention of such a symbol indicates a reference to a United Nations document.

The opinions expressed in this technical material are those of the authors and do not necessarily reflect the views of the Secretariat of the United Nations.

E/ESCWA/EDID/2016/1
ISSN: 0255-5123
ISBN: 978-92-1-128386-0
e-ISBN: 978-92-1-058315-2

16-00181

UNITED NATIONS PUBLICATION
Sales No. E.16.II.L.6

Acknowledgements

This report was prepared under the overall direction and guidance of Moctar Mohamed El Hacene, Director of the Economic Development and Integration Division (EDID) at the Economic and Social Commission for Western Asia (ESCWA). Mohamed Hedi Bchir, Chief of the Modeling and Forecasting Section at EDID, led the report team, which included Nathalie Khaled, Maroun Laoun, John Sloan and Yasuhisa Yamamoto.

The team would like to acknowledge the contributions of the following colleagues: Tarik Alami, Director of the Emerging and Conflict-related Issues Division (ECRI), Rabi Bashour, Valentina Calderon Mejia, Fernando Cantu-Bazaldua, Youssef Chaitani and Sofia Palli (ECRI); Mehrinaz El Awady, Director of the ESCWA Center for Women; Wafa Aboul Hosn, Chief of the Economic Statistics Section at the Statistics Division (SD), Hussam Al Zoubi, Roy Doumit, Wassim Hammoud and Majed Skaini (SD); Frederico Neto, Director of the Social Development Division (SDD), Rania Al Jazairi, Rouba Arja, Jozef Bartovic and Viridiana Garcia (SDD). Bassel Kaghadou, Coordinator of the National Agenda for the Future of Syria (NAFS) project, and Ahmad Shikh Ebid (NAFS), also contributed to the report.

Mohamad Bizri and Zeinab Hassan (EDID) provided research assistance. Arpy Atamian (EDID) provided administrative support.

The following members of an expert group reviewed the report and made valuable comments and suggestions: Hamoud Ali Al-Najar, Khaled Bohsali, Rima Younes El Khatib, Hana S. El-Gallal, Wissam Harake, Musa Shteiwi and Mohamed Habib Zitouna.

A team from the Conferences Services Section at ESCWA edited and designed the report.

Executive Summary

The economic and political uncertainty that has characterized the Arab region in the wake of the 2011 transitions and upheaval continues to restrain the region's prospects for growth, job creation and stability. Economic expansion remains stalled, with persistently low global oil prices adding a further burden to the regional economy and constraining the growth and fiscal balances of those countries that had been top performers due to energy exports. While some progress on social indicators such as gender representativeness can be noted, countries in and affected by political transition and conflict have regressed on a plethora of socioeconomic indicators. These trends can be noted for the past five years and, with this in mind, the 2015-2016 Survey will utilize recent data in order to take stock of the impact of instability and conflict, and address the foregone growth and output and destructive effects of this period. It also draws on recent research by the Economic and Social Commission for Western Asia (ESCWA) on migration, social developments, the impact of conflict, women's empowerment and specific country-level analysis.

In chapter 1, we analyse global and regional economic developments in the reporting period from January 2015 to March 2016. The global economic landscape in 2015 has affected the Arab region's prospects. Developed countries have experienced extremely low, and in some cases negative, interest rates, declining inflation and a savings glut, and are under deflationary pressures. Developing countries, on the other hand, are increasingly short of funds, and most are under balance-of-payments and fiscal constraints. International investors are becoming more risk-averse, with uncertainty stemming from a number of sources, including political instability, a still fragile global economic recovery, the monetary policy of the United States of America and Chinese economic prospects. The world economy has thus shown a trend towards polarization between developed and developing countries. Social developments remained grim as more people were displaced internally and externally and employment improved only in a limited number of countries. International commodity prices, including for oil, natural gas and phosphates, declined and are projected to stay much lower than previous levels. The resulting cut in oil revenues has had a major impact on the Arab region. It became a net importer in 2015 and total foreign reserves also declined as they were used to finance external deficits.

In chapter 2, we interpret the performance of the Arab region and the effect of the global environment, specifically of natural resource commodities markets, on the region as a whole and on its subregions and individual countries. Estimates have placed the average growth rate of gross domestic product (GDP) in the Arab region in real terms at 0.9 per cent in 2015, unchanged from 2014. The economies of the countries of the Gulf Cooperation Council (GCC), which had led the region's growth for the past few years, slowed in 2015, reflecting weak domestic demand expansion. The oil price decline since mid-2014 had an adverse influence on Arab economies, combined with other negative factors such as the persistence, and indeed spread, of armed conflict in the region. In addition to the loss of oil export revenues and weaker business confidence, GCC countries faced challenges concerning the direction of their economic diversification strategies.

Reforms, including of subsidies, indicated the seriousness of policy efforts to cope with falling oil prices, which did not benefit energy-importing Arab countries as much as had been expected. Import bills went down, but nominal export revenues also declined in most countries owing to declines in export unit prices, reflecting weak demand abroad. Furthermore, security incidents in the region had a negative impact on tourism and services exports. Balance-of-payments conditions tightened in Arab economies, particularly Egypt, the Sudan, the Syrian Arab Republic, Tunisia and Yemen. This has restricted domestic demand expansion and lowered living standards.

GDP in the region is forecast to grow by 1.5 per cent in 2016. Economic expansion in GCC countries is projected to continue decelerating, as further cuts to public expenditure are expected. The anticipated monetary tightening by the United States and an increase in debt issuance by GCC Governments are likely to discourage investment. Other Arab subregions will also experience weak growth due to geopolitical factors, the prospect of weak demand from China and Europe and tightening balance-of-payments conditions.

Chapter 2 also features a regional gender overview and country gender profiles covering all ESCWA member states. Developments are analysed using different research lenses, including humanitarian development, political representation, labour market representation, and other dimensions such as domestic work. Women in the Arab region still suffer from inequality at all levels. According to the Gender Inequality Index, the Arab region continues to rank fifth out of six comparable regions of the world. The Arab region also ranked last according to the Gender Gap Index, having closed only 60 per cent of the gender gap. On the political indicator, 17.5 per cent of parliamentarians in the region are now women, compared with the 14 per cent average of last year. Algeria, Tunisia

and the Sudan are leading the way in that regard. Enforcing quota systems remains the most effective means of increasing women's participation and representation in decision-making. Female participation in the labour market is still very low, with an average of 23.4 per cent compared with 75 per cent participation rate for males in 2014. Unemployment is high for men and women, but the gender gap is also wide. Unemployment among young women in the region increased from 31.8 per cent in 2002 to 46.1 per cent in 2013 and those with higher education face still higher unemployment than others. The Arab region will need to do more to foster more and quality jobs for women and improve social protection systems and labour laws. Domestic work, mostly involving women migrants, accounts for 5.6 per cent of total employment in the region. Some Arab States have enacted laws to protect domestic workers, but enforcement and monitoring mechanisms are needed.

The thematic third chapter of this year's Survey addresses the cumulative effects of the political changes and conflicts that began in 2011, and the impact that these have had on the region's prospects. The transition of Arab countries, initiated in 2011 by sociopolitical events collectively known as the Arab Spring, has resulted in instability and, in several cases, war. The adverse affects have been felt not only in those countries enduring armed violence to varying degrees, such as Iraq, Libya, the Syrian Arab Republic and Yemen, but also in neighbouring countries. The occupation of Palestine continues to prevent access of Palestinians to economic opportunities, social mobility and self-determination. Against policy efforts for regional Arab integration, the socioeconomic situation of the region was increasingly discussed in terms of humanitarian crises, economic disruption and displaced populations. The Survey provides an overall economic and social assessment for the entire region. Recent literature on the impact of conflict in the region has focused on country- and conflict-specific effects and has provided neither a region-wide assessment of impact on macroeconomic variables, nor a deep analysis of the impact on neighbouring countries. The Survey finds that – as compared with projections made before 2011 – conflicts in the region have led to a net loss of $613.8 billion in economic activity, and an aggregate fiscal deficit of $243.1 billion. Conflicts have worsened other economic and social indicators, such as debt, unemployment, corruption and poverty. The international refugee crisis has placed a strain on communities that have lost populations, on countries coping with refugee influxes, and above all on the refugee populations themselves, which suffer from poor health and malnutrition, and have limited access to employment and education. Crisis affects everyone, but women have faced the most adverse effects. Greater policy interventions are needed to address these issues and to prevent the rise of a "lost generation" of Arab youth affected by conflict.

Analysis of the impact of conflict has been undertaken on four Arab countries. We look first at the Syrian Arab Republic, a country experiencing the dire human and economic toll of civil war, but for which rebuilding plans are ready to be implemented when the conflict ends. We then take stock of the direct and indirect effects of the Syrian crisis on Lebanon, particularly regarding the movement of people and impact on the domestic economy, trade portfolio and the Government's fiscal balances. We examine Tunisia as it faces the consequences of its transition and the effects of civil war in neighbouring Libya. Finally, we review the ongoing adverse effects of the occupation of Palestine.

The Survey concludes with a number of policy recommendations for Arab Governments to draw on in responding to these many issues facing the region. It is the hope of ESCWA that policymakers will recognize the great need to address a host of economic, social and security concerns. Only through concerted action by the Arab and international communities might the regional economy acquire the means to diversify and grow, create adequate and secure jobs, especially for women and the young, and tackle other adverse effects of conflict through short-term humanitarian assistance and long-term economic revitalization and social inclusion.

Contents

List of Figures

List of Boxes

Abbreviations and Explanatory Notes

ACU	Arab Customs Union
AfDB	African Development Bank
BIS	Bank for International Settlements
Btu	British thermal unit
CAPMAS	Central Agency for Public Mobilization and Statistics (Egypt)
Cedigaz	International Association for Natural Gas
CFTC	Commodity Futures Trading Commission (United States)
CGE	computable general equilibrium
CPI	consumer price index
DAP	diammonium phosphate
ECB	European Central Bank
EIA	Energy Information Administration (United States)
EIBOR	Emirates Interbank Offered Rate
ECA	Economic Commission for Africa
EIU	Economist Intelligence Unit
ESCAP	Economic and Social Commission for Asia and the Pacific
ESCWA	Economic and Social Commission for Western Asia
EU	European Union
FNC	Federal National Council (of the United Arab Emirates)
FYP	five-year plan
GAFTA	Greater Arab Free Trade Area
GBV	gender-based violence
GCC	Gulf Cooperation Council
GDP	gross domestic product
GGI	Gender Gap Index
GII	Gender Inequality Index
HDI	Human Development Index
HDR	Human Development Report
IDPs	internally displaced persons
IEA	International Energy Agency
IFA	International Fertilizer Industry Association
IFC	International Finance Corporation
IFS	international financial statistics
ILO	International Labour Organization
IMF	International Monetary Fund
INS	National Statistics Institute (Tunisia)
IPU	Inter-Parliamentary Union
JODI	Joint Organizations Data Initiative
JODIBOR	Jordan Interbank Offered Rate

KIBOR	Kuwait Interbank Offered Rate
KLIM	Key Indicators of the Labour Market (ILO)
LDC	least developed country
LIBOR	London Interbank Offered Rate
MDGs	Millennium Development Goals
MENA	Middle East and North Africa
MERCOSUR	Mercado Común del Sur (Southern Common Market)
NAFS	National Agenda for the Future of Syria
NCA	National Constituent Assembly
ODA	official development assistance
OECD	Organisation for Economic Co-operation and Development
OPEC	Organization of Petroleum Exporting Countries
SCPR	Syrian Centre for Policy Research
SDGs	Sustainable Development Goals
SVAR	structural vector autoregression
UAE	United Arab Emirates
UNDP	United Nations Development Programme
UNESCO	United Nations Educational, Scientific and Cultural Organization
UNHCR	United Nations Office of the High Commissioner for Refugees
UNRWA	United Nations Relief and Works Agency for Palestine Refugees in the Near East
UNSD	United Nations Statistics Division
UN Women	United Nations Entity for Gender Equality and the Empowerment of Women
UNWTO	World Tourism Organization
WDI	World Development Indicators
WEF	World Economic Forum
WHO	World Health Organization
WTI	West Texas Intermediate

References to dollars ($) are to United States dollars, unless otherwise stated. Other currencies are abbreviated as defined in ISO4217 currency code:

CNY	Chinese Yuan Renminbi
EGP	Egyptian Pound
JPY	Japanese Yen
SDG	Sudanese Pound
SYP	Syrian Pound
TND	Tunisian Dinar
YER	Yemeni Rial

The following subregional groupings are used in this report, taking into account a combination of per capita income levels, geographical proximity and similarities in economic and social characteristics and conditions: Gulf Cooperation Council (GCC) countries: Bahrain, Kuwait, Oman, Qatar, Saudi Arabia, the United Arab Emirates; Arab Mashreq countries: Egypt, Iraq, Jordan, Lebanon, the State of Palestine, the Syrian Arab Republic; Arab Maghreb countries: Algeria, Libya, Morocco, Tunisia; Arab Least Developed Countries (LDCs): the Comoros, Djibouti, Mauritania, Somalia, the Sudan, Yemen.

International support measures are increasingly vital to efforts to alleviate macroeconomic constraints and create a solid foundation for sustainable economic and social development.

1. Global Context and its Implications for the Arab Region

A. Global context

The world economy reflects growing complexities and uncertainties. The complexities stem from the consequences of extreme monetary easing in Europe and Japan, the diverging monetary policy stances of the United States of America and other developed economies and the growing savings gluts in the developed economies, compared with funds shortages in developing economies. The complexities amplify the uncertainties, as there are increasing signs of a global economic slowdown. In 2015, deflationary pressures became a major policy concern in many developed countries and certain developing countries, including China, as they faced economic stagnation due to weak domestic demand expansion. To cope with the deflationary pressures and the prospect of weak demand, central banks in major developed countries, with the exception of the United States, pushed their monetary easing policies to the extreme, with very low interest rates and other measures in Europe and Japan aimed at encouraging economic expansion. However, investment activities did not expand in response to historically low financing costs, pointing to a significant savings glut in Europe and Japan (box 1.1) Deposit interest rates reached levels close to zero in some countries in Europe and in Japan, where negative interest rates became a reality for short-term government bonds. Although the world economy is forecast to maintain moderate growth in 2016 on average, deflationary pressures remain.

Table 1.1 Growth and inflation 2014-2017: world and regional averages (percentage)

	Real GDP growth rate				Consumer price inflation rate			
	2014	2015[a]	2016[a]	2017[a]	2014	2015[b]	2016[b]	2017[b]
Arab region	1.5	1.5	2.4	3.8	7.3	5.1	4.9	4.4
World	2.6	2.4	2.4	2.8				
Developed economies	1.7	1.9	1.8	1.9	1.2	0.3	1.2	1.9
United States of America	2.4	2.4	2.2	2.5	1.3	0.2	1.6	2.3
European Union	1.4	1.9	1.9	2.0	0.6	0.1	1.0	1.7
Japan	-0.1	0.5	0.5	0.5	2.7	0.7	0.5	1.1
Economies in transition	0.9	-2.8	-1.2	1.1	7.8	16.1	10.5	7.1
Developing economies	4.4	3.8	3.8	4.4	6.7	7.7	8.3	6.0
Africa	3.8	3.0	2.8	3.4	7.0	7.5	6.7	6.3
East and South Asia	6.1	5.7	5.7	5.8	3.5	2.5	3.1	3.3
Latin America and the Caribbean	1.0	-0.6	-0.6	1.5	11.7	20.1	21.4	12.2

Sources: Figures for Arab region are ESCWA staff calculations (see table 1.1 in the appendix for details). Other figures are from United Nations Department of Economic and Social Affairs (DESA), *World Economic Situation and Prospects 2016 Update as of mid-2016* (May 2016) and *World Economic Situation and Prospects 2016* (January 2016). The country grouping is based on World Economic Situation and Prospects 2016, pp.159-160 (tables A, B, and C).
[a] DESA Estimations/projection in part of Project LINK as of May 2016 (with the exception of the Arab region, which is an ESCWA staff estimation).
[b] DESA Estimations/projection in part of Project LINK as December 2015 (with the exception of the Arab region, which is an ESCWA staff estimation).

Box 1.1 Savings glut hypotheses

Nominal interest rates in developed economies, and some developing economies, have recorded historical lows.

In 2015, the European Central Bank (ECB) and the central banks of Japan, Switzerland, Sweden and Denmark adopted negative policy interest rates for deposits. Had the demand for investment spending been high relative to the savings available for lending, market interest rates would have remained high. However, monetary easing by central banks in developed economies brought market rates down in parallel. Consequently, lending rates also dropped in developed economies. Lower interest rates, however, have not boosted investment. Rather, rates stayed low. This phenomenon can be understood as an excess supply of available funds (savings) against a weak demand for them (investment), also known as savings glut.

The global savings glut was a key theme for the then Governor of Federal Reserve, Ben Bernanke, in 2005.[a] The glut resulted from increased savings on the part of ageing populations in developed countries and enforced domestic savings mobilization of developing countries after a series of financial crises (Mexico, Asia and Russia) in the 1990s. The increased savings were directed to assets of the United States, such as Treasury bonds, to accumulate foreign reserves, rather than to domestic physical investment in each country. The resulting increase in capital inflows to the United States caused a wider current account deficit, while many other countries maintained current account surpluses. The economy of the United States went deeper into debt but, awash with funds, dollar interest rates went down. Bernanke also saw the global savings glut and resulting property booms as among the causes of the 2008 global financial crisis.

Bernanke's argument, however, does not explain the current savings glut in countries where current accounts are in surplus. Moreover, the definition of savings is net rather than gross savings. Under net savings, no distinction is made between savings for asset accumulation and savings for debt repayment.

Another line of research focuses on gross savings of the corporate sector (corporate savings glut hypothesis). It shows that the corporate sector of major developed countries has increased savings and reduced investment expenditures to strengthen the balance sheet since mid-2000.[b] Similarly, if a household needs to strengthen its balance sheets, for example negative mortgage equity, it must save to pay off the mortgage. In short, an extensive debt overhang may result in a savings glut.

In both cases, the situation can be resolved by increasing domestic demand so that a sufficient profit incentive can work for physical investment. However, monetary policy has been ineffective and many countries are reluctant to take active fiscal measures given their priority of fiscal consolidation. In the meantime, the more developing economies are short of funds for sustainable development, mainly due to tightening balance-of-payments conditions. Markets have failed to act as an intermediary to direct funds from developed to developing economies, and so an alternative framework is necessary to solve this serious global imbalance.

[a] Bernanke, 2005.
[b] Gruber and Kamin, 2015.

The United States stood out as the only major developed country to emerge from the deflationary danger zone, with robust economic expansion and consistent growth in private consumption and physical investment.[1] Continuing growth in the value of residential and commercial real estate since 2010 underlined the strength of the private sector, and the Federal Government's fiscal consolidation rendered the contribution of public expenditure to the expansion of domestic demand negligible. Given the resilience of economic recovery over the past few years, the Federal Reserve normalized its monetary policy stance by raising its key interest rate by 0.25 percentage points in December 2015 (figure 1.1A). Market interest rates, benchmarked by yields on government bonds, responded weakly to the hike in the policy rate. The benchmark 2-year bond yield had risen consistently up to December 2015, but it declined upon the policy rate rise. The benchmark 10-year bond yield kept declining into the first quarter of 2016. Those responses indicated a trend in deposit rates, whereby the 3-month LIBOR leapt by more than 0.25 percentage points and the TED spread (between the 3-month LIBOR and 3-month United States Treasury Bill yield rate), showed only a moderate increase in December 2015 (figure 1.1B). The interest rate dynamics of the

dollar indicate that the United States was also influenced by a savings glut, although to a lesser extent than other developed economies.

The economies of the European Union (EU) achieved moderate growth in 2015 (table 1.1). Although investment remained weak, private consumption sustained the expansion of domestic demand, owing to improved household purchasing power resulting from low oil prices.[2] The ECB continued to encourage investment by lowering its key lending rate (main refinancing operation rate) from 0.05 per cent to zero in March 2016 (figure 1.1C), while drastically cutting the policy deposit rate (deposit facility rate) to -0.4 per cent in March 2016. The market interest rates, benchmarked by the yields of German government bonds, declined to extremely low levels. The 2-year German government bond yield went further into negative territory,

Figure 1.1 Interest rates: United States (US) dollar and euro, 2011-2016

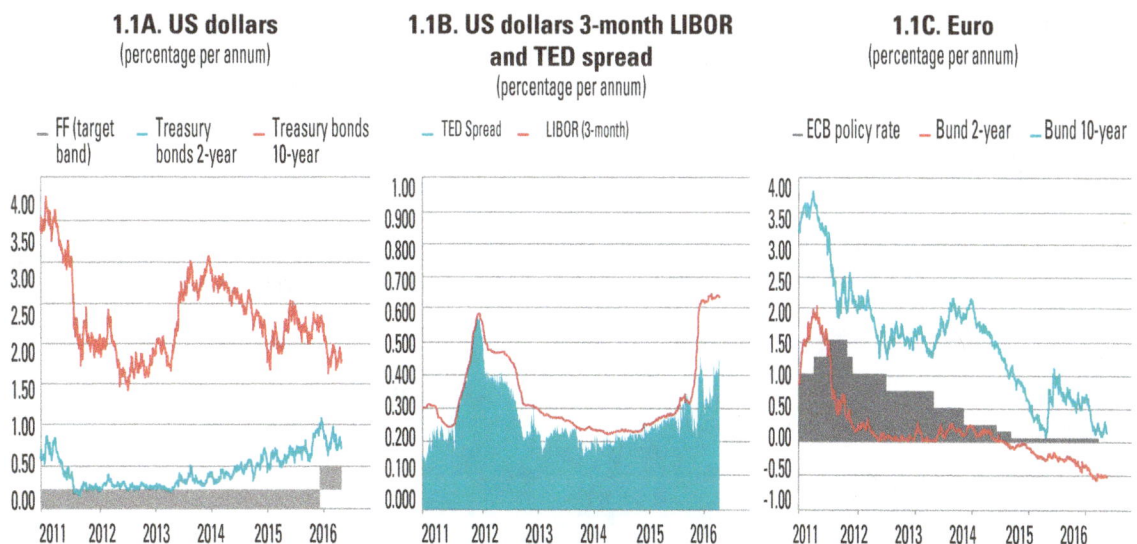

1.1A. US dollars
(percentage per annum)

— FF (target band) — Treasury bonds 2-year — Treasury bonds 10-year

Source: Board of Governors of the Federal Reserve System. Available from www. federalreservegov/releases/h15/data.htm.

1.1B. US dollars 3-month LIBOR and TED spread
(percentage per annum)

— TED Spread — LIBOR (3-month)

Sources: ICE Benchmark Administration Limited (IBA), 3-Month London Interbank Offered Rate (LIBOR), based on U.S. Dollar© [USD3MTD156N], retrieved from FRED, Federal Reserve Bank of St. Louis; https://fred.stlouisfed.org/series/USD3MTD156N and Federal Reserve Bank of St. Louis, TED Spread [TEDRATE], retrieved from FRED, Federal Reserve Bank of St. Louis; https://fred.stlouisfed.org/series/TEDRATE.

1.1C. Euro
(percentage per annum)

— ECB policy rate — Bund 2-year — Bund 10-year

Sources: Deutsche Bundesbank, https://www.bundesbank.de/Redaktion/EN/Downloads/Statistics/Money_Capital_Markets/Interest_Rates_Yields/stat_geldmarkts.pdf?__blob=publicationFile and https://www.bundesbank.de/Redaktion/EN/Downloads/Statistics/Money_Capital_Markets/Interest_Rates_Yields/stat_zinsstruktur_bwp.pdf?__blob=publicationFile.

while the 10-year bond yield dropped close to zero in the first quarter of 2016. The same interest rates structure was observed in some other European countries, namely Denmark, Sweden and Switzerland. However, the need of commercial banks in several EU economies to further improve balance sheets kept financing costs higher than those policy rates indicated.

The new United States monetary stance is expected to result in widening differences in interest rates between the dollar and other major currencies — rates in the United States are expected to rise while rates in other developed countries remain low. At first, this was expected to cause a further appreciation of the dollar against other major currencies, including the euro and the Japanese yen. Indeed, the euro and the yen remained weak against the dollar throughout 2015 (figures 1-2A and 1-2B). However, no further appreciation of the dollar was observed in the first half of 2016, which was attributed to the low dollar deposit rates and associated corrections of net speculative positions. The latter, calculated on data from the Commodity

Futures Trading Commission (CFTC), showed that short positions were unwound rapidly in the euro and yen after the US policy rate hike in December 2015.

Relatively strong growth continued in East and South Asia with the exception of Japan (table 1.1). Lower oil prices were a boon, as most countries in the region are net energy importers. Robust growth in the United States, the region's primary export destination, also sustained regional economic growth. Recent fiscal consolidation measures in Japan slowed domestic demand expansion as the country came under severe deflationary pressure. Although the Chinese economy showed more signs of slowing down, it kept up a relatively high growth margin due to active public investment and resilient domestic demand growth. However, speculation on the health of the financial sector's balance sheets was fuelled by a weakening yuan against the dollar (figure 1.2C) and declining foreign reserves. The Indian economy recorded strong growth as external constraints were largely lifted. As the terms of trade improved, the country

Figure 1.2 Foreign exchange rates of major world currencies, 2011-2016

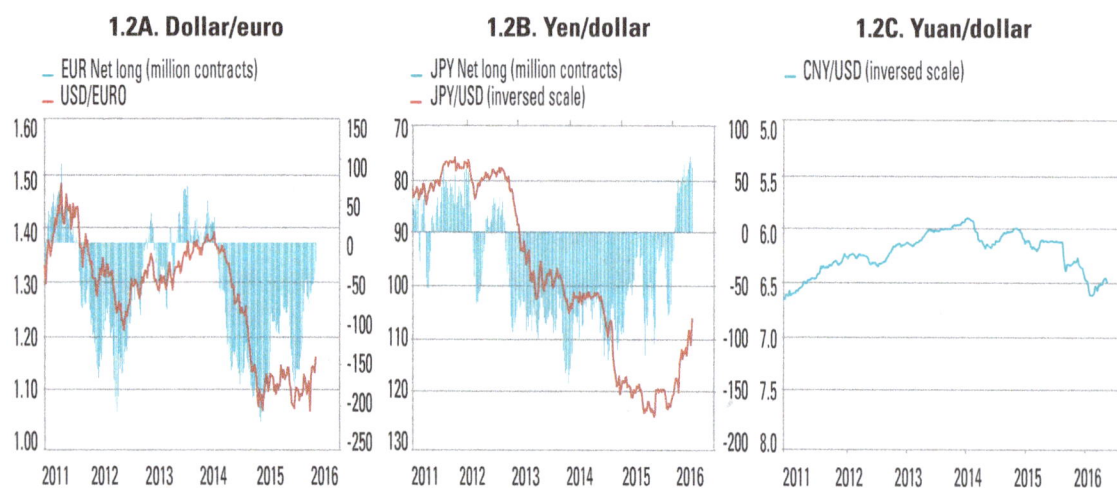

Sources: Exchange rates are from the Board of Governors of the Federal Reserve System. Available from www.federalreserve.gov/releases/h10/hist/. Net long positions are ESCWA staff calculations based on CFTC "Commitments of Traders" Traders in Financial Futures; Futures Only Reports. Available from www.cftc.gov/MarketReports/CommitmentsofTraders/HistoricalCompressed/index.htm.

experienced lower inflation rates and current account deficits, and an accumulation of foreign reserves at a stable exchange rate. India can afford to adopt growth-oriented fiscal and monetary policies and is expected to lead the region's growth.

India is a rare exception. Developing economies, particularly in Latin America and the Caribbean and Africa, face growing challenges as prospects have weakened rapidly (table 1.1). A substantial decline in commodity prices hit commodity-dependent economies, including major oil exporters, with declining fiscal revenues and tightening balance-of-payments constraints. In most cases, low commodity prices failed to improve balance-of-payment constraints for commodity importers in a significant way, as the terms of trade for those countries did not improve as expected. As the United States interest rate prospects discouraged the flow of funds to developing economies, more developing economies became prone to balance-of-payments crises. By the first quarter of 2016, several developing economies, mostly those in which exports were dominated by commodities, had requested balance-of-payments support from international financial institutions. This is another paradoxical consequence of the current world economic situation, in which savings gluts in developed economies are in sharp contrast to a growing lack of funds in developing economies.

Employment creation remained stagnant during 2015 with the exception of a few developed economies, including Germany, Japan, the United Kingdom and the United States. The margin of improvement in those developed economies did not offset the deteriorating employment situation in developing economies,[3] and unemployment increased globally in 2015. Weak employment prospects caused sociopolitical tensions in many parts of the world amid unprecedented movements of refugees and migrants across the Mediterranean to Europe. The refugee and migrant crisis gave rise to political debates, underlining often radically opposing views on the socioeconomic role of refugees and migrants in host countries. The divergence between the employment situations in developed and developing economies is likely to widen in 2016. Sociopolitical tensions related to employment, asylum and migration are projected to continue in developed and developing economies.

Unemployment is the core global labour policy challenge, but the problems of job quality, informal employment and working poverty compelled policymakers to aim to provide decent work. Sustainable Development Goal (SDG) 8, on "sustained, inclusive and sustainable economic growth, full and productive employment and decent work for all", is a core driver for eradicating poverty by 2030 (box 1.2). Mainstreaming labour policy on "decent work" is expected to bring coordinated international policy efforts to alleviate unemployment and poverty.

The growth in displaced populations, both internally and externally, continued in 2015. According to a report by the Office of the United Nations High Commissioner for Refugees (UNHCR),[4] 65.3 million individuals were displaced by the end of 2015 (59.5 million at the end of 2014). With East and Central Africa, the Arab region remained a major source of refugees. The Syrian Arab Republic was the source country with the most refugees: more than 5 million by the end of 2015. In the Arab region, Iraq, Somalia and the Sudan were the other main source countries of refugees. Egypt, Iraq, Jordan and Lebanon are among the main host countries for Syrian refugees, and the Sudan hosted refugees mainly from African countries. The complexity of population displacement is exemplified in the cases of Iraq and the Sudan, which are both source and host countries on a significant scale. UNHCR estimated that the Syrian Arab Republic held the second largest internally displaced persons (IDP) population in the world, following Colombia, with 6.6 million at the end of 2015. Other Arab countries also have sizable IDP populations: Iraq (4.4 million); Yemen (2.5 million); and the Sudan (2.1 million).

Box 1.2 Sustainable Development Goals

In September 2015, the Member States of the United Nations adopted the Sustainable Development Goals (SDGs) and the 2030 Agenda for Sustainable Development (A/RES/70/1). The 17 goals and many targets thereunder will serve as a policy guide to eradicate all forms of poverty, alleviate inequalities, combat climate change and achieve sustainable socioeconomic development around the world. The goals are:

Goal 1. End poverty in all its forms everywhere

Goal 2. End hunger, achieve food security and improved nutrition and promote sustainable agriculture

Goal 3. Ensure healthy lives and promote well-being for all at all ages

Goal 4. Ensure inclusive and equitable quality education and promote lifelong learning opportunities for all

Goal 5. Achieve gender equality and empower all women and girls

Goal 6. Ensure availability and sustainable management of water and sanitation for all

Goal 7. Ensure access to affordable, reliable, sustainable and modern energy for all

Goal 8. Promote sustained, inclusive and sustainable economic growth, full and productive employment and decent work for all

Goal 9. Build resilient infrastructure, promote inclusive and sustainable industrialization and foster innovation

Goal 10. Reduce inequality within and among countries

Goal 11. Make cities and human settlements inclusive, safe, resilient and sustainable

Goal 12. Ensure sustainable consumption and production patterns

Goal 13. Take urgent action to combat climate change and its impacts

Goal 14. Conserve and sustainably use the oceans, seas and marine resources for sustainable development

Goal 15. Protect, restore and promote sustainable use of terrestrial ecosystems, sustainably manage forests, combat desertification, and halt and reverse land degradation and halt biodiversity loss

Goal 16. Promote peaceful and inclusive societies for sustainable development, provide access to justice for all and build effective, accountable and inclusive institutions at all levels

Goal 17. Strengthen the means of implementation and revitalize the Global Partnership for Sustainable Development

B. Developments in natural resource commodities

1. Oil

According to the Organization of the Petroleum Exporting Countries (OPEC), total estimated world demand for oil in 2015 was 92.98 million barrels per day on average, an increase of 1.54 million barrels per day compared with 2014.[5] OPEC projects that demand will grow further in 2016, to 94.23 million barrels per day. It also estimates the total supply of crude oil at 95.09 million barrels per day on average in 2015, an increase of 2.65 million barrels per day compared with 2014.[6] The global demand for crude oil has not collapsed, but rather remains on a path of moderate growth. Meanwhile, supply growth has surpassed demand growth over the past few years. It came mostly from non-OPEC countries, in particular in North America, where production recently peaked. In December 2015, the United States lifted a ban on crude oil exports that had been in place for more than 40 years. The market is estimated to have had an oversupply of one million barrels per day in 2014, with the margin widening to 2.1 million barrels per day in 2015.[7]

In past oil price decline phases, OPEC has acted promptly. For example, it cut its production quota by 4.2 million barrels per day in December 2008, when the market experienced a sharp drop in oil prices. OPEC production behaviour was once determined in relation to its target price band, which might give rise to the expectation that it would act to bring about a concerted reduction in production to address the present supply glut. However, coordination of production has proved difficult in the current market (box 1.3). Without a bold, enforceable agreement involving all major oil-producing countries, the fear of losing market share prevents any oil-producing country from instituting voluntary production cuts. Even with a successfully

Figure 1.3 Oil prices

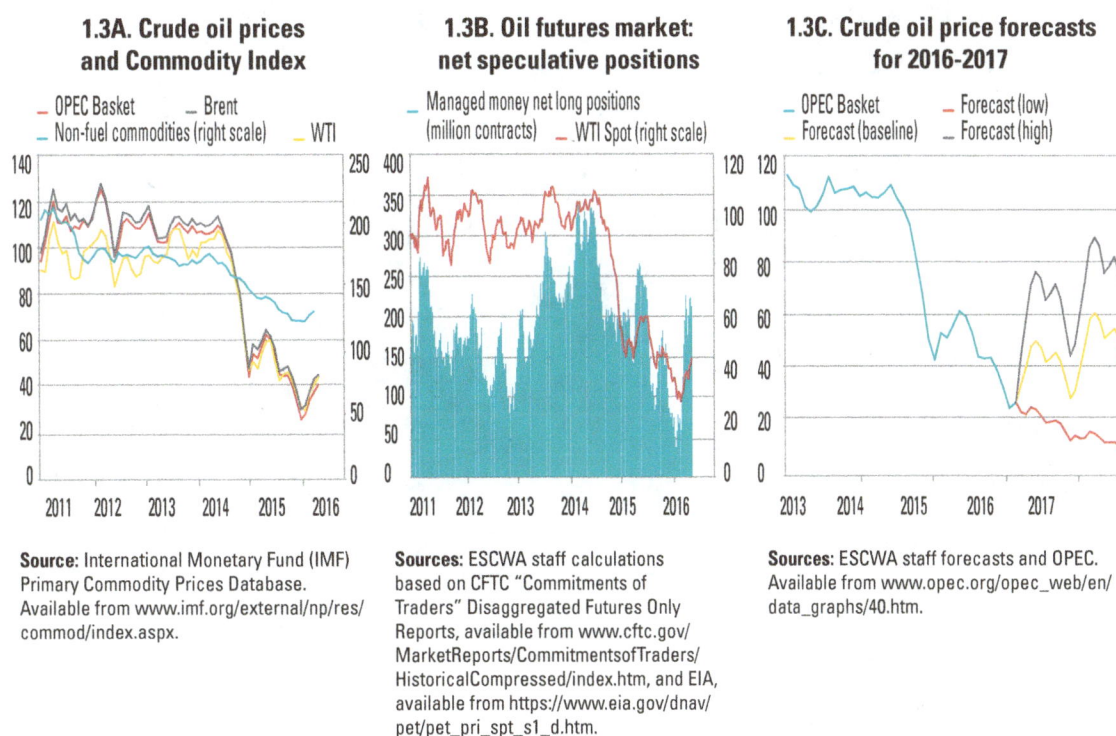

1.3A. Crude oil prices and Commodity Index

— OPEC Basket   — Brent
— Non-fuel commodities (right scale)   — WTI

1.3B. Oil futures market: net speculative positions

— Managed money net long positions (million contracts)   — WTI Spot (right scale)

1.3C. Crude oil price forecasts for 2016-2017

— OPEC Basket   — Forecast (low)
— Forecast (baseline)   — Forecast (high)

Source: International Monetary Fund (IMF) Primary Commodity Prices Database. Available from www.imf.org/external/np/res/commod/index.aspx.

Sources: ESCWA staff calculations based on CFTC "Commitments of Traders" Disaggregated Futures Only Reports, available from www.cftc.gov/MarketReports/CommitmentsofTraders/HistoricalCompressed/index.htm, and EIA, available from https://www.eia.gov/dnav/pet/pet_pri_spt_s1_d.htm.

Sources: ESCWA staff forecasts and OPEC. Available from www.opec.org/opec_web/en/data_graphs/40.htm.

Table 1.2 Crude oil price estimation and forecast (OPEC Reference Basket: US dollars per barrel)

Year	Minimum	Maximum	Annual average	Forecasted annual average		
				Lower	Baseline	Higher
2013	96.35	114.94	105.87			
2014	52.00	110.48	96.29			
2015	30.74	64.96	49.49			
2016				23.7	41.5	59.3
2017				14.8	49.3	72.2

Sources: OPEC for 2012-2014. Figures for 2016 and 2017 are ESCWA staff forecasts as of March 2016.

Table 1.3 Oil production in the Arab region, 2012-2017 (thousands of barrels per day)

Country/subregion	2012	2013	2014	2015[a]	2016[b]	2017[b]
Bahrain	46	48	49	42	52	52
Kuwait	2 977	2 922	2 869	2 621	2 891	2 888
Oman	923	947	949	986	1 007	1 012
Qatar	734	724	709	656	674	677
Saudi Arabia	9 765	9 634	9 714	10 189	9 769	9 808
United Arab Emirates	2 657	3 048	3 036	3 189	3 165	3 157
GCC countries	17 102	17 323	17 327	17 684	17 559	17 594
Egypt	672	669	672	682	672	674
Iraq	2 950	2 977	3 133	3 499	3 742	4 111
Syrian Arab Republic	170	31	0	0	0	0
Mashreq	3 792	3 677	3 784	4 181	4 414	4 785
Algeria	1 113	1 217	1 209	1 072	1 197	1 197
Libya	1 450	993	480	404	420	450
Morocco	0.5	0.5	0.5	0.5	0.5	0.5
Tunisia	67	61	54	49	47	45
Maghreb	2 631	2 271	1 744	1 526	1 664	1 692
Mauritania	7	7	6	5	5	5
Sudan	82	85	85	87	100	110
Yemen	180	159	111	40	0	0
Arab LDCs	269	251	202	132	105	115
Arab region total	23 793	23 522	23 057	23 523	23 742	24 186

Sources: ESCWA staff calculations based on JODI database (available from https://www.jodidata.org/oil/), with the exception of Mauritania, Morocco, the Syrian Arab Republic, the Sudan and Yemen. For those countries, the source is OAPEC Databank (available from http://www.oapecorg.org/Home/DataBank).
[a] ESCWA staff estimates as of March 2016.
[b] ESCWA staff projections as of March 2016.

Box 1.3 What drives oil price changes?

The speed and magnitude of the oil price fall since mid-2014 gave rise to questions regarding the drivers of oil prices. Oil prices are determined through market transactions, by which an excess supply is the main driver of oil price falls. However, while actual crude oil production and demand make up the fundamental supply-demand relationship, commodity futures markets create additional supply and demand even for speculators who do not trade actual crude oil. In commodity futures markets, a trader can trade a future-date contract of purchasing crude oil (long position) or a future-date contract of selling crude oil (short position). Before the contracted delivery date, however, speculators unwind their positions. By doing so, a long-positioned speculator gains when oil prices are rising, and a short-positioned speculator gains when they are declining. Speculators' behaviour in commodity futures markets amplifies the margin of price fluctuations. For example, an excess of short selling drives oil prices down more than the fundamental oversupply can justify.

Kilian (2009) popularized the use of model-based analyses to investigate the nature of oil price fluctuations. He used the historical decomposition method on a structural vector auto-regression (SVAR) model to show that rising demand drove the significant oil price growth until the mid-2000s. By applying the same methodology, but with a different data set for a different sample period, the characteristic of recent oil price dynamics was investigated. The historical decomposition method was used on a simple three-variable SVAR model with a recursive causal ordering. The variables used are: physical crude oil supply; world industrial production index (as a proxy of fundamental demand for crude oil); and nominal spot price of Brent. The main purpose of this modelling exercise was to decompose unexpected oil price changes (defined as "de-trended oil price changes") into the factors of causal shocks (supply, demand and others).

A preliminary result shows that the extent of the present oil price plunge cannot be explained only by the fundamental relationship of crude oil trading (see figure). The fundamental oversupply of crude oil, caused by rapidly growing crude oil supply and slowly growing crude oil demand, contributed to only about a third of oil price changes. About two thirds of contributing factors are from non-fundamental sources. This stands in contrast with the previous price collapse in 2008-2009, which was driven by demand shocks. "Other shocks" include not only speculation, but also factors such as the change in demand for storage. They are related more to expectations on oil prices than to physical supply and demand.

Historical decomposition of de-trended oil price changes

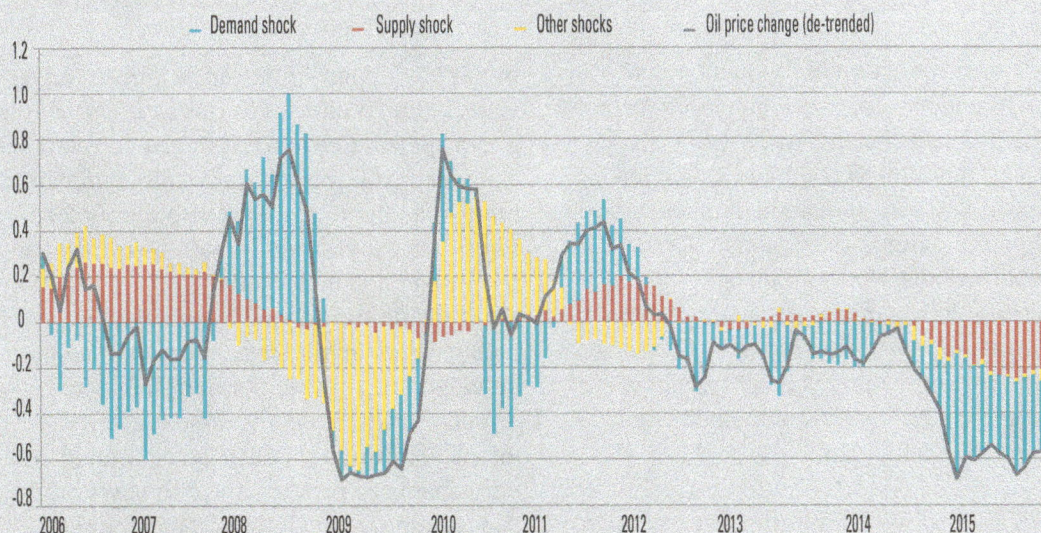

Source: ESCWA staff calculations.

Table 1.4 Gross oil export revenues in the Arab region, 2012-2017 (billions of US dollars)

Country/subregion	2012	2013	2014	2015[a]	2016[b]	2017[b]
Bahrain	15.0	15.1	14.3	7.0	6.9	7.8
Kuwait	112.5	108.5	97.6	51.4	48.7	59.4
Oman	31.7	32.5	30.5	16.6	15.2	19.5
Qatar	34.4	32.4	28.8	13.2	10.3	11.0
Saudi Arabia	337.5	321.9	284.4	153.3	130.0	163.5
United Arab Emirates	112.8	116.5	99.0	53.4	47.0	58.7
GCC countries	643.8	627.0	554.6	295.0	258.1	319.9
Egypt	12.8	13.1	10.9	6.5	5.4	6.4
Iraq	93.8	89.6	83.8	48.4	43.4	56.7
Syrian Arab Republic	--	--	--	--	--	--
Mashreq	106.6	102.6	94.7	54.9	48.8	63.1
Algeria	43.5	40.1	35.4	19.5	19.8	25.5
Libya	59.8	44.4	18.1	9.3	8.1	10.3
Morocco	0.9	1.1	0.8	0.3	0.3	0.3
Tunisia	2.8	2.6	2.2	1.0	0.8	0.9
Maghreb	107.0	88.2	56.5	30.2	29.0	37.1
Mauritania	0.3	0.2	0.2	0.1	0.1	0.1
Sudan	1.0	1.7	1.4	0.6	0.5	0.5
Yemen	6.3	6.5	4.5	0.8	--	--
Arab LDCs	7.6	8.5	6.0	1.5	0.5	0.6
Arab region total	865.0	826.3	711.9	381.6	336.5	420.7

Source: ESCWA staff estimates based on national statistical sources (see appendix).
[a] ESCWA staff estimates as of March 2016.
[b] ESCWA staff projections as of March 2016.

coordinated reduction in production, the extent to which it could bring about a recovery in oil prices remains unclear. If oil prices are not elastic enough to respond to changes in supply, any such reduction in production would not maximize oil revenues. Amid those difficulties, North American crude oil production has begun to decline, owing to the closure of non-profitable wells. It is projected that the current supply glut will be eliminated in the second half of 2017, but global supply in 2016 remains uncertain.

Oil prices bounced back from a recent low in the first half of 2016 (figure 1.3A). While chronic excess supply has dominated the markets, oil prices have been significantly influenced by speculation in oil futures markets. The changes in net speculative long positions correlate with changes in oil prices (figure 1.3B) and caused high volatility in oil prices throughout 2015. Prices are expected to remain below the long-term trend line in 2016 and 2017. Speculative short selling has recently pushed oil prices below the estimated fundamental price floor of between $35 and $40 per barrel. Speculation-driven price fluctuations are expected to intensify throughout 2016, as oil market participants remain sensitive to news on the excess supply condition and its prospects (figure 1.3C). Given those factors and the slow but growing demand for crude oil, the OPEC

Reference Basket price is forecast to be $41.5 per barrel on average in 2016 and $49.3 per barrel on average in 2017 (table 1.2).

Total crude oil production in the Arab region is estimated to have been 23.5 million barrels per day on average in 2015, an increase of 0.5 million barrels per day compared with the rate in 2014 (table 1.3). GCC countries are estimated to have produced 17.7 million barrels per day in 2015, with no significant change over the previous year. Crude oil production in Iraq continued to grow as more facilities were expanded in the south. Libya managed to sustain production at 400,000 barrels per day in 2015, in spite of armed conflict and political instability. Production in Yemen ceased in April 2015 amid intensifying military operations. Present trends are expected to continue into 2016. GCC producers are expected to maintain the present production level, while production in Iraq is projected to reach 4 million barrels per day by the end of 2017. Production in the Sudan is also projected to increase moderately, owing to recent foreign investment. Low oil prices are preventing other non-GCC Arab oil producers from increasing capital expenditure to enhance production.

Total gross oil export revenues for the region are estimated at $382 billion in 2015, a 46 per cent drop over the previous year (table 1.4). That is due mostly to lower oil prices but to a lesser extent also reflects increasing domestic demand in the oil exporters. Domestic demand for fuel products continued to grow in the Arab region, and GCC countries strengthened local refining capacity to cater for domestic needs. It is expected that they will step up those efforts as part of economic diversification strategies. Traditionally Arab oil producers exported crude oil and imported fuel products from European and Asian countries. That traditional pattern is changing. Total gross oil export revenues are set to slide by 12 per cent to $337 billion in 2016, representing a 61 per cent decline since the peak of 2012. Revenues are expected to bounce back in 2017 to $421 billion.

2. Natural gas

Natural gas has developed rapidly into a key export for Arab countries in the past few years. Algeria, Egypt, Libya, Qatar and the United Arab Emirates are members of the Gas Exporting Countries Forum, and Iraq and Oman are observers. Yemen also became a gas exporter in 2009. Lebanon, the Syrian Arab Republic and the State of Palestine have been planning offshore gas exploration for a number of years. However, in April 2015, fighting brought Yemen's gas production to a halt and geopolitical risks have prevented eastern Mediterranean countries from making progress in their gas exploration plans. Despite instability, Libya has managed to export natural gas through the Greenstream pipeline to Italy. Iraq and Saudi Arabia are expected to invest more effort into natural gas exploration and production. Qatar remained among the most influential gas exporters, along with Australia and the Russian Federation.

The growing awareness in European countries of their dependency for gas on the Russian Federation has led them to look to Arab gas exporters as alternative suppliers. It has been recognized that the Arab region needs greater infrastructure investment in this sector in order to increase natural gas exports through the pipelines or liquefied natural gas facilities.

According to the International Association for Natural Gas (Cedigaz), there was oversupply in the global gas market in 2015. That trend is likely to last until 2022, particularly in the liquefied natural gas sector.[8] Weak demand prospects, overcapacity in liquefied natural gas facilities and increasingly competitive alternative energy sources caused a global supply glut. The natural gas market is segmented but geographical benchmark prices showed a trend of convergence towards a lower level in late 2015 (figure 1.4A). As of January 2016, the benchmark price for

Figure 1.4 Natural gas prices, phosphate prices and exports

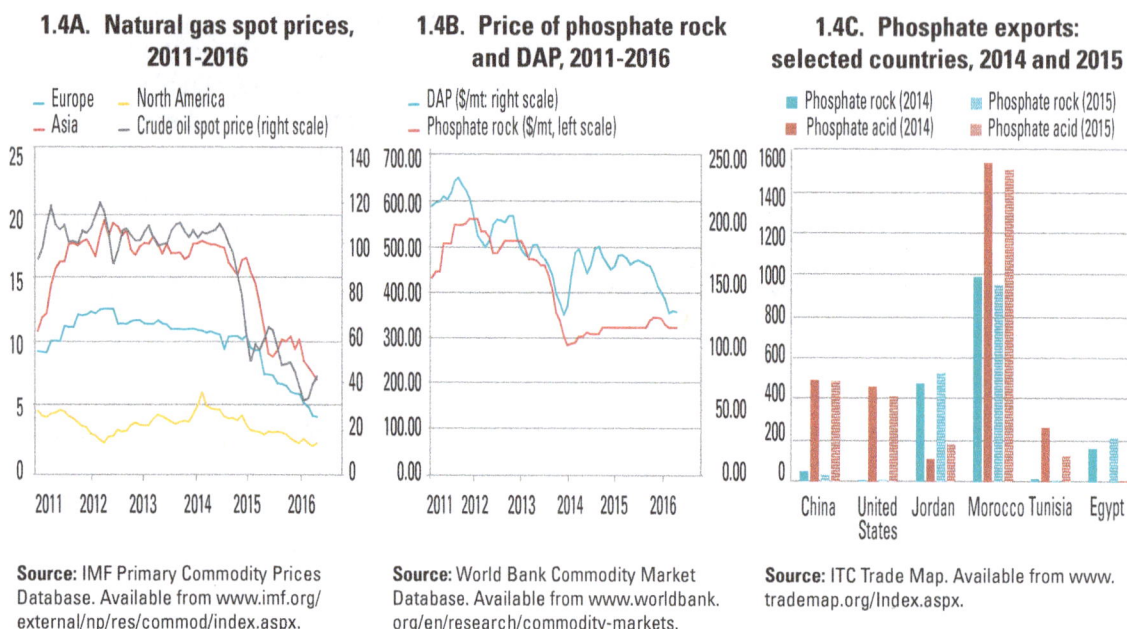

1.4A. Natural gas spot prices, 2011-2016

Legend: Europe, North America, Asia, Crude oil spot price (right scale)

1.4B. Price of phosphate rock and DAP, 2011-2016

Legend: DAP ($/mt: right scale), Phosphate rock ($/mt, left scale)

1.4C. Phosphate exports: selected countries, 2014 and 2015

Legend: Phosphate rock (2014), Phosphate rock (2015), Phosphate acid (2014), Phosphate acid (2015)

Countries: China, United States, Jordan, Morocco, Tunisia, Egypt

Source: IMF Primary Commodity Prices Database. Available from www.imf.org/external/np/res/commod/index.aspx.

Source: World Bank Commodity Market Database. Available from www.worldbank.org/en/research/commodity-markets.

Source: ITC Trade Map. Available from www.trademap.org/Index.aspx.

Europe stood at $5.09 per million metric British thermal units (Btu), the benchmark price for Japan stood at $9.0 per million Btu, and the benchmark price for the United States stood at $2.27 per million Btu.[9] There have been institutional developments to improve gas transactions and overcome market segmentation. For example, the recent introduction of futures markets for liquefied natural gas in Singapore is expected to create flexible spot pricing, which would benefit gas-exporting and gas-importing countries. However, the market situation is expected to remain challenging for gas exporters in terms of increasing spot transactions, given the projected long-term structural supply glut.

3. Phosphate

The phosphate sector continues to be strategically important in the Arab region. Despite persistent weak demand in global fertilizer markets, interregional partnerships were developed involving foreign direct investment. According to estimates from the International Fertilizer Industry Association,

in the 2015-2016 crop season, global fertilizer demand will drop by 0.1 per cent, or 183.4 million tons, and demand for phosphorus will decline by 0.9 per cent, or 41.1 million tons, compared with the previous crop season.[10] Low crop prices continued to dampen global fertilizer demand, and weak demand growth is projected for the next crop season. Meanwhile, the supply capacity for diammonium phosphate, one of the most widely used phosphorus fertilizers, continued to grow. Most notably, the expansion of a fertilizer plant in Jorf Lasfar contributed to the increasing supply capacity of Morocco and positioned the country as a leading exporter.

The price of phosphate rock stabilized after a 51 per cent decline from the peak of 2011 (figure 1.4B). The average yearly price edged up from $110.2 per metric ton in 2014 to $117.5 in 2015.[11] Meanwhile, the price of diammonium phosphate (DAP) declined by 26 per cent from the peak of $485.24 per metric ton reached in February 2015. The price of phosphate rock is expected to remain at its current level, and the price of DAP is projected to stabilize in 2016. No substantial rise in prices is expected in this sector as structural excess supply continues globally in 2016.

The value of phosphate product exports declined in 2015 due to the decrease in the unit prices, while export volumes marked moderate growth. Morocco led global phosphate markets (figure 1.4C) and Jordan saw rapid growth in exports of phosphate products in terms of value and volume. Egypt also increased exports of phosphate rocks and has potential for downstream development into exports of phosphate acid and DAP. Tunisia experienced a substantial drop in phosphate rocks production due to a series of labour disputes in the Gafsa region. Its exports of phosphate acid dropped considerably in 2015 as a result.

C. Financial and trade linkages to the Arab region

Global economic developments impacted the Arab region through its financial and trade linkages in several ways. The drastic decline in the value of exports was seen not only in oil and other natural resources but also other non-oil sector products. As a result, more Arab countries started experiencing current account deficits in 2015. Meanwhile, the inflow of capital, which had financed the current account deficits, also stagnated. International investors became increasingly selective in forming their global portfolio in a situation where relatively higher yields were assured in one of the safest financial assets, US Treasury bonds. As the Arab region remained prone to economic and geopolitical risks, capital inflows were seen more as a result of "pull" factors, such as increasing international bond issuance by GCC Governments. Most Arab countries running current account deficits had to choose between currency depreciation or running down foreign reserves.

In parallel to declining oil revenues, the value of financial wealth in GCC countries, as measured by market capitalization of stock markets, contracted in 2015 (figure 1.5A). The margin of contraction, however, was moderate compared with lost oil export revenues and to the stock market crashes of 2006 and 2008. This pattern indicates the resilience of the financial sector in GCC countries, unlike in 2008 and 2009, when several financial institutions in GCC countries were bailed out.

Figure 1.5B shows the total cross-border claims on and liabilities to Arab countries' clients by the reporting banks of the Bank for International Settlements (BIS). Total liabilities, namely Arab clients' deposits with main international banks, have been declining, while total claims, namely borrowings by Arab clients from main international banks, have been on the increase. The Arab region in total, owing to the strong external financial wealth of GCC countries, remained a net lender to main international banks, although its margin narrowed in 2015.

Financing costs, as measured by 3-month money market rates, rose in 2015 in GCC countries in parallel with the rise of the US dollar 3-month LIBOR (figure 1.5C). Financing costs in Jordan continued to decrease, reflecting policy rate cuts in 2015. However, the declining trend was stalled in the second half of 2015 before reaching the level of spread it held over GCC countries before 2008. While GCC countries have experienced a moderate rise in financing costs, other Arab countries, such as Egypt, Lebanon, Morocco and Tunisia, faced much tighter financing conditions.

The Arab region became a net importer in 2015 (figure 1.6A), with total exports estimated at $844 billion and imports at $892 billion. The total net value of imports was thus $48 billion in 2015, as opposed to the $250 billion net value in exports of the previous year. Net outflow of financial

Figure 1.5 Global financial linkages in the Arab region

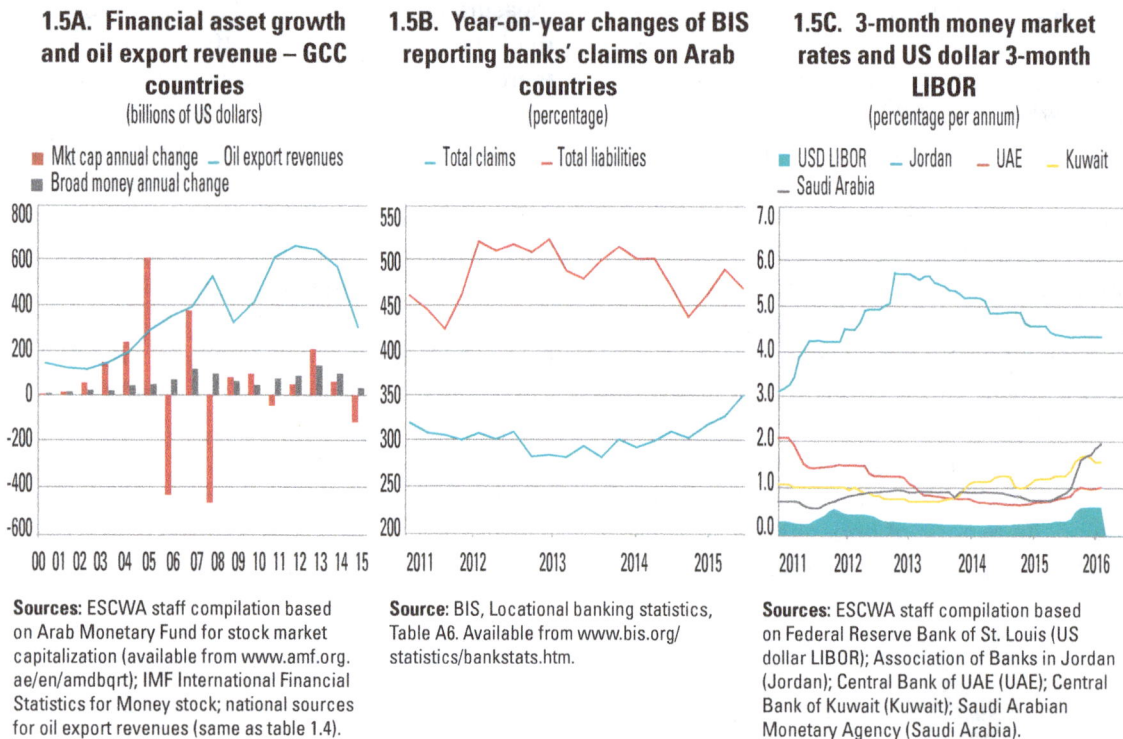

1.5A. Financial asset growth and oil export revenue – GCC countries
(billions of US dollars)

- Mkt cap annual change
- Broad money annual change
- Oil export revenues

1.5B. Year-on-year changes of BIS reporting banks' claims on Arab countries
(percentage)

- Total claims
- Total liabilities

1.5C. 3-month money market rates and US dollar 3-month LIBOR
(percentage per annum)

- USD LIBOR
- Jordan
- UAE
- Kuwait
- Saudi Arabia

Sources: ESCWA staff compilation based on Arab Monetary Fund for stock market capitalization (available from www.amf.org.ae/en/amdbqrt); IMF International Financial Statistics for Money stock; national sources for oil export revenues (same as table 1.4).

Source: BIS, Locational banking statistics, Table A6. Available from www.bis.org/statistics/bankstats.htm.

Sources: ESCWA staff compilation based on Federal Reserve Bank of St. Louis (US dollar LIBOR); Association of Banks in Jordan (Jordan); Central Bank of UAE (UAE); Central Bank of Kuwait (Kuwait); Saudi Arabian Monetary Agency (Saudi Arabia).

wealth has been ongoing since 2014. Foreign reserves declined by $171 billion in 2015, following a $32 billion decrease in 2014, as a result of weak exports in goods and services, and stagnating capital inflows.

The geographical pattern of trade by Arab countries in total reflected the change in terms of trade (figure 1.6B). The unit price of oil, gas and other natural resources declined more than for other goods in 2015. The geographical pattern of export destinations changed significantly, given that oil and other natural resources were the main export items for certain regions, while the pattern of import origins barely changed as most import items are non-energy products. In 2015, 53 per cent of merchandise exports from the Arab region were shipped to the Asia-Pacific region, a drop from the previous year's share of 58.1 per cent. Europe accounted for 14.5 per cent of total Arab exports in 2015, a slight decline from 14.8 per cent in the previous year. North America

accounted for 5.2 per cent of total Arab exports, dropping from 7.3 per cent in 2014. The share of Arab exports to Africa stood at 2.5 per cent and 1.2 per cent to Latin America and the Caribbean.

The share of imports from the Asia-Pacific region decreased slightly to 39.3 per cent in 2015 from 40.1 per cent in the previous year, while Europe's share was 32.2 per cent, down from 32.3 per cent (figure 1.6C). Imports from North America, Latin America and the Caribbean, and Africa accounted for 8.8 per cent, 2.7 per cent and 0.8 per cent, respectively.

The share of intraregional trade is estimated at 15.2 per cent of total gross exports (10.8 per cent in 2014) and 15.5 per cent of total gross imports in 2015. The growth in intraregional exports can be interpreted as a result of changing terms of trade, but also as an indication of the resilience of economic

Figure 1.6 Global trade linkages in the Arab region

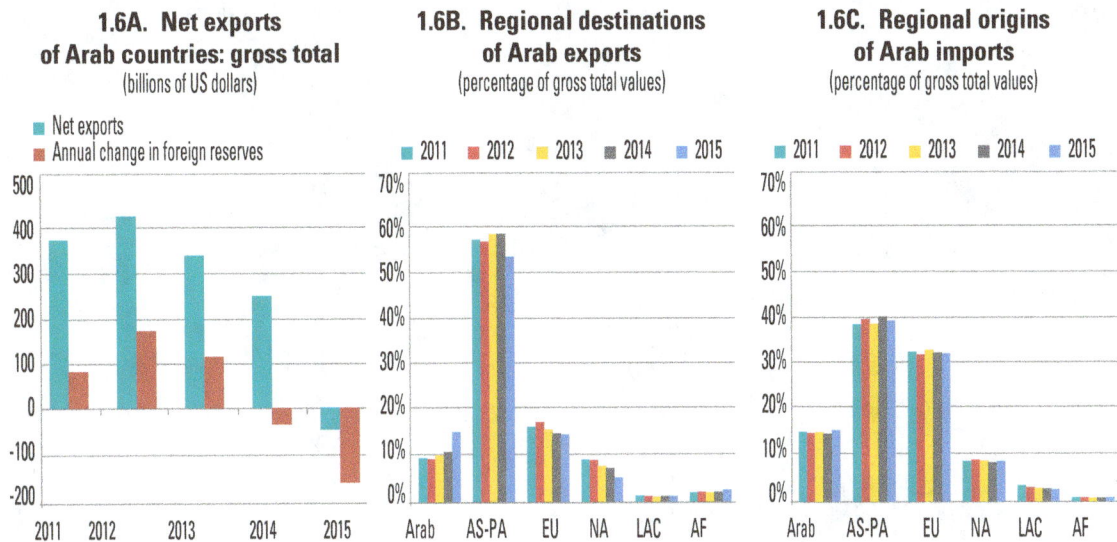

1.6A. Net exports of Arab countries: gross total
(billions of US dollars)

- Net exports
- Annual change in foreign reserves

1.6B. Regional destinations of Arab exports
(percentage of gross total values)

■ 2011 ■ 2012 ■ 2013 ■ 2014 ■ 2015

1.6C. Regional origins of Arab imports
(percentage of gross total values)

■ 2011 ■ 2012 ■ 2013 ■ 2014 ■ 2015

Sources: ESCWA staff calculations based on IMF, Directions of Trade Statistics and International Financial Statistics. Available from www.imf.org/en/Data.
Abbreviations: Arab, Arab countries; AS-PA, Asia and the Pacific; EU, Europe; NA, North America; LAC, Latin America and the Caribbean; AF, Africa excluding Arab countries.

activities in the region, despite the conflicts afflicting key overland commercial routes in the Mashreq.

D. Concluding remarks

With the savings glut in developed economies on the one hand, and the tightening of balance-of-payments conditions in developing economies on the other, the world economy is becoming increasingly polarized.

Market mechanisms appear to have failed to balance the availability of funds for development between developed and developing economies. In this situation, lower oil prices converted the Arab region into a net importer of goods and services. The ample financial cushion represented by the major

oil exporters has deflated rapidly. In the past, intraregional financial assistance, usually from GCC countries to other Arab countries, prevented major balance-of-payments crises, except in case of war, conflict or economic sanctions. As lower oil prices have reversed the region's process of oil-based financial accumulation, some Arab countries have developed balance-of-payment problems. In the year marking the launch of the SDGs, the uneven distribution of funds, represented by the global savings glut, must be tackled. Excess available savings must be invested and utilized to alleviate balance-of-payments pain in developing economies, including those of the Arab region. International support measures are increasingly vital to efforts to alleviate macroeconomic constraints and create a solid foundation for sustainable economic and social development in those countries.

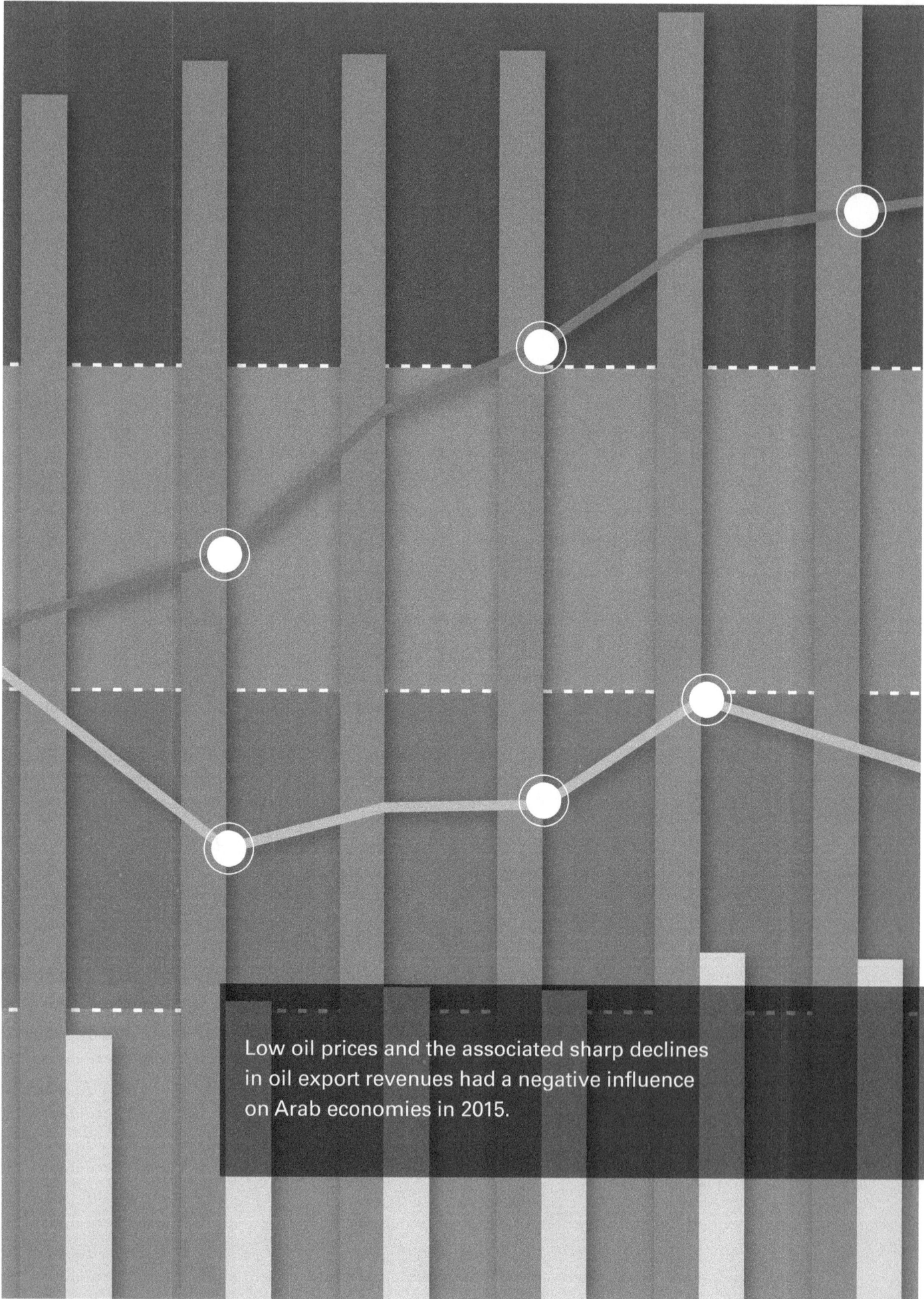

Low oil prices and the associated sharp declines in oil export revenues had a negative influence on Arab economies in 2015.

2. Socioeconomic Trends and Developments in the Arab Region

A. Economic situation and prospects

1. Overview

Low oil prices and the associated sharp declines in oil export revenues had a negative influence on Arab economies in 2015. Real GDP growth on average in the Arab region was 0.9 per cent in 2015 (table 2.1: left columns) and is forecast to be 1.5 per cent in 2016. The major fluctuating factor is the negative growth estimates for Libya, the Syrian Arab Republic and Yemen. Despite falling oil prices, GCC countries remained the growth centre of the Arab region in 2015. Armed conflicts and violence in Iraq, Libya, the Syrian Arab Republic, Yemen and Palestine continued to have an adverse effect on socioeconomic development, with consequences not only for those countries, but also neighbouring Egypt, Jordan, Lebanon and Tunisia. Tourism in the Mashreq and Maghreb dwindled in the face of heightened security risks. Balance-of-payments conditions have generally tightened in the region, reflecting the lack of foreign funds available to countries with current account deficits.

Average annual inflation as reflected in the regional consumer price index is estimated at 5.4 per cent in 2015, compared with 5.2 per cent in 2014 (table 2.1: right columns). In GCC countries, weak international commodity prices dampened other inflationary pressures, such as the rising price of utilities, owing to subsidy reforms. Low inflation in the eurozone had an impact on several countries, including Jordan, Lebanon and Mauritania. Jordan and Lebanon recorded negative inflation rates in 2015. Inflation was contained in Iraq and Palestine, but low inflation rates did not indicate functioning supply chains in either country. Both countries' economic activities faced conflict-related logistical difficulties. In Egypt, a trend of high inflation continued as a result of expanding money stock. The Syrian Arab Republic and Yemen suffered from conflict-related hyperinflation. Libya also experienced a rapid increase in its consumer price index towards the end of 2015. In the Sudan, hyperinflation showed signs of stabilization in 2015.

The average inflation rate is forecast to remain unchanged in 2016. International commodity prices will remain weak, keeping inflation low in most Arab countries. Price rises on housing-related items, including utilities, due to further subsidy reforms in GCC countries, are expected to have a moderate impact on prices. Inflation in the Sudan is expected to stabilize at its 2015 level. Inflation in Libya is projected to accelerate, following the trend in 2015. Inflation in the Syrian Arab Republic is expected to remain high owing to severe constraints on foreign exchange. The expected high level of monetary expansion is likely to pin the inflation rate in Egypt at the 10 per cent mark for 2016. Yemen is set to suffer from hyperinflation as a result of its severe balance-of-payments situation and monetary factors.

A gradual depreciation of the national currencies of Algeria, Libya, Mauritania, Morocco and Tunisia continued against the United States dollar in 2015, mainly due to the weakening euro, against which those countries' currencies have traditionally maintained stable exchange rates. The currency of Kuwait, which is pegged to a basket of currencies, including the euro, also remained weak against the dollar. GCC countries, as well as Djibouti, Iraq,

Table 2.1 Real GDP growth rate and consumer price inflation rate, 2013-2017 (annual percentage change)

Country/subregion	Real GDP growth rate					Consumer price inflation rate				
	2013[a]	2014[a]	2015[b]	2016[c]	2017[c]	2013	2014	2015[b]	2016[c]	2017[c]
Bahrain	5.4	4.5	2.9	2.4	2.7	3.3	2.7	1.8	2.6	2.0
Kuwait	1.2	-1.6	0.4	1.4	3.0	2.6	2.9	3.3	3.3	3.6
Oman	3.9	2.9	3.3	2.1	2.7	1.3	1.0	0.1	1.7	2.0
Qatar	4.6	4.0	4.2	3.5	4.1	3.1	3.0	1.8	1.3	1.5
Saudi Arabia	2.7	3.6	3.4	1.7	2.4	3.5	2.7	2.2	2.1	1.7
United Arab Emirates	4.3	4.6	3.0	2.4	2.9	1.1	2.2	4.2	2.3	2.7
GCC countries	3.3	3.4	3.0	2.1	2.8	2.7	2.5	2.6	2.2	2.2
Egypt[d]	2.1	3.5	2.1	2.6	3.1	9.5	10.1	10.4	9.2	10.0
Iraq	7.6	-0.6	-2.8	1.5	5.4	1.9	2.2	1.4	1.8	2.0
Jordan	2.8	3.1	2.4	1.9	2.4	4.8	2.9	-0.9	1.1	1.5
Lebanon	3.0	2.1	1.3	1.4	1.9	5.7	1.7	-3.7	0.5	1.2
State of Palestine	2.2	-0.2	3.5	3.1	3.8	1.7	1.7	1.4	1.2	1.7
Syrian Arab Republic[e]	-16.9	-11.6	-8.1	-6.5	-5.0	87.7	24.3	37.3	44.0	35.7
Mashreq	1.5	0.5	-0.3	1.1	2.7	15.9	8.5	9.3	10.1	9.6
Algeria	2.8	3.8	3.2	1.7	2.2	4.1	3.9	4.4	3.9	4.3
Libya	-30.8	-47.7	-22.0	-5.2	-3.3	2.6	2.4	8.6	11.0	10.0
Morocco	4.7	2.4	4.3	2.7	2.9	1.9	0.4	1.6	1.2	1.7
Tunisia	2.4	2.3	0.8	1.6	2.4	5.8	4.9	4.9	4.2	4.0
Maghreb	-3.1	-6.4	-1.6	0.7	1.4	3.5	2.9	4.5	4.6	4.7
Comoros	3.5	3.9	3.6	4.0	4.2	1.6	1.4	2.2	2.0	2.2
Djibouti	5.0	6.0	4.7	5.0	5.0	2.5	3.0	2.7	2.2	2.5
Mauritania	5.7	6.4	3.7	3.4	3.5	4.1	3.5	0.5	1.2	2.0
Somalia[f]	--	3.7	2.7	3.4	4.3	4.5	1.3	4.0	3.2	2.9
Sudan	5.3	2.5	3.2	3.6	4.0	36.5	36.9	16.9	15.1	14.6
Yemen	3.2	1.5	-34.6	-11.1	-7.5	11.0	8.0	30.0	35.0	32.5
Arab LDCs	4.5	2.5	-7.3	-0.5	0.8	26.5	25.7	19.2	19.4	18.4
Arab region total[g]	1.8	0.9	0.9	1.5	2.4	7.2	5.2	5.4	5.4	5.2

Source: National sources.

[a] GDP figures for 2013 and 2014 are from national sources unless otherwise indicated.

[b] March 2016 estimates.

[c] March 2016 forecasts.

[d] For GDP growth rates of Egypt, the figures are for the country's fiscal year, which ends in June.

[e] GDP growth rates of the Syrian Arab Republic for 2013-2015 are estimates from the ESCWA National Agenda for the Future of Syria (NAFS) project.

[f] GDP growth rates and consumer price inflation rates for Somalia are from the International Monetary Fund (2015) Staff Report for the 2015 Article IV Consultation. Available from https://www.imf.org/external/pubs/ft/scr/2015/cr15208.pdf.

[g] Figures for country groups are weighted averages, where weights for each year are based on GDP in 2010.

Jordan and Lebanon, continue to peg their currencies to the dollar. Egypt managed an orderly depreciation of the Egyptian pound (EGP) from EGP 7.60 to EGP 8.8 to the dollar. The Sudan also managed to set a gradual depreciation of its national currency, the Sudanese pound (SDG), to SDG 6.45 to the dollar. The value of the Syrian pound (SYP) continued to weaken, from SYP 198 to the dollar in January 2015 to SYP 580 to the dollar in May 2016. Armed conflict caused a significant devaluation of the Yemeni rial (YER), from YER 215 to the dollar in March 2015 to YER 280 to the dollar in March 2016. Further devaluations of national currencies against the dollar are forecast for Egypt, Libya, the Sudan, the Syrian Arab Republic, Tunisia and Yemen in 2016.

2. GCC Countries

The GCC countries subregion is estimated to have had GDP growth of 3 per cent in 2015, compared with 3.4 per cent in the previous year (table 2.1). The variation in growth rates among GCC countries reflects the performance of the non-oil sector as well as the depth of the oil sector. Refining activities retained more value added in the oil sector in real terms as demand for fuel products persisted. The growth of the non-oil sector has increased consistently, albeit at a slower rate, throughout the GCC countries. The value of financial assets and real estate has declined, reflecting weakening business sentiment and low oil prices. Broad money growth has stagnated as a result of weak credit growth. The financial sector in GCC countries maintained healthy balance sheets despite the rise in financing costs, which affected the sector's profitability. Estimated growth rates for 2015 are 2.9 per cent for Bahrain; 0.4 per cent for Kuwait; 3.3 per cent for Oman; 4.2 per cent for Qatar; 3.4 per cent for Saudi Arabia; and 3 per cent for the United Arab Emirates.

The value of total exports from GCC countries dropped significantly in 2015 due to low oil prices. The value of imports also came down,

partly due to declining commodity prices and stagnating domestic demand. As a result, net merchandise exports decreased in the third consecutive year from the estimated value of $461 billion in 2013 to $102.6 billion in 2015 (figure 2.1A). The margin of surplus in the merchandise trade account was not sufficient to offset deficits in services trade, and primary and secondary income accounts. The resulting current account deficits were partly financed by capital inflows, including repatriation of foreign assets, foreign borrowing and foreign direct investments, and partly by the sale of foreign reserves. Total foreign reserves in the subregion are estimated to have dropped by $110 billion in 2015.

The share of exports from GCC countries to, and imports from, the Asia-Pacific region decreased in 2015 to 60.5 per cent and 43.7 per cent respectively (figure 2.1B). The share of exports from GCC countries to, and imports from, Europe rose slightly to 7.5 per cent and 27.9 per cent respectively. Exports to North America, Latin America and the Caribbean, and Africa accounted for 7.5 per cent, 0.9 per cent, and 2.6 per cent respectively. Imports from those areas accounted for 11.2 per cent, 1.9 per cent, and 0.8 per cent respectively. The share of intra-Arab trade surged in 2015, from 9.3 per cent to 13.2 per cent in terms of exports and from 12.7 per cent to 13.7 per cent in terms of imports.

In 2015, all GCC countries recorded surpluses in merchandise trade. However, as the surplus margins were insufficient for Bahrain, Oman and Saudi Arabia to offset deficits in service trade, and primary and secondary income accounts, those countries are estimated to have recorded current account deficits (figure 2.2). It is estimated that Kuwait, Qatar and the United Arab Emirates maintained current account surpluses in 2015. Bahrain, Oman and Saudi Arabia are projected to experience current account deficits in 2016 and 2017, albeit cushioned by gradually recovering oil prices. Despite current account deficits, GCC countries

Figure 2.1 Geographical trade structure: GCC countries

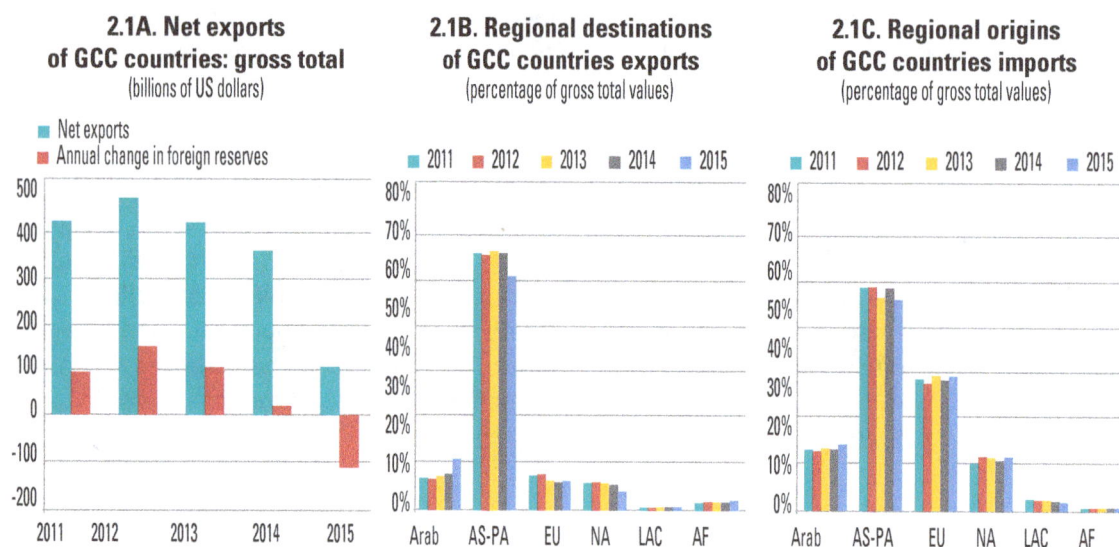

2.1A. Net exports of GCC countries: gross total (billions of US dollars)

2.1B. Regional destinations of GCC countries exports (percentage of gross total values)

2.1C. Regional origins of GCC countries imports (percentage of gross total values)

Sources: ESCWA staff calculations based on IMF, Directions of Trade Statistics and International Financial Statistics. Available from www.imf.org/en/Data.

Abbreviations: Arab, Arab countries; AS-PA, Asia and the Pacific; EU, Europe; NA, North America; LAC, Latin America and the Caribbean; AF, Africa excluding Arab countries.

are not expected to suffer serious balance-of-payments constraints because they have accumulated sufficient foreign assets.

Foreign reserves dwindled in Kuwait, Qatar and Saudi Arabia, and accumulation in Bahrain, Oman and the United Arab Emirates stagnated (figure 2.3). Those countries operate fixed exchange rates. However, as central banks are not primary managers of foreign assets in GCC countries, foreign reserve dynamics may reflect factors other than flows of funds, such as the transactions of sovereign wealth funds and financial institutions in the private sector. The dent in the asset side of central bank balance sheets, namely foreign reserves, can be seen in parallel with weak growth in the liability side of each country's financial sector, namely broad money stock. Serious signs of weak domestic demand appeared in Kuwait, Qatar and Saudi Arabia, where year-on-year growth of broad money stock fell close to zero towards the end of 2015. Bahrain, Oman and the United Arab Emirates kept broad money growth in positive

territory, albeit subdued compared with recent peaks.

Reflecting the drastic decline in revenues, all GCC countries but Qatar are estimated to have experienced fiscal deficits in 2015 (figure 2.4). Government expenditure remains moderately positive in terms of GDP, which implies that public spending was vital to sustained positive growth in GCC countries in 2015. Their fiscal stance in the budgets covering 2016 is expected to be neutral to tightening, but not to the extent that it could be considered "fiscal austerity". Fiscal reforms on the revenue and expenditure sides will accelerate but their impact will be limited in the near future. Nevertheless, the introduction of taxation, such as value-added tax (VAT), is part of policy reform plans. In Bahrain, the estimated budget deficit of 11.5 per cent of GDP in 2015 is forecast to rise to 12.6 per cent in 2016. The respective figures for Kuwait, Qatar, Saudi Arabia and the United Arab Emirates are: 16.7 per cent (18.8 per cent in 2016); 21.8 per cent (19.8 per cent in 2016); 15 per cent (13.1 per cent in 2016) and 5.2 per cent

Figure 2.2 Trade and current account balances: GCC countries

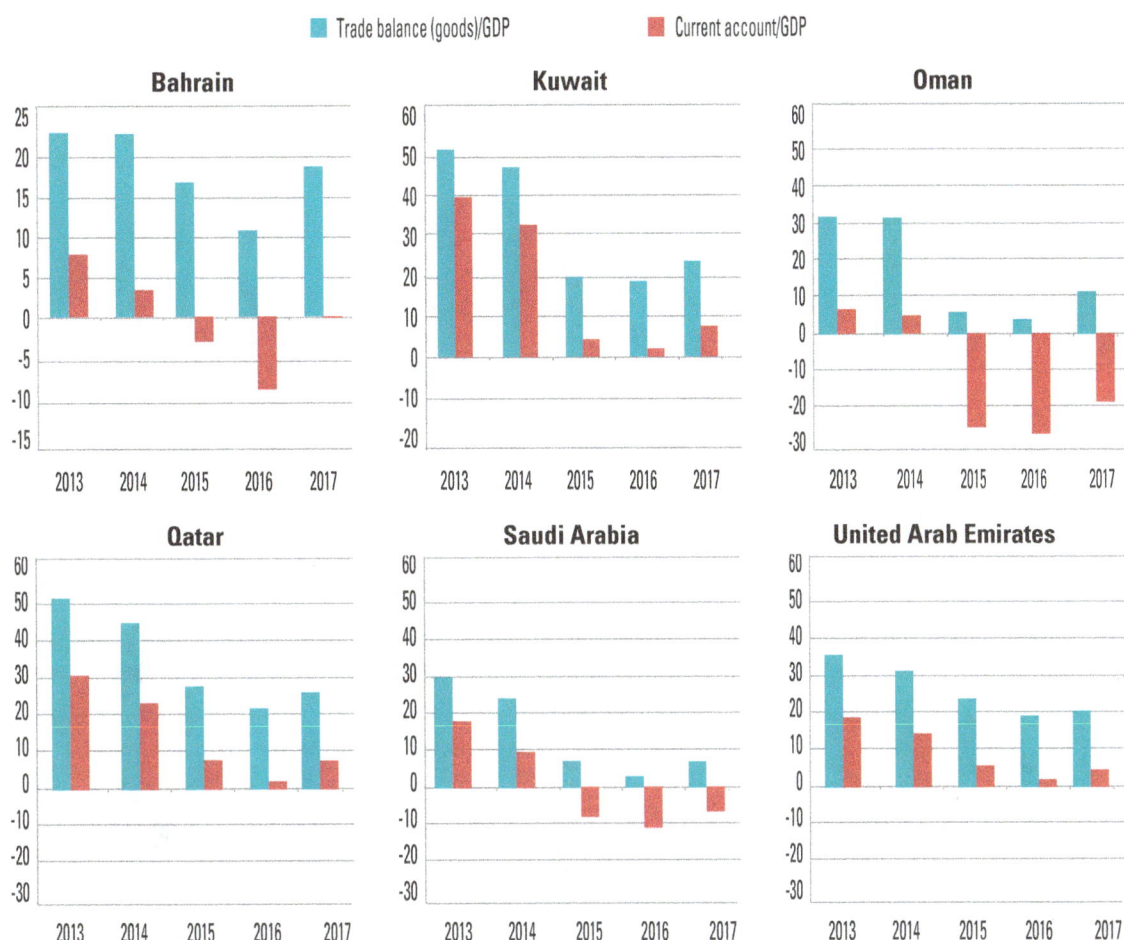

■ Trade balance (goods)/GDP   ■ Current account/GDP

Sources: ESCWA staff calculations based on national sources. Figures for 2015, 2016 and 2017 are ESCWA staff estimates/projections.

(4.5 per cent in 2016). It is estimated that Qatar ran a budget surplus of 4.5 per cent of GDP in 2015, which is forecast to drop to a deficit of 2.1 per cent in 2016.

In 2016, slower GDP growth still is forecast in the GCC countries. Financing costs are expected to rise, influenced by probable interest rate hikes in the United States. Financing costs will also be affected by the crowding-out effects of the expected increase in the debt issuance of GCC Governments. Public spending cuts are likely to weaken domestic demand in Bahrain, Oman, Saudi Arabia and the United Arab Emirates. Kuwait and Qatar are likely to maintain their fiscal

spending levels in terms of nominal GDP. Decelerating Chinese growth is expected to have a negative impact, but strong growth in India is likely to sustain the GCC non-oil sector. The average real GDP growth rate of the subregion is projected to be 2.1 per cent in 2016. Bahrain, Oman, Qatar and the United Arab Emirates are projected to grow faster than the subregional average. Saudi Arabian growth is projected to slow, owing mainly to a significant cut in capital spending and the rise in financing costs. Kuwait is projected to register consistent growth, setting the stage for expansion in its domestic demand. The forecast growth rates for 2016 are 2.4 per cent for Bahrain, 1.4 per cent for Kuwait, 2.1

Figure 2.3 Monetary indicators: GCC countries

▨ Total reserves excluding gold (US$ million: right scale)　　— Broad money (year-on-year growth %: left scale)

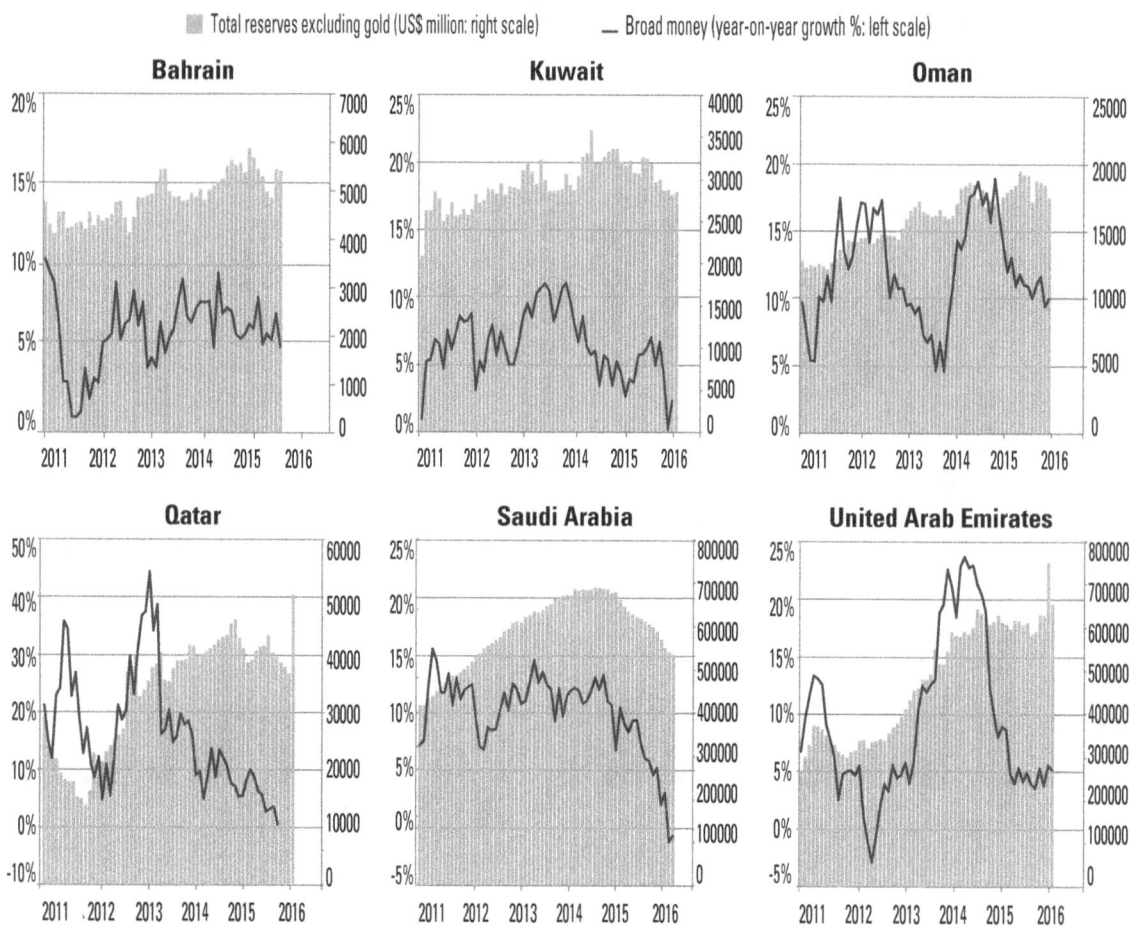

Source: ESCWA staff calculations based on IMF International Financial Statistics. Available from www.imf.org/en/Data.

per cent for Oman, 3.5 per cent for Qatar, 1.7 per cent for Saudi Arabia and 2.4 per cent for the United Arab Emirates.

3. Mashreq countries

It is estimated that the economies in the Mashreq subregion contracted by an average of 0.3 per cent in 2015, after registering 0.5 per cent growth in 2014 (table 2.1). The main factor affecting the subregion's growth is the dire economic situation in Iraq and the Syrian Arab Republic. Conflict there and the continued Israeli occupation in Palestine severely hampered economic activities. The ongoing blockade of the Gaza Strip prevented

reconstruction of economic infrastructure and production facilities destroyed in 2014.[1] The expansion in domestic demand in Jordan and Lebanon slowed, thus partly contributing to consumer price deflation. Growth was insufficient to maintain standards of living in those two countries, given the significant number of Syrian refugees residing in them. A severe balance-of-payments situation continued in Egypt, hampering its economic recovery. Estimated growth rates for 2015 are: 2.1 per cent for Egypt; 2.4 per cent for Jordan; 1.3 per cent for Lebanon; and 3.5 per cent for Palestine. It is estimated that the Iraqi and Syrian economies contracted by 3.8 per cent and 8.1 per cent respectively.

Figure 2.4 Fiscal positions: GCC countries

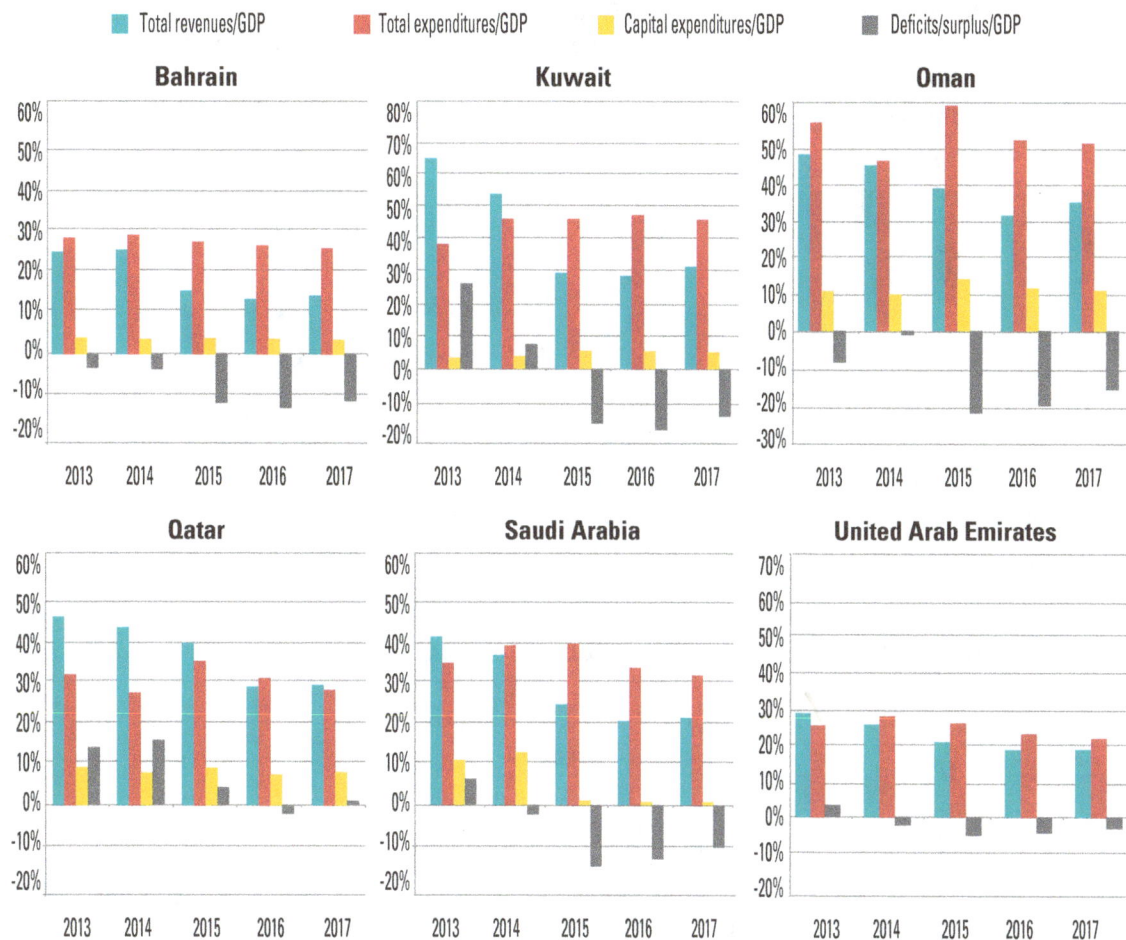

Legend: ■ Total revenues/GDP ■ Total expenditures/GDP ■ Capital expenditures/GDP ■ Deficits/surplus/GDP

Bahrain, Kuwait, Oman, Qatar, Saudi Arabia, United Arab Emirates (2013–2017)

Sources: ESCWA staff calculations based on national sources (see appendix). Figures for 2015, 2016 and 2017 are ESCWA staff estimates/projections.

The falling value of energy exports also affected the subregion's geographical trade pattern. As the value of oil exports to the Asia-Pacific region, mainly from Iraq, declined, the share of merchandise exports to the region eased to 38.9 per cent (figure 2.5B). Exports to Europe, North America, Africa, and Latin America and the Caribbean stood at 20.4 per cent, 7.4 per cent, 2.1 per cent and 0.7 per cent respectively. The greatest share of imports, at 36.3 per cent, came from the Asia-Pacific, followed by Europe (31.3 per cent), North America (5.4 per cent), Latin America and the Caribbean (3.7 per cent) and Africa (0.8 per cent). The

share of intra-Arab trade in the subregion surged to 29.6 per cent in terms of exports and 22.5 per cent in terms of imports. Indeed, intra-Arab trade, which is vital to the Mashreq, showed remarkable resilience in the face of conflict and the closure of several main border crossings.

Egypt, Jordan, Lebanon and Palestine remained net importers of goods in 2015, while Iraq just hung on as a net exporter (figure 2.6). Some of the main items that traditionally finance trade deficits showed stagnation. Trade in services, such as tourism, was affected by security concerns and spillover from

Figure 2.5 Geographical trade structure: Mashreq countries

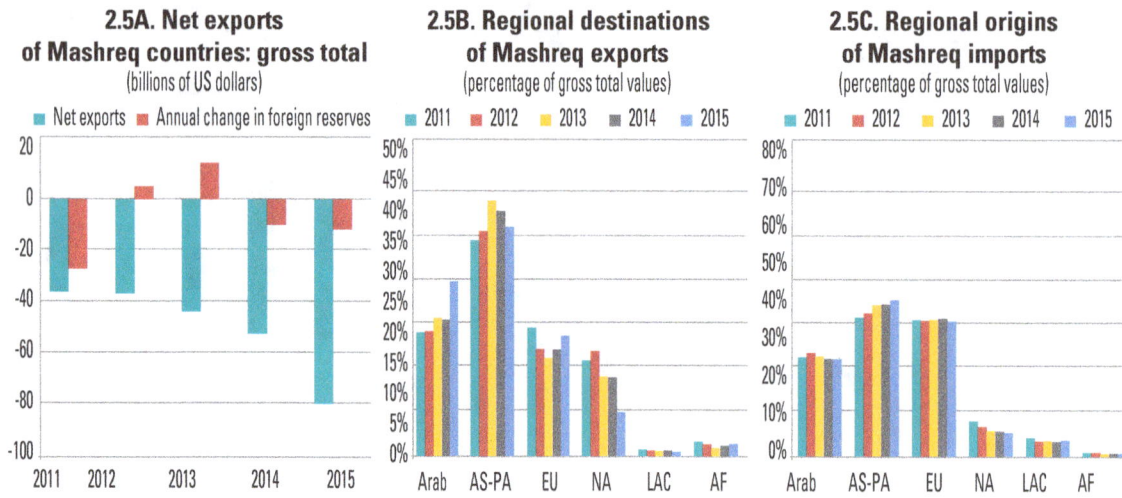

2.5A. Net exports of Mashreq countries: gross total
(billions of US dollars)

- Net exports
- Annual change in foreign reserves

2.5B. Regional destinations of Mashreq exports
(percentage of gross total values)

- 2011
- 2012
- 2013
- 2014
- 2015

2.5C. Regional origins of Mashreq imports
(percentage of gross total values)

- 2011
- 2012
- 2013
- 2014
- 2015

Sources: ESCWA staff calculation based on IMF, Directions of Trade Statistics and International Financial Statistics. Available from www.imf.org/en/Data.
Abbreviations: Arab, Arab countries; AS-PA, Asia and the Pacific; EU, Europe; NA, North America; LAC, Latin America and the Caribbean; AF, Africa excluding Arab countries.

Figure 2.6 Trade and current account balances: Mashreq countries

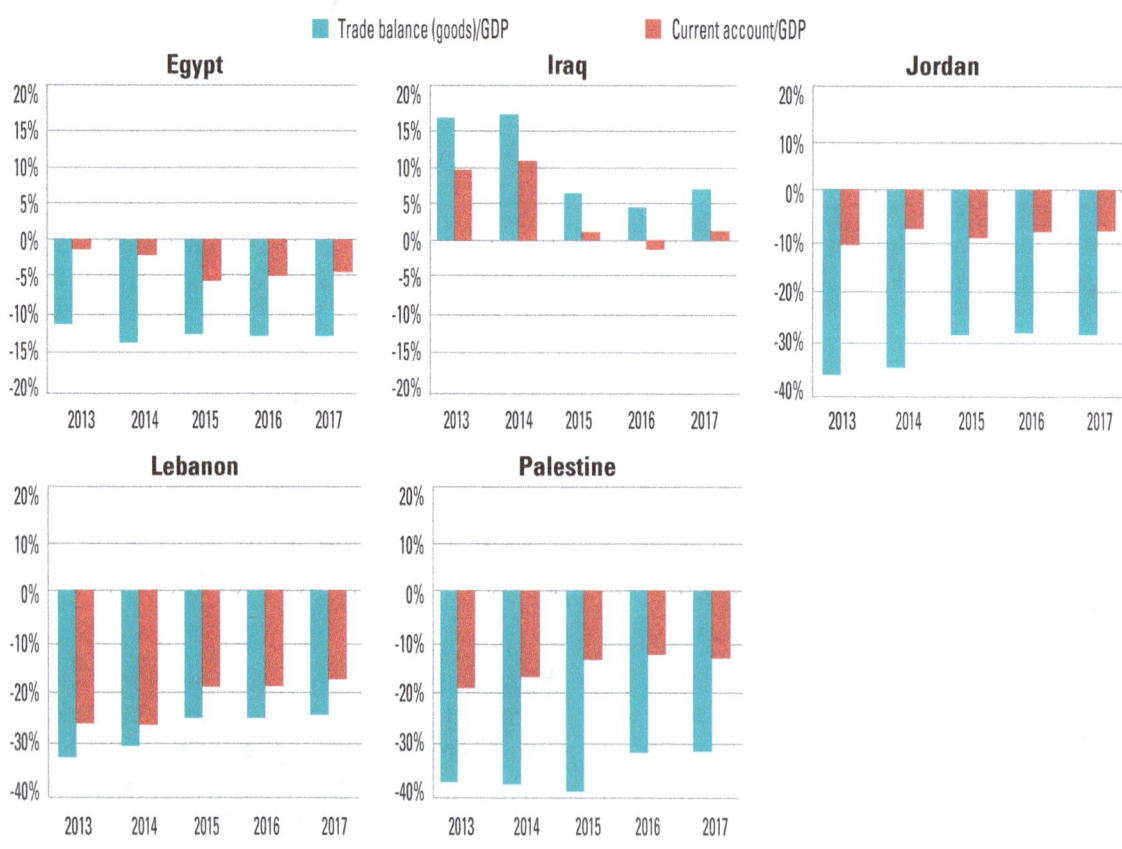

- Trade balance (goods)/GDP
- Current account/GDP

Egypt

Iraq

Jordan

Lebanon

Palestine

Sources: ESCWA staff calculations based on national sources (see appendix). Figures for 2015, 2016 and 2017 are ESCWA staff projections.
Note: Due to the lack of official statistics, figures for the Syrian Arab Republic are not estimated.

Figure 2.7 Monetary indicators: Mashreq countries

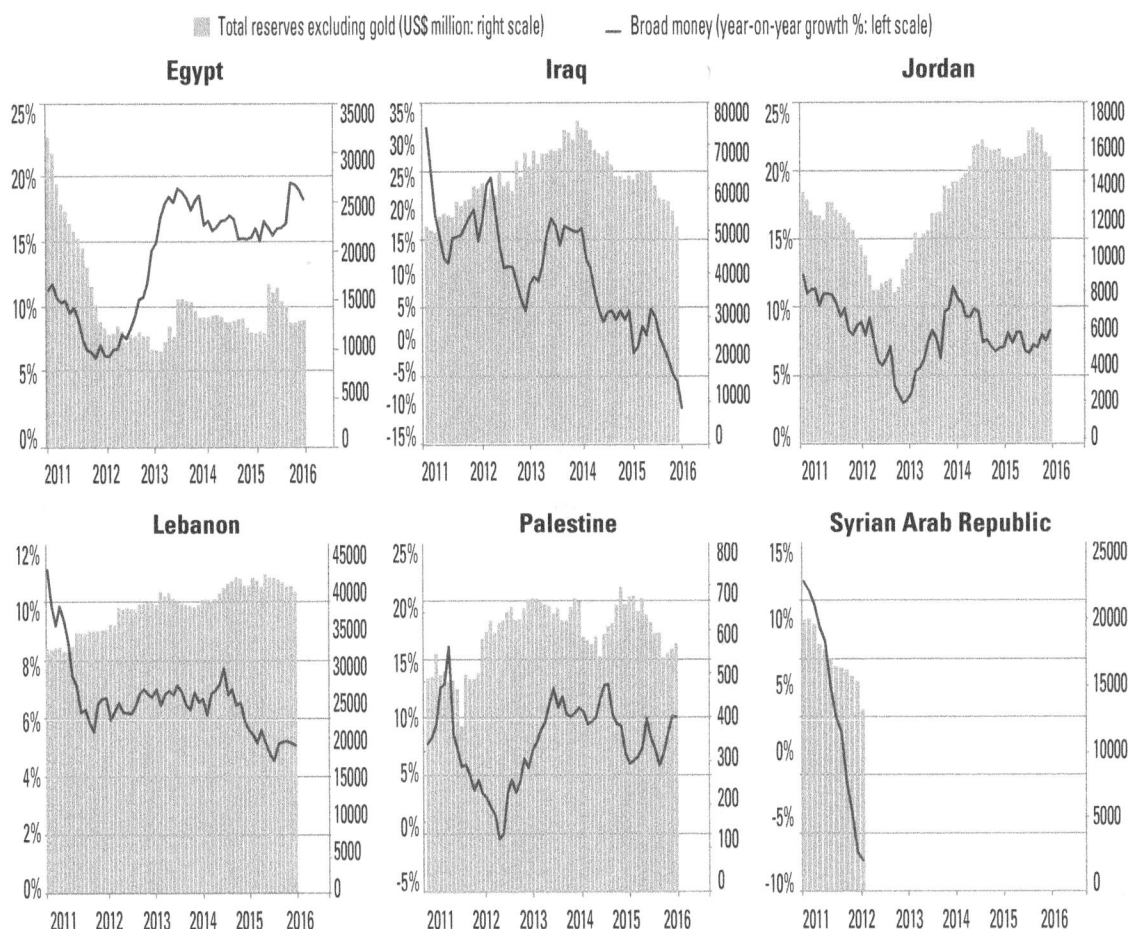

Total reserves excluding gold (US$ million: right scale) — Broad money (year-on-year growth %: left scale)

Egypt · Iraq · Jordan · Lebanon · Palestine · Syrian Arab Republic

Source: ESCWA staff calculations based on IMF International Financial Statistics. Available from www.imf.org/en/Data.

conflicts in neighbouring countries. Cross-border remittance inflows faltered as growth slackened off in host countries. Capital inflows into Mashreq countries slowed down because of the subregion's increasing downside risk. Consequently, the earlier tendency to accumulate foreign reserves was reversed (figure 2.7), and monetary expansion in Iraq, Jordan and Lebanon stagnated as a result. Domestic demand growth is increasingly subject to tighter external constraints. Iraq has been experiencing monetary contraction since mid-2015, indicating a serious implosion of domestic demand. Strong monetary expansion in Egypt is exceptional, but the country has sustained domestic demand

expansion at a cost of accelerated inflation. The Syrian Arab Republic has not issued official balance of payments figures, but it is likely that the situation has deteriorated further.

The fiscal stance of Mashreq countries is fragile, with weak domestic revenue underlining the need for foreign aid to sustain government expenditure. Despite repeated requests from Jordan and Lebanon, international financial support for their spending on Syrian refugees has been slow in coming. Reconstruction in the Gaza Strip since 2014 has accelerated only gradually, even though the disbursement rate stood at

Figure 2.8 Fiscal positions: Mashreq countries

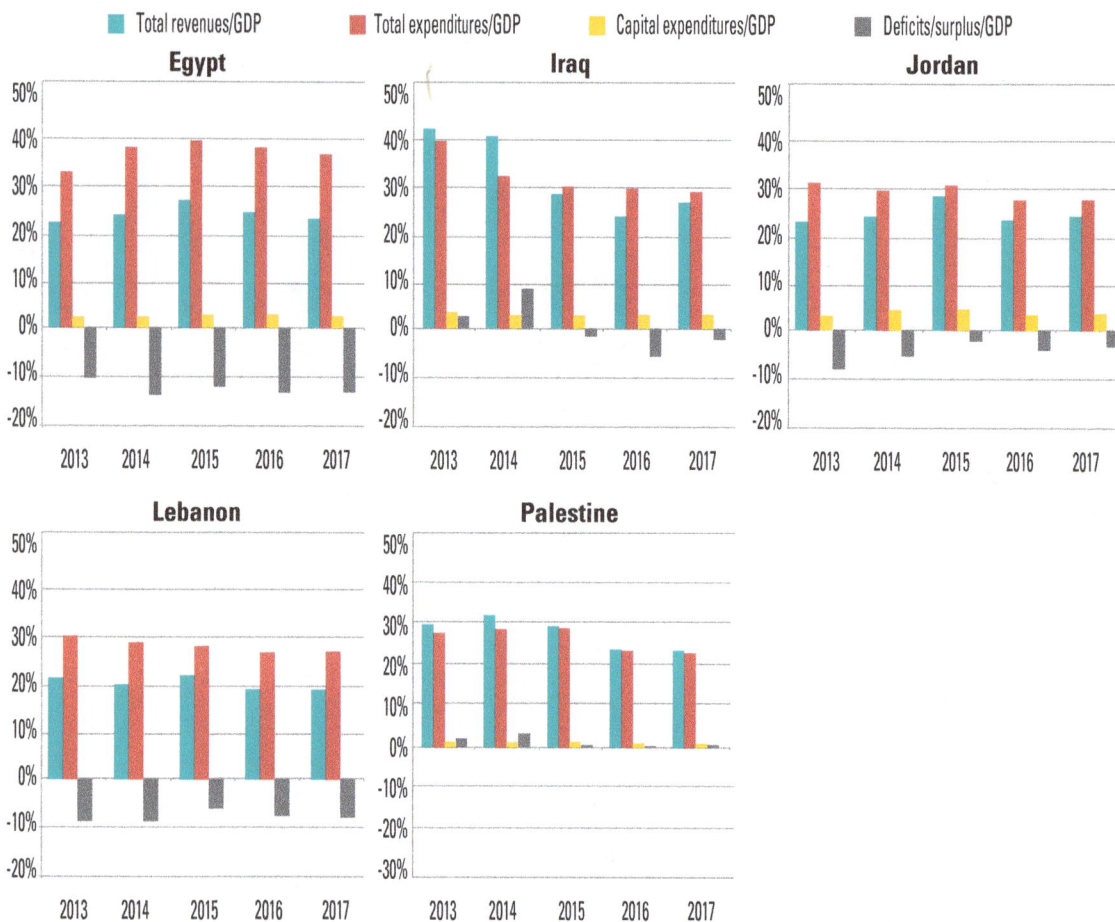

Legend: ■ Total revenues/GDP ■ Total expenditures/GDP ■ Capital expenditures/GDP ■ Deficits/surplus/GDP

Sources: ESCWA staff calculations based on national sources (see appendix). Figures for 2015, 2016 and 2017 are ESCWA staff estimates/projections.
Note: Jordan and Palestine's total revenues include foreign grants. Due to the lack of official statistics, figures for the Syrian Arab Republic are not estimated.

40 per cent of the aid pledged by international donors by the end of March 2016.[2] It is estimated that government expenditure shrank in Egypt, Iraq, Jordan, Lebanon and Palestine in 2015 (figure 2.8), reflecting tight revenue conditions and fiscal prudence. The budget deficit of Egypt is estimated at 13.8 per cent of GDP in 2015 and is set to narrow slightly to 13.7 per cent in 2016. The respective figures for Iraq, Jordan and Lebanon are 1.7 per cent (5.9 per cent in 2016), 4.2 per cent (3.5 per cent in 2016 and 7.8 per cent (8.1 per cent in 2016). Palestine ran a budget deficit estimated at 0.5 per cent of GDP in 2015. It could narrow to 0.3 per cent in 2016 if the pledged amount in foreign aid is disbursed smoothly.

In 2016, it is projected that the Mashreq economies will grow by 1.1 per cent on average. It is predicted that the severity of the economic contraction in the Syrian Arab Republic will ease. Crude oil production in Iraq is expected to rise further, compensating for weak domestic demand caused by conflict. Growth in Lebanon and Jordan will remain weak as geopolitical factors weigh on their economic prospects. Rising financing costs are expected to hamper investment in both countries. Egypt is likely to maintain its current growth level, as its potential is capped by the severe balance-of-payments situation. Palestine will experience moderate growth, but it will fall far short of what is needed to rebuild the Gaza Strip. The forecast growth rates for 2016 are: 2.6 per cent for Egypt; 1.5 per cent for Iraq; 1.9 per cent for Jordan; 1.4 per cent for Lebanon; and 3.1 per cent for Palestine. The Syrian Arab Republic is set to undergo a 6.5 per cent economic contraction.

4. Maghreb countries

It is estimated that the economies of the Maghreb subregion contracted by an average of 1.6 per cent in 2015, after a contraction of 6.4 per cent in 2014. The situation in Libya, where the economy is set to continue contracting for three consecutive years, weighed heavily on the subregional figures. Domestic demand in Libya has crashed in the wake of political instability and armed conflict. A degree of oil and gas production was maintained, but it was insufficient to prevent the Libyan economy from shrinking. An increase in agricultural output gave a boost to growth in Morocco,

while other sectors maintained stable growth. Tunisia experienced a severe deceleration as a worsening balance of payments hampered expansion in domestic demand. A series of security incidents hit the tourism sector, thus contributing to a significant decline in services exports. Public investment remained high in Algeria, which sustained domestic demand growth despite declining oil and gas revenues. Estimated growth rates for 2015 are 3.2 per cent for Algeria; 4.3 per cent for Morocco; and 0.8 per cent for Tunisia. The Libyan economy is estimated to have contracted by 22 per cent.

A relative decline in the price of energy compared with other goods impacted the geographical pattern of trade in the subregion. Trade links with Europe remained strong but the value of total exports to Europe declined significantly (figure 2.9B) due to falling energy exports from Algeria and Libya. Europe accounted for an estimated 64.8 per cent of the subregion's gross total exports in 2015, followed by the Asia-Pacific region (11.4 per cent), North America (6.9

Figure 2.9 Geographical trade structure: Maghreb countries

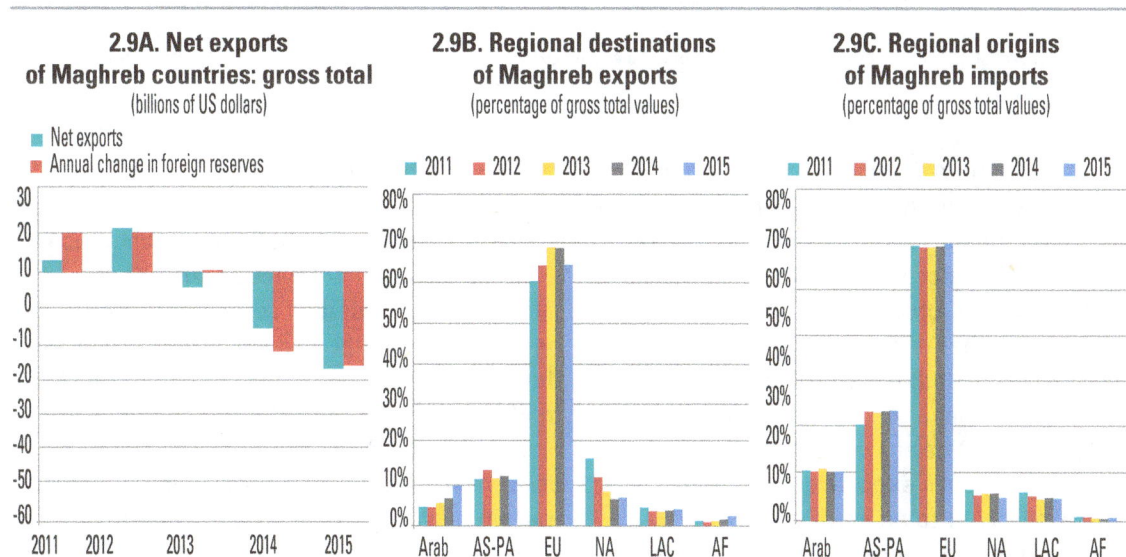

2.9A. Net exports of Maghreb countries: gross total (billions of US dollars)

2.9B. Regional destinations of Maghreb exports (percentage of gross total values)

2.9C. Regional origins of Maghreb imports (percentage of gross total values)

Sources: ESCWA staff calculations based on IMF, Directions of Trade Statistics and International Financial Statistics. Available from www.imf.org/en/Data.

Abbreviations: Arab, Arab countries; AS-PA, Asia and the Pacific; EU, Europe; NA, North America; LAC, Latin America and the Caribbean; AF, Africa excluding Arab countries.

Figure 2.10 Trade and current account balances: Maghreb countries

■ Trade balance (goods)/GDP   ■ Current account/GDP

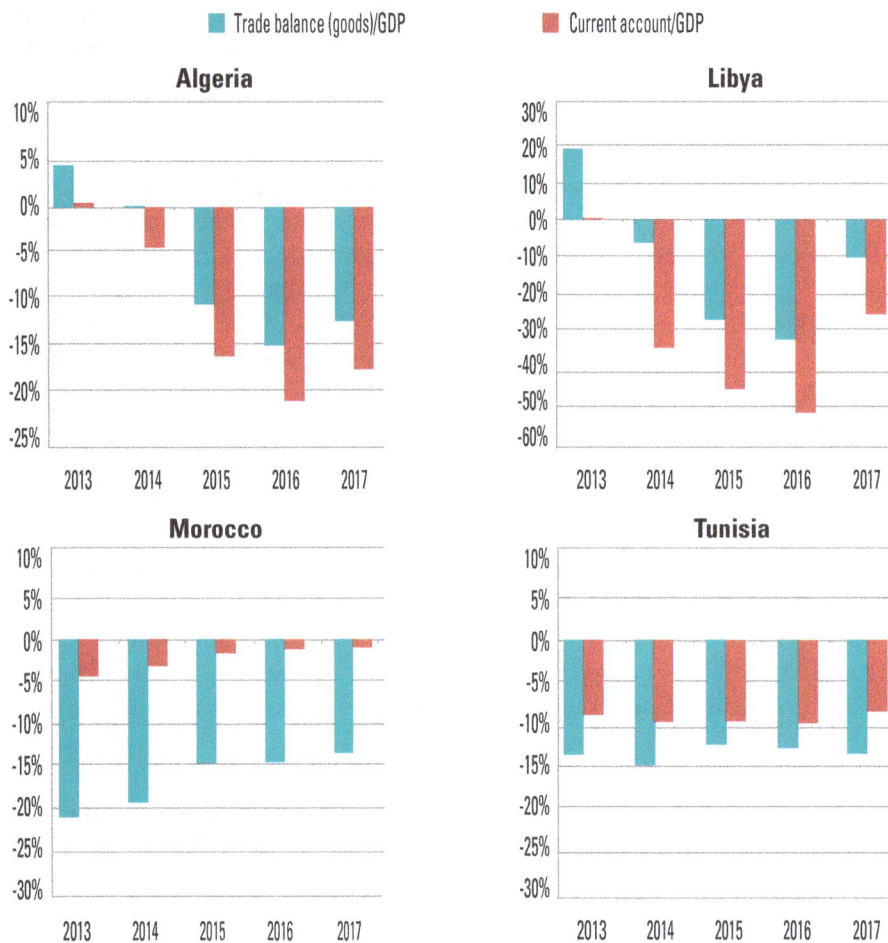

Sources: ESCWA staff calculations based on national sources (see appendix). Figures for 2015, 2016 and 2017 are ESCWA staff estimates/projections.

per cent), Latin America and the Caribbean (4.1 per cent) and Africa (2.4 per cent). Europe remained the largest source of imports to the subregion, accounting for an estimated 56.9 per cent of gross total imports in 2015, followed by the Asia-Pacific (22.6 per cent), North America (4.8 per cent), Latin America and the Caribbean (4.6 per cent) and Africa (0.8 per cent). The share of intra-Arab trade in the subregion's exports grew from 6.7 per cent in 2014 to an estimated 10 per cent in 2015, mainly owing to changing terms of trade. The share of intra-Arab trade in terms of imports crept up from 10 per cent in 2014 to 10.1 per cent in 2015.

The Maghreb remained a net importer in 2015 (figure 2.9A). However, a moderate inflow of funds resulting from merchandise trade deficits that were less marked than falling foreign reserves somewhat offset net resources outflows. The current account deficits of Algeria and Libya widened quickly in 2015 because of the sharp fall in energy exports (figure 2.10). The trade and current accounts of Morocco improved as the deficit margin narrowed significantly in 2015. Morocco benefited more than other countries from improved terms of trade due to lower energy prices. Tunisia also saw an improved trade balance, but its current

Figure 2.11 Monetary indicators: Maghreb countries

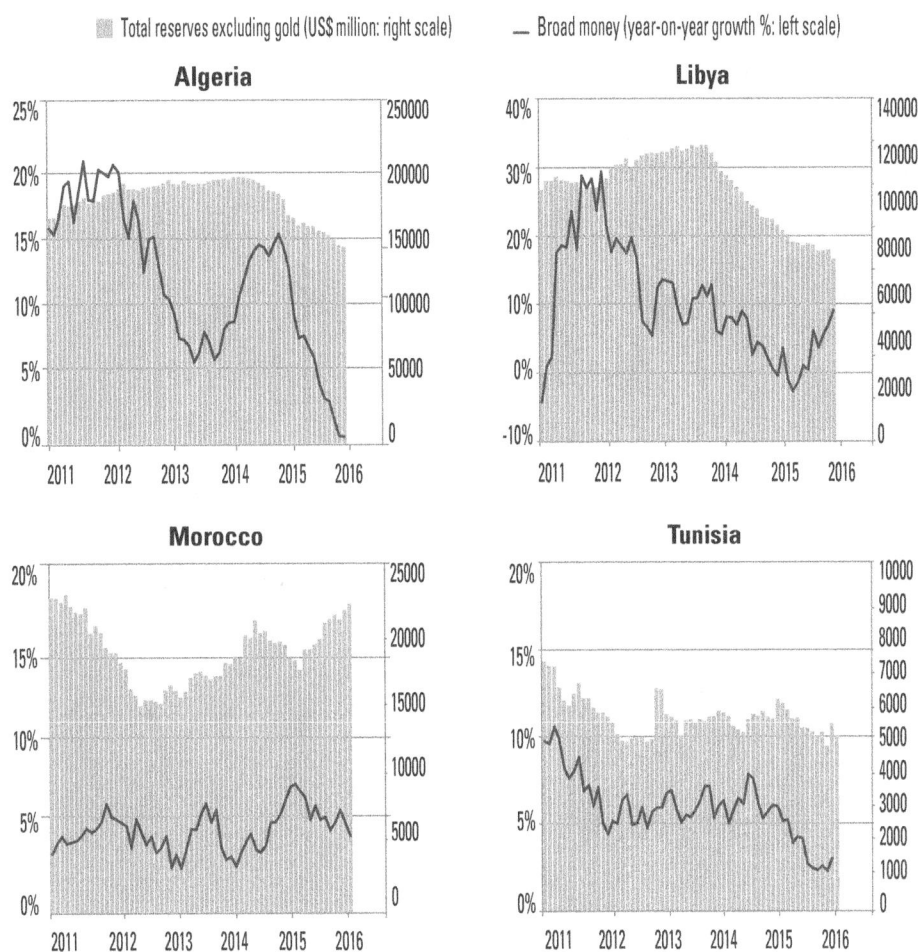

Total reserves excluding gold (US$ million: right scale) — Broad money (year-on-year growth %: left scale)

Algeria

Libya

Morocco

Tunisia

Source: ESCWA staff calculations based on IMF International Financial Statistics. Available from www.imf.org/en/Data.

account deficits remained high due to dwindling tourism.

With reduced current account deficits and consistent capital inflows, Morocco was an exception in the region, experiencing sizeable foreign reserves accumulation in 2015 (figure 2.11). Although broad money growth stagnated, Morocco maintained healthy domestic demand expansion. That was not so in Tunisia, where foreign reserves and broad money stock growth declined, or Algeria, where lower foreign reserves and decelerating broad money growth indicate a slowdown in private sector activities. In spite of quickly

depleting foreign reserves, broad money growth actually accelerated in Libya. However, that coincided with creeping inflation towards the end of 2015, which does not necessarily contribute to growth in domestic demand.

In 2015, government revenues in terms of GDP are estimated to have increased in Algeria and Libya, and declined moderately in Morocco and Tunisia (figure 2.12). Government expenditure grew in Algeria, and shrank in Libya, Morocco and Tunisia in terms of GDP. Although aiming at consolidation, Algeria maintained an active fiscal stance, while Morocco and Tunisia took more cautious

Figure 2.12 Fiscal positions: Maghreb countries

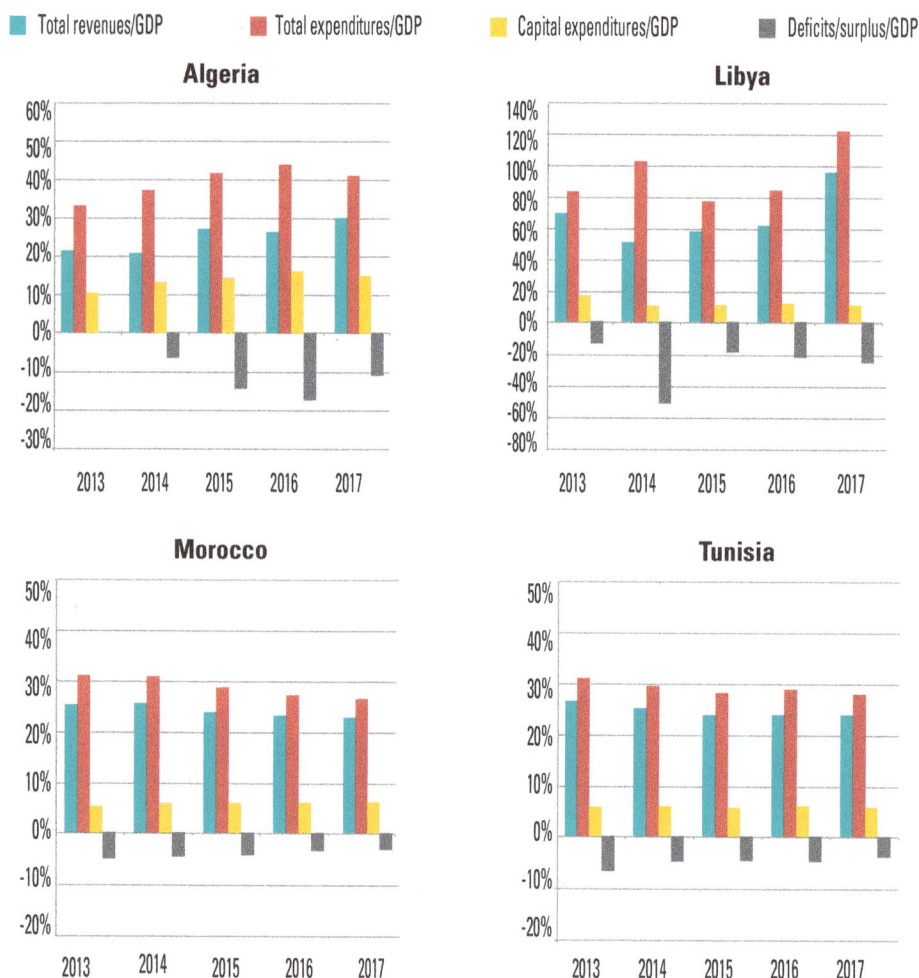

Sources: ESCWA staff calculations based on national sources. Figures for 2015, 2016 and 2017 are ESCWA staff estimates/projections.

fiscal stances. The 2015 budget deficit for Algeria is estimated at 15.8 per cent of GDP, with a forecast of 19.1 per cent in 2016. Deficit estimates/projections for Libya, Morocco and Tunisia are 19 per cent (22.4 per cent in 2016), 4.4 per cent (3.5 per cent in 2016) and 4.8 per cent (5 per cent in 2016).

The Maghreb as a whole is projected to experience 0.7 per cent economic growth in 2016. The continuing contraction in the Libyan economy will lose pace. Although Libya is not under tight financial constraint, the political situation may preclude policymakers from utilizing funds efficiently to tackle balance-of-payments and fiscal constraints. Morocco is set to see slower growth as agricultural production loses steam compared with the previous year. Nevertheless, it may benefit from the space it has created for domestic demand expansion. Such space is likely to remain limited in Tunisia as its severe balance-of-payments situation persists. However, any improvement in the Libyan crisis is likely to benefit Tunisia by a surge of trade and tourism. An active public sector will probably offset dampened private sector activities in Algeria. Like GCC countries, Algeria needs to do more

Figure 2.13 Geographical trade structure: Arab LDCs

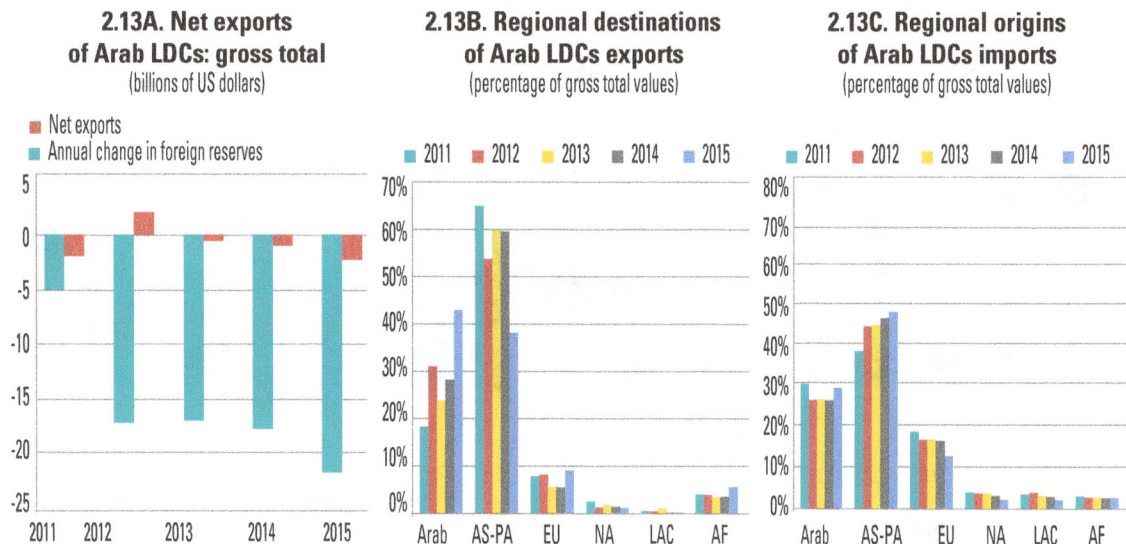

**2.13A. Net exports
of Arab LDCs: gross total**
(billions of US dollars)

**2.13B. Regional destinations
of Arab LDCs exports**
(percentage of gross total values)

**2.13C. Regional origins
of Arab LDCs imports**
(percentage of gross total values)

Sources: ESCWA staff calculations based on IMF, Directions of Trade Statistics and International Financial Statistics. Available from www.imf. org/en/Data.

Abbreviations: Arab, Arab countries; AS-PA, Asia and the Pacific; EU, Europe; NA, North America; LAC, Latin America and the Caribbean; AF, Africa excluding Arab countries.

to diversify the economy. For 2016, the forecast growth rates are 1.7 per cent for Algeria, 2.7 per cent for Morocco and 1.6 per cent for Tunisia. The Libyan economy is projected to contract by 5.2 per cent.

5. Arab least developed countries

The economies of the Arab least developed countries (LDCs) are estimated to have contracted by an average of 7.3 per cent in 2015. The Sudan managed to maintain economic expansion despite an ongoing severe balance-of-payments situation. Progress was made on export diversification, and the economy appeared more resilient following the instability that had prevailed since 2012. Growth in Mauritania stagnated as iron ore prices slumped. Mineral-related investment slowed, and growth in the agricultural and fishery sectors was insufficient to maintain the level of domestic demand expansion experienced in previous years. The Comoros maintained a path of low, stable growth in 2015, in line with its

long-term trend. Busy port-related activity driven by the booming Ethiopian economy buoyed growth in Djibouti. Violence in Yemen caused a serious economic contraction as oil and gas production came to a halt in April. Infrastructure was severely damaged in the fighting. Estimated growth rates for 2015 are: 3.6 per cent for the Comoros; 4.7 per cent for Djibouti; 3.7 per cent for Mauritania; 2.7 per cent for Somalia; and 3.2 per cent for the Sudan. It is estimated that the economy in Yemen shrank by 34.6 per cent.

As elsewhere in the Arab region, falling energy prices left their mark on geographical trade patterns. Intra-Arab trade (43 per cent) surpassed that of the Asia-Pacific region (38.2 per cent) in terms of exports in 2015. This can be attributed primarily to a rise in the share of exports from Somalia, the Sudan and Yemen to GCC countries. However, the value of natural resources exports from Mauritania, the Sudan and Yemen fell as unit prices slumped. The Asia-Pacific region remained the largest source of imports (figures 2.13B

Figure 2.14 Trade and current account balances: Arab LDCs

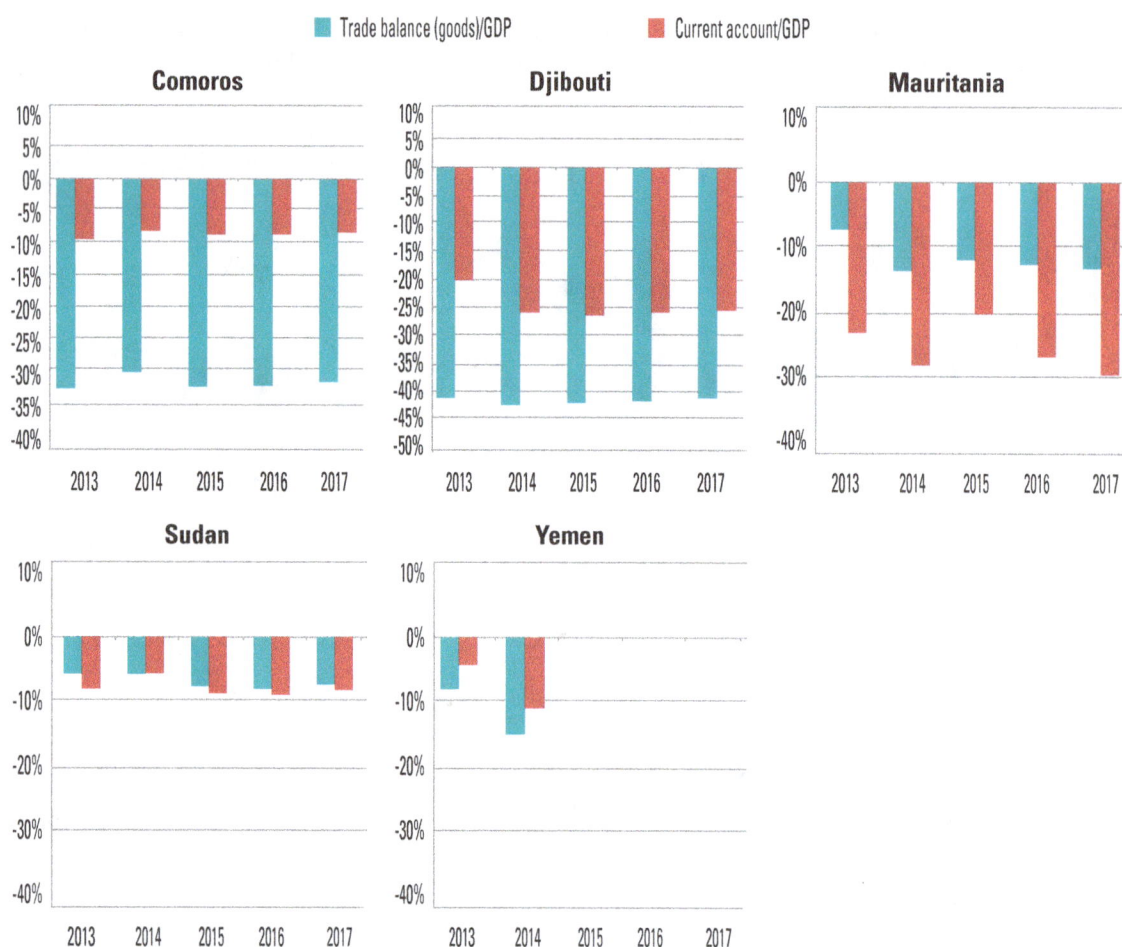

■ Trade balance (goods)/GDP   ■ Current account/GDP

Source: ESCWA staff calculations based on national sources (see appendix): figures for 2015, 2016 and 2017 are ESCWA staff projections.

and 2.13C), accounting for 47.3 per cent, as opposed to 29 per cent of imports coming through intra-Arab trade. Europe accounted for 8.9 per cent of exports from the subregion, followed by Africa (5.4 per cent) and North America (1 per cent). Exports to Latin America and the Caribbean were negligible. Europe accounted for 12.6 per cent of imports into the subregion, followed by Africa (2.6 per cent), North America (2.1 per cent) and Latin America and the Caribbean (also 2.1 per cent).

Arab LDCs are net importers and trade deficits widened in 2015. Other resource flows, such as remittances and foreign aid,

were essential to staving off balance-of-payments crises (figure 2.13A), but latitude for stable domestic demand expansion remained limited. Although better terms of trade benefited Mauritania by narrowing the deficit margin, the high level of domestic demand expansion needed to maintain per capita consumption could easily lead to ballooning external deficits as exports stagnate (figure 2.14). Balance-of-payments constraints tightened in the Comoros and Mauritania and broad money growth dropped sharply (figure 2.15). Given low inflation, high broad money growth in Djibouti indicates a resilience in domestic demand expansion

Figure 2.15 Monetary indicators: Arab LDCs

Total reserves excluding gold (US$ million: right scale) — Broad money (year-on-year growth %: left scale)

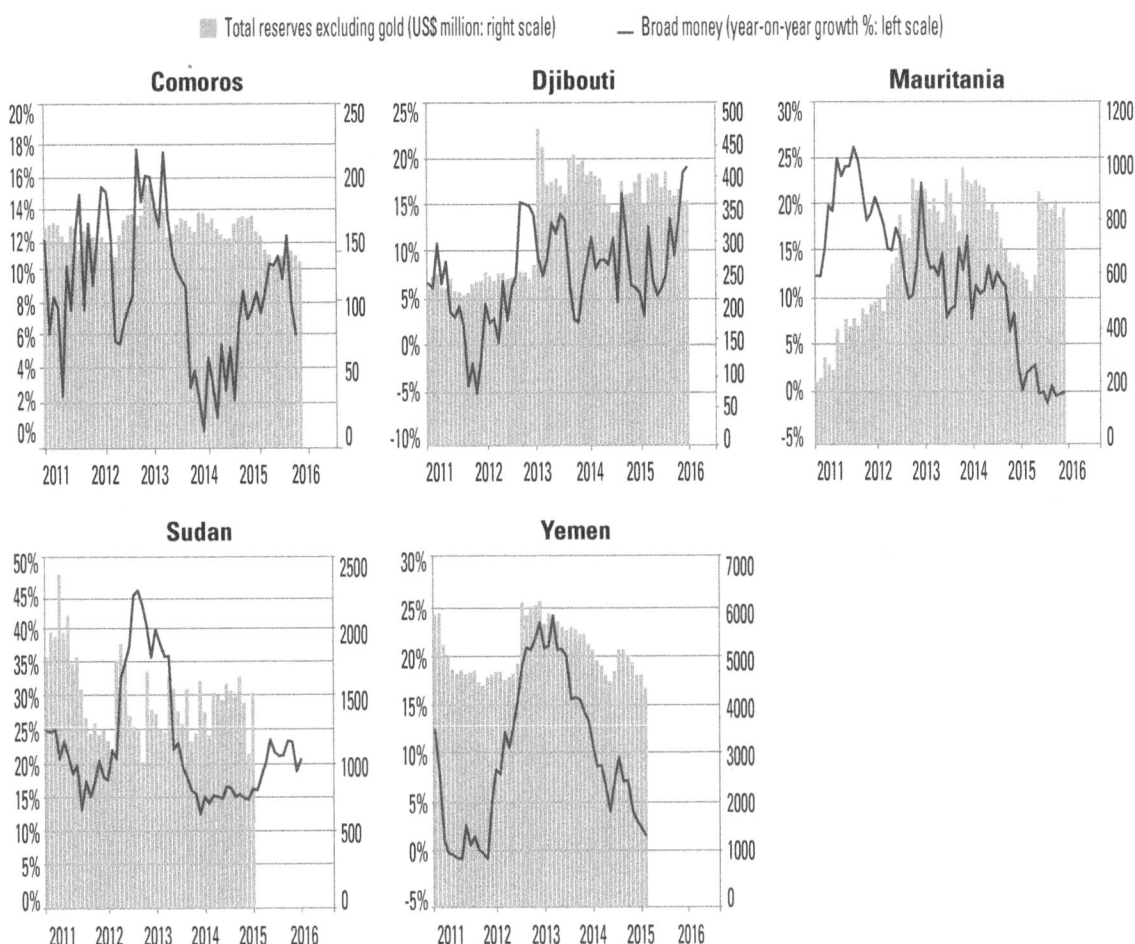

Source: ESCWA staff calculations based on IMF International Financial Statistics. Available from www.imf.org/en/Data.

(table 2.1). In the Sudan, on the other hand, high broad money growth points to money-led inflation as consumer inflation remained high. Domestic demand in Yemen collapsed to subsistence level in 2015. There are mounting difficulties in the delivery of essential goods and signs of hyperinflation.

Government revenues in terms of GDP declined in all Arab LDCs (figure 2.16) but Mauritania, which recorded a moderate increase. The Comoros enjoyed a budget surplus, including foreign grants, in 2015 estimated at 6.7 per cent of GDP. That figure is expected to slip to 4.1 per cent in 2016. Deficit estimates/projections for Djibouti, Mauritania

and the Sudan are: 3.1 per cent (2.8 per cent in 2016); 3.7 per cent (2.3 per cent in 2016); and 3.7 per cent (4.3 per cent in 2016) respectively. In Yemen, the Ministry of Planning estimates the budget deficit at 15.4 per cent of GDP in 2015, up from 4.7 per cent in 2014.[3] According to the Ministry, 84 per cent of the deficit was financed through an overdraft from the Central Bank of Yemen. In Somalia, reconstruction accelerated in 2015, with more State institutions rebuilt, and the budget process became more transparent. Government expenditure has grown from $151 million in 2014 to $246 million in 2016.[4] Some 43 per cent of revenue for that period came from international

Figure 2.16 Fiscal positions: Arab LDCs

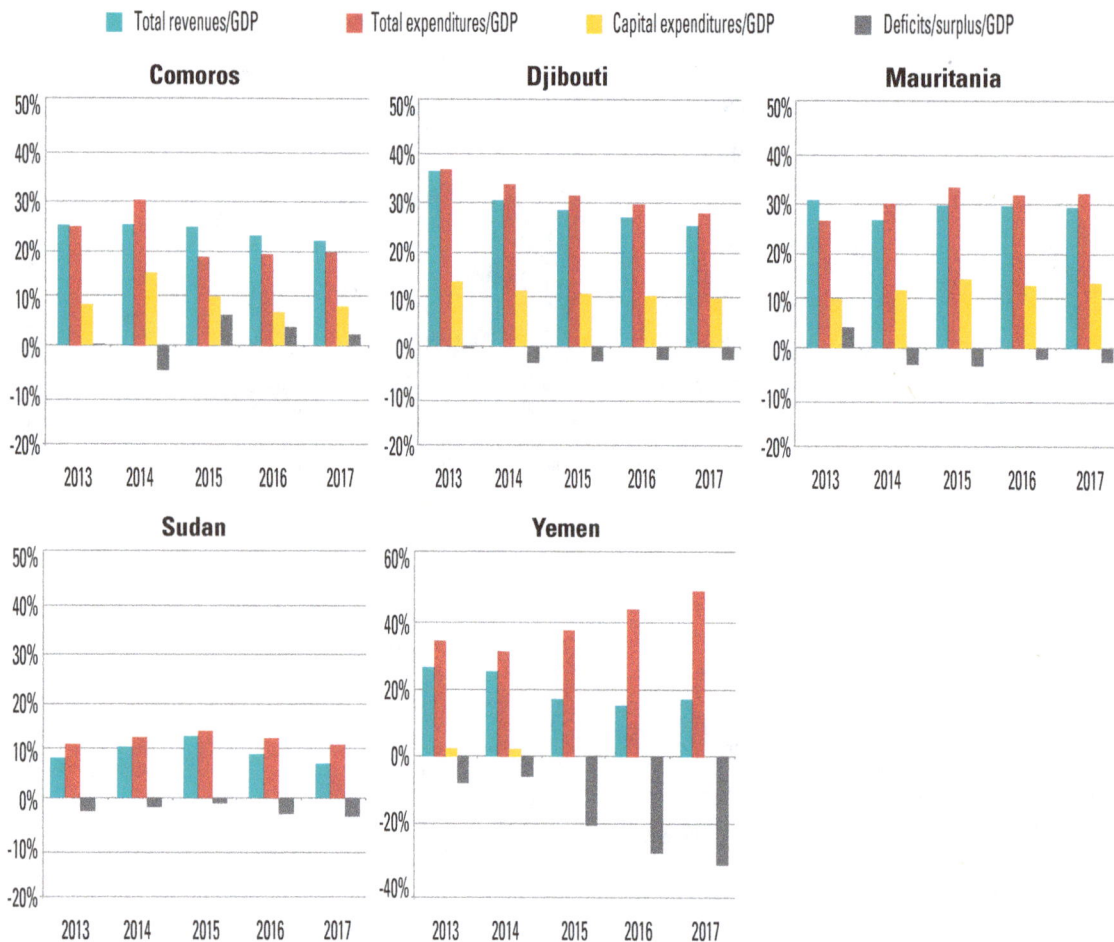

Legend: ■ Total revenues/GDP   ■ Total expenditures/GDP   ■ Capital expenditures/GDP   ■ Deficits/surplus/GDP

Charts: Comoros, Djibouti, Mauritania, Sudan, Yemen (2013–2017)

Sources: ESCWA staff calculations based on national sources (see appendix).
Note: Figures include foreign grants. Figures for 2015, 2016 and 2017 are ESCWA staff estimates/projections.

donors, but ongoing reconstruction and emerging economic activities are expected to broaden the Government's revenue base.

The real GDP of the Arab LDCs is forecast to slip by 0.5 per cent on average in 2016. More space for an expansion in domestic demand is likely to open up for the Sudan, as its balance-of-payments situation improves moderately. Economic expansion in Mauritania will decelerate as a result of weak domestic demand growth and a continuing decline in foreign capital inflows. The poor prospects for iron ore prices are weighing on the balance of

payments, which in turn will hamper domestic demand expansion. In Yemen, the implosion of domestic demand and destruction of infrastructure will lead to negative growth. The scale of the problem will depend on developments in the security situation. Djibouti will maintain a high growth path based on increased port activities and trade with neighbouring Ethiopia and Somalia. A moderate boost in infrastructure building in the Comoros should encourage a mild increase in growth. Reconstruction of infrastructure is expected to continue in Somalia. The forecast GDP growth rates in 2016 are: 4 per cent for the

Comoros, 5 per cent for Djibouti, 3.4 per cent for Mauritania, 3.4 per cent for Somalia and 3.6 per cent for the Sudan. The Yemeni economy is projected to contract by 11.1 per cent in real GDP terms.

B. Policy challenges

Policymakers in the Arab region continued to face substantial constraints in 2015, preventing them from acting to stimulate domestic demand. A tighter monetary stance, paired with rising financing costs, particularly in GCC countries, would brake growth in the region considerably, given that the fiscal side was already tightened following the oil price plunge last year.

The United States Federal Reserve decided on 16 December 2015 to raise interest rates by 0.25 percentage points, shifting the target band for the federal funds rate from a range of 0 to 0.25 per cent to a range of 0.25 to 0.5. That had an impact on the monetary policy of countries in the region that peg their currencies, officially or unofficially, to the dollar: Bahrain, Djibouti, Jordan, Lebanon, Oman, Qatar, Saudi Arabia and the United Arab Emirates. That also applied to monetary policy in Kuwait, where the currency is pegged to a basket of currencies in which the dollar is significantly weighted. The central banks of Bahrain, Kuwait, Saudi Arabia and the United Arab Emirates thus raised their deposit rates by 0.25 percentage points following the rate rise in the United States (figure 2.17).

The impact of those policy changes, however, was limited in the first half of 2016, in part because the financial markets in the United States and the Arab region had anticipated the changes. However, several worrying signs were observed. Despite the deposit rate hike, Bahrain, Kuwait, Saudi Arabia and the United Arab Emirates maintained their current lending

policy rates, thereby aiming to avoid an undue tightening of their monetary stances and maintain stable exchange rate pegs. However, money market lending rates in GCC countries crept up during the first half of 2016. Financing costs are expected to rise further in GCC countries in line with United States monetary policy and due to the "crowding out" effect of the expected increase in government bonds issuance.

In 2015, key interest rates were lowered in Egypt (in January), Jordan (in January, February and July) and Tunisia (in October) as inflationary pressures receded owing to lower prices for commodities, including energy and food items. In 2016, Morocco followed that trend and lowered its policy interest rate (March). However, a deteriorating balance-of-payments situation forced Egypt to reverse its monetary stance by raising its policy interest rates in December 2015, March 2016 and June 2016. Considering the recent turbulent international financial environment, it is unlikely that Arab central banks will adopt monetary easing measures in the near future. Egypt and Tunisia may indeed tighten their monetary stances to cope with tight balance-of-payments situations.

Under these difficult circumstances, policymakers in the region will be looking at diversifying revenues sources, including through the strategic use of debt issuances. GCC countries are expected to issue more sovereign bonds in international capital markets in 2016, following successful issuances in 2015. Applying active assets-liability management may keep the borrowing cost down while maintaining the value of assets. As reflected in the Saudi Vision 2030 plan, coordination between monetary, fiscal and asset management will be important in GCC countries. Diversification of revenue sources is equally important in the other subregions, but needs to be approached in such a way so as not to adversely affect the poorer segments of society.

Figure 2.17 Policy interest rates 2009-2016: selected Arab countries

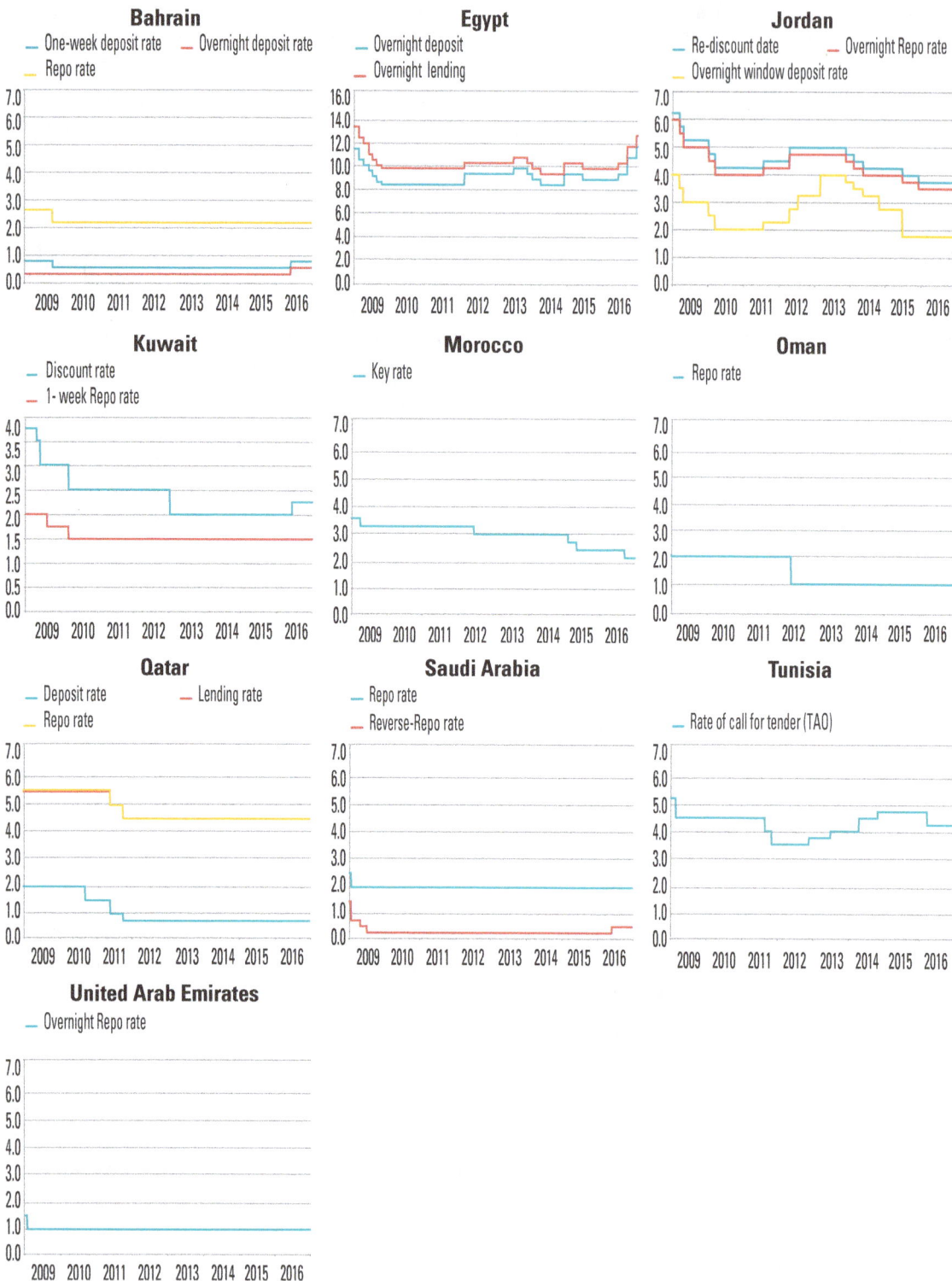

Bahrain
— One-week deposit rate   — Overnight deposit rate
— Repo rate

Egypt
— Overnight deposit
— Overnight lending

Jordan
— Re-discount date   — Overnight Repo rate
— Overnight window deposit rate

Kuwait
— Discount rate
— 1- week Repo rate

Morocco
— Key rate

Oman
— Repo rate

Qatar
— Deposit rate   — Lending rate
— Repo rate

Saudi Arabia
— Repo rate
— Reverse-Repo rate

Tunisia
— Rate of call for tender (TAO)

United Arab Emirates
— Overnight Repo rate

Sources: Bahrain, Central Bank of Bahrain; Egypt, Central Bank of Egypt; Jordan, Central Bank of Jordan; Kuwait, Central Bank of Kuwait; Morocco, Bank Al-Maghreb; Oman, Central Bank of Oman; Qatar, Qatar Central Bank; Saudi Arabia, Saudi Arabian Monetary Agency; Tunisia, Central Bank of Tunisia; United Arab Emirates, Central Bank of the United Arab Emirates.

C. Socioeconomic developments and gender dynamics

1. Introduction

The situation of women in the Arab region has been examined from social, economic, humanitarian and political angles. Women account for 45 per cent of the population of the region[5] and the advancement of Arab countries will depend greatly on their involvement in the economy and society.

Improving the situation of women in terms of education, health, employment and political representation has a direct impact on the economic and development performance of society. Providing women with equal access to education and economic opportunities can improve productivity and competitiveness. Including women in the policymaking process broadens representation and thereby contributes to healthier policy choices.

Women in the Arab region are subject to various infringements of their rights and freedoms. Although progress towards gender equality has been achieved, obstacles born of tradition or the misinterpretation of religion continue to stand in the way of change.

In this section, we focus on the situation of women with regard to humanitarian development, political representation and labour market representation.

2. Gender Inequality Index and Gender Gap Index

The United Nations Development Programme (UNDP) uses the Gender Inequality Index (GII) to measure gender disparity in its yearly Human Development Report.[6] According to the GII, progress on gender inequality has been slight in recent years, with a GII value of 0.537 in 2014 compared with 0.564 in 2013. In 2014, the Arab region ranked fifth out of six regions, with sub-Saharan Africa at the bottom and

Europe and Central Asia at the top of the chart (figure 2.18).

In the Arab region, Libya, the United Arab Emirates and Tunisia have the most positive rankings. Yemen continues to rank worst (figure 2.19) and, with a score of 0.744, ranked last out of the 155 countries measured in the 2014 index. In Yemen, women hold only 0.7 per cent of seats in parliament, and only 8.6 per cent of adult women receive at least a secondary school education, compared with 26.7 per cent of their male counterparts. For every 100,000 live births, 270 women die of causes related to pregnancy; the adolescent birth rate is 47 births per 1,000 women aged 15-19; and female participation in the labour market is 25.4 per cent, compared with 72.2 for men.

Libya has a GII value of 0.134, ranking it 27th out of 155 countries in the 2014 index and the top performer in the Arab region. In Libya, 16 per cent of parliamentary seats are held by women, and 55.5 per cent of adult women receive at least a secondary school education, compared with 41.9 per cent of their male counterparts. For every 100,000 live births, 15 women die of pregnancy-related causes; the adolescent birth rate is 2.5 births per 1,000 women aged 15-19; and female participation in the labour market is 30 per cent, compared with 76.4 per cent for men.

Elsewhere in the Maghreb, Tunisia ranks 48th and Morocco ranks 117th, with a GII value of 0.525. In Morocco, women hold 11 per cent of seats in parliament, and 20.7 per cent of adult women receive at least a secondary school education, as opposed to 30.2 per cent of their male counterparts. Female participation in the labour market is 26.5 per cent, compared with 75.8 for men.

Among the GCC countries, Kuwait, with a GII score of 0.387, ranks 79th in the 2014 index. In Kuwait, 55.6 per cent of adult women receive at least a secondary school education, compared with to 56.3 per cent of their male counterparts. Women hold 1.5 per cent of seats in parliament.[7] For every 100,000 live births, 14 women die of causes related to pregnancy;[8] female participation in the labour market is 43.6 per cent, compared with 83.1 for men. By way of comparison, Oman ranks 53rd and Qatar 116th.

Figure 2.18 Gender Inequality Index 2014: by region

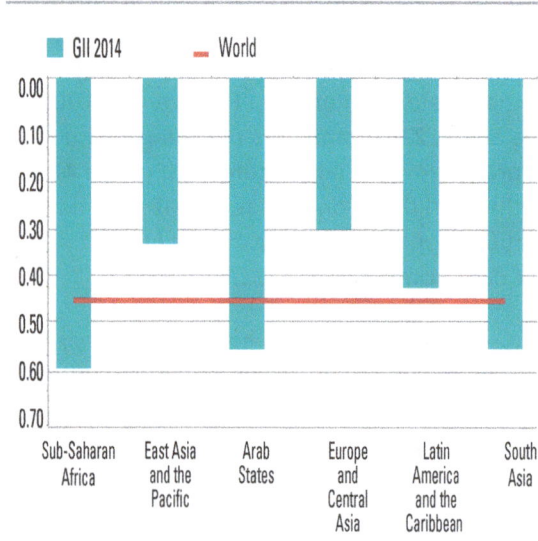

Source: ESCWA staff calculations based on UNDP, *Human Development Report 2015*, pp. 224-227, table 5.

The World Economic Forum Gender Gap Index (GGI) reveals gaps in access to resources between men and women regardless of the level of available resources.[9] In 2015, 145 countries were measured using the index.

At the regional level, North America held the top spot on the overall Global Gender Gap Index in 2015, followed by Europe and Central Asia, Latin America and the Caribbean, sub-Saharan Africa, Asia and the Pacific and, lastly, the Middle East and North Africa (figure 2.20).

Iceland held the top spot in the 2015 GGI report, followed closely by Norway and Finland. The bottom three were the Syrian Arab Republic, Pakistan and Yemen.

There was little change between 2014 and 2015 in the Arab region, which continues to rank last (figure 2.20), having closed 60 per cent of its gender gap.[10] Kuwait and the United Arab Emirates remain the top performers, with the GGI rankings of 117th and 119th place respectively. Yemen has been the lowest-ranked country in the index since 2006,

Figure 2.19 Gender Inequality Index: by country, 2013 and 2014

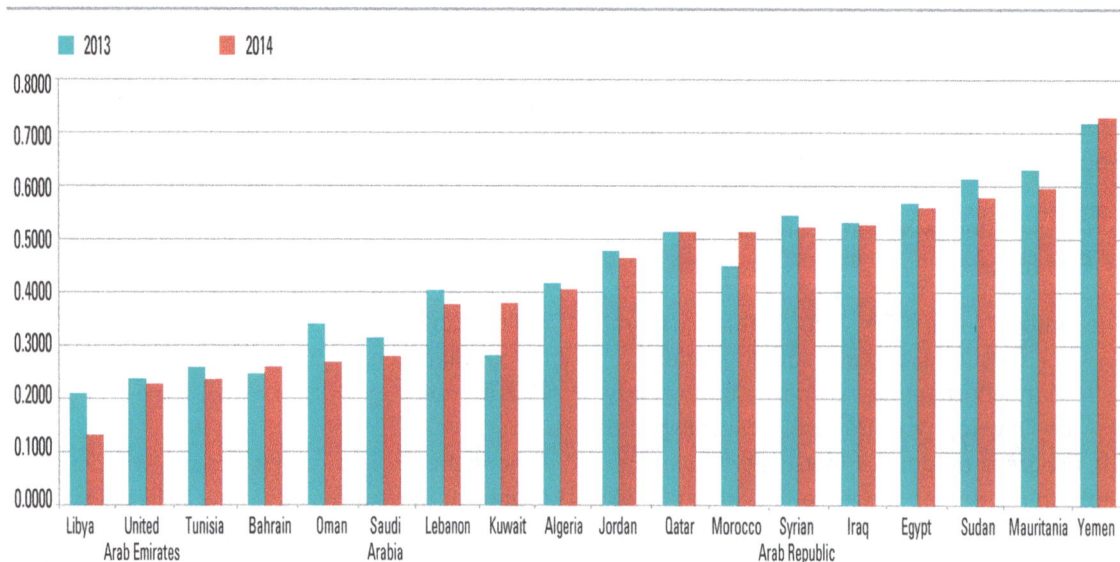

Source: ESCWA staff calculations based on UNDP, *Human Development Report 2015*, pp. 224-227, table 5.

despite having closed more than 48 per cent of its gender gap during the past decade.

Qatar occupies the highest spot among Arab countries in the economic participation

Figure 2.20 Gender Gap Index 2015: by region

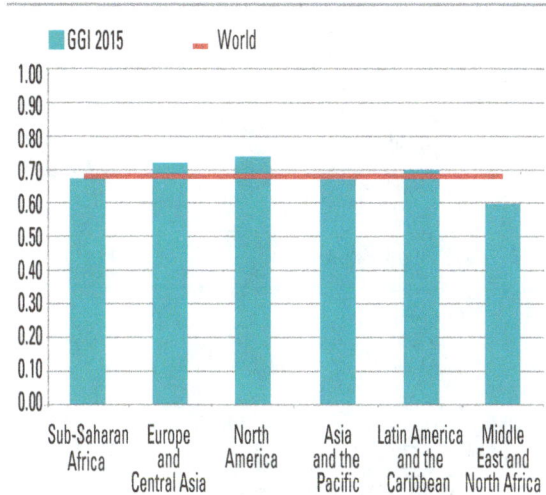

Source: ESCWA staff calculations based on WEF, *The Global Gender Gap Report 2015*. Available from reports.weforum.org/global-gender-gap-report-2015/.
Note: Regional average scores are weighted by population using population data from the World Bank's World Development Indicators online database.

subindex (figure 2.21), ranking 97th. On the political subindex, Algeria ranks highest among Arab countries in 55th place. Kuwait tops Arab countries on the education subindex, ranking 77th. On the health subindex, Mauritania takes first place among the Arab countries, in 87th place.

GGI 10-year analysis concluded that Saudi Arabia was the most improved country relative to its starting point on the economic participation and opportunity subindex, while the United Arab Emirates was the most improved on the political empowerment subindex. In contrast, Jordan lost the most ground relative to its past performance on economic participation.

Gender equality reforms in some countries have not necessarily contributed to closing the gender gap. Egypt ranked 136th out of 145 countries in 2015, compared with 125th in 2013, despite constitutional and legal reforms carried out in 2014. This shows that the gender gap will continue to widen without proper institutional reinforcement mechanisms to activate and implement reforms.[11]

Figure 2.21 Gender Gap Index 2015 subindices

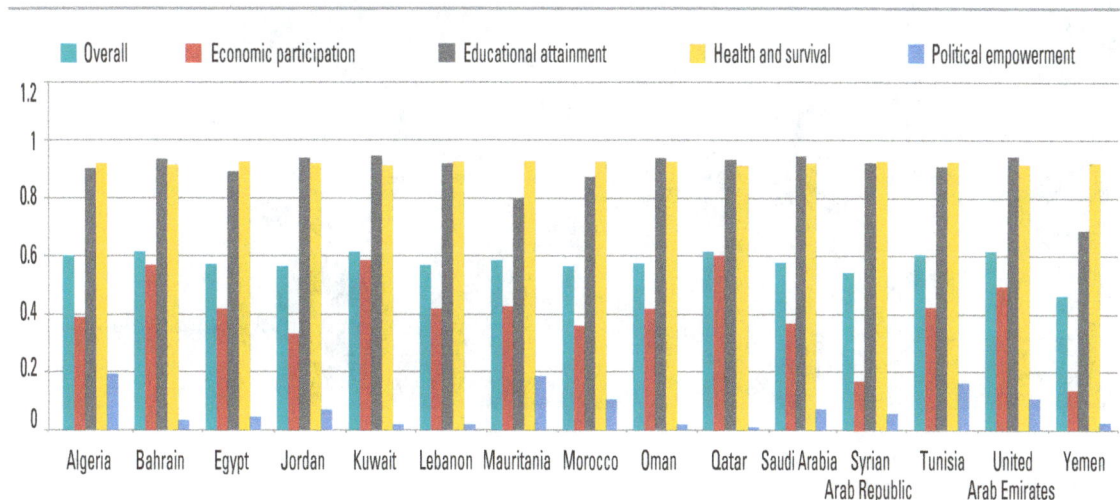

Source: ESCWA staff calculations based on WEF, *The Global Gender Gap Report 2015*. Available from reports.weforum.org/global-gender-gap-report-2015/.

Table 2.2 Women in national parliaments: comparison 2015 – 2016

	Country	As at 1 January 2015				As at 1 February 2016			
		Lower or Single House				Lower or Single House			
		Elections	Seats[a]	Women	Percentage of women	Elections	Seats[a]	Women	Percentage of women
1	Algeria[b]	5/2012	462	146	31.60	5/2012	462	146	31.60
2	Bahrain	11/2014	40	3	7.50	11/2014	40	3	7.50
3	Comoros	12/2009	33	1	3.00	1/2015	33	1	3.00
4	Djibouti[b]	2/2013	55	7	12.70	2/2013	55	7	12.70
5	Egypt[c]	-	-	-	-	10/2015	596	89	14.90
6	Iraq[b]	4/2014	328	87	26.50	4/2014	328	87	26.50
7	Jordan[b]	1/2013	150	18	12.00	1/2013	150	18	12.00
8	Kuwait	7/2013	65	1	1.50	7/2013	65	1	1.50
9	Lebanon	6/2009	128	4	3.10	6/2009	128	4	3.10
10	Libya	6/2014	188	30	16.00	6/2014	188	30	16.00
11	Mauritania	11/2013	147	37	25.20	11/2013	147	37	25.20
12	Morocco[b]	11/2011	395	67	17.00	11/2011	395	67	17.00
13	Oman	10/2011	84	1	1.20	10/2015	85	1	1.20
14	State of Palestine[c]	-	-	-	-	-	-	-	-
15	Qatar	7/2013	35	0	0.00	7/2013	35	0	0.00
16	Saudi Arabia	1/2013	151	30	19.90	1/2013	151	30	19.90
17	Sudan[b]	4/2010	354	86	24.30	4/2015	426	130	30.50
18	Syrian Arab Republic	5/2012	250	31	12.40	5/2012	250	31	12.40
19	Tunisia[b]	10/2014	217	68	31.30	10/2014	217	68	31.30
20	United Arab Emirates	9/2011	40	7	17.50	9/2011	40	9	22.50
21	Yemen	4/2003	301	1	0.30	4/2003	300	0	0.00

Source: Inter-Parliamentary Union, women in national parliaments as of 1 January 2015 and 1 February 2016. Available from www.ipu.org/wmn-e/arc/classif010115.htm and www.ipu.org/wmn-e/arc/classif010216.htm.

[a] Figures correspond to the number of seats currently filled in parliament.
[b] Quota system in place to reserve number of seats for women in parliament.
[c] Data are unavailable or not separately reported.

3. Political participation

The gradual trend to growing participation by women in parliamentary life in the Arab region continued in 2015, with 17.5 per cent of seats in parliament held by women, compared with 14 per cent in the previous year. In Algeria, the Sudan and Tunisia, the international minimum target of 30 per cent of decision-making positions occupied by women established under the Beijing Declaration and Platform for Action was exceeded. Nevertheless, the region as a whole retains one of the poorest records in this respect and is below the international average of 22.5 per cent.

In 2015, Algeria added an article to the Constitution on balancing representation in elected assemblies. In 2011, a clause was added to the electoral law of Tunisia on gender parity in elections, requiring political parties to nominate equal numbers of men and women.

Box 2.1 Promotion of gender equality: from MDGs to SDGs

Goal 5 of the SDGs ("Achieve gender equality and empower all women and girls") follows on from the Millennium Development Goal (MDG) 3, which aimed to promote gender equality and empower women. Development issues as they affect women are also addressed as indicators of progress in several other SDGs (including those related to hunger, poverty, health and education). Under Goal 3 of the MDGs, there has been considerable progress in terms of primary education for women, especially in Oman and Yemen, where female primary school enrolment rose by 5 per cent and 7.9 per cent between 2005 and 2014 respectively. Oman and Mauritania achieved more than 50 per cent enrolment of female students in primary education. Most countries had filled the gap between girls and boys in primary education by 2015, with exceptions, such as Morocco and Yemen. Significant progress was made on the political indicator for women in most countries across the region, but the opposite was true with regard to female participation in the labour force. Goal 5 of the SDGs is more comprehensive than its MDG predecessor and includes nine targets ranging from the elimination of child, early and forced marriage through to recognition of unpaid domestic work and equal opportunities for participation in decision-making.

Figure A Ratio of girls to boys in primary education

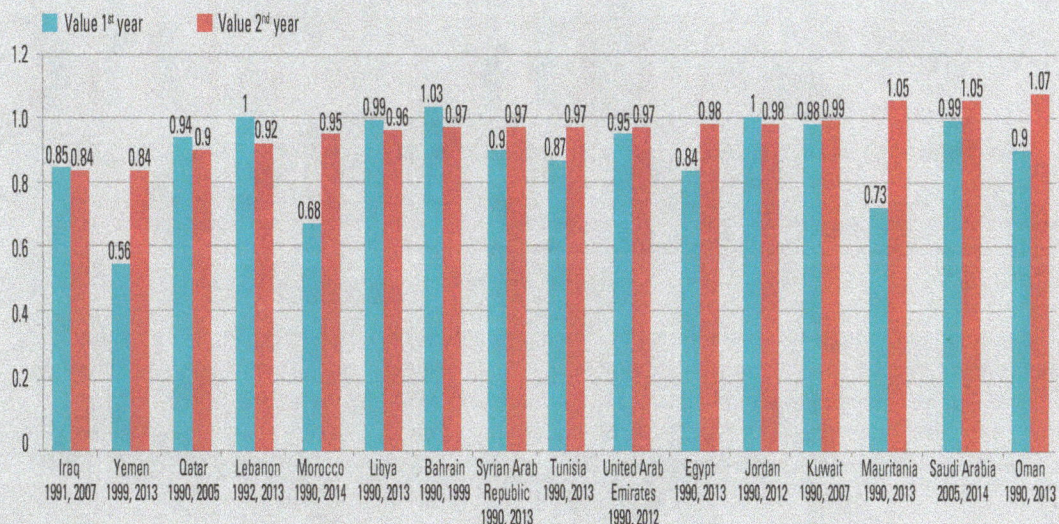

Figure B Share of women in wage employment in the non-agricultural sector (percentage)

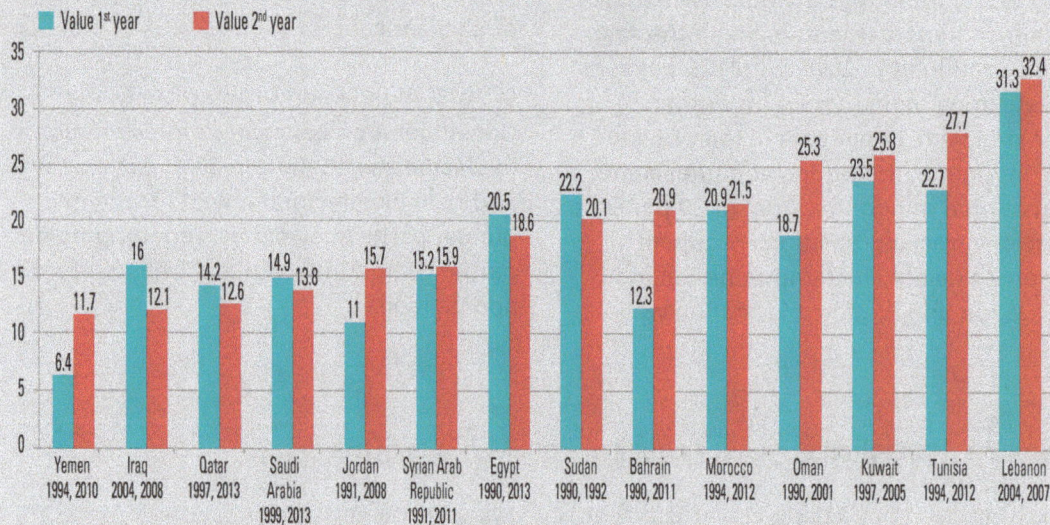

Legend: ■ Value 1st year ■ Value 2nd year

Country / years	Value 1st year	Value 2nd year
Yemen 1994, 2010	6.4	11.7
Iraq 2004, 2008	16	12.1
Qatar 1997, 2013	14.2	12.6
Saudi Arabia 1999, 2013	14.9	13.8
Jordan 1991, 2008	11	15.7
Syrian Arab Republic 1991, 2011	15.2	15.9
Egypt 1990, 2013	20.5	18.6
Sudan 1990, 1992	22.2	20.1
Bahrain 1990, 2011	12.3	20.9
Morocco 1994, 2012	20.9	21.5
Oman 1990, 2001	18.7	25.3
Kuwait 1997, 2005	23.5	25.8
Tunisia 1994, 2012	22.7	27.7
Lebanon 2004, 2007	31.3	32.4

Figure C Proportion of seats held by women in national parliament (single or lower house only – percentage)

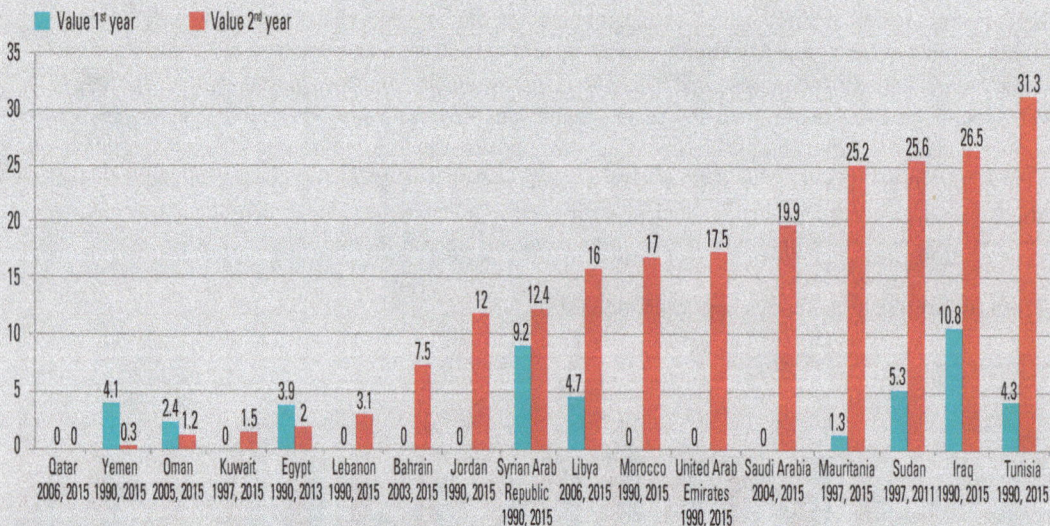

Legend: ■ Value 1st year ■ Value 2nd year

Country / years	Value 1st year	Value 2nd year
Qatar 2006, 2015	0	0
Yemen 1990, 2015	4.1	0.3
Oman 2005, 2015	2.4	1.2
Kuwait 1997, 2015	0	1.5
Egypt 1990, 2013	3.9	2
Lebanon 1990, 2015	0	3.1
Bahrain 2003, 2015	0	7.5
Jordan 1990, 2015	0	12
Syrian Arab Republic 1990, 2015	9.2	12.4
Libya 2006, 2015	4.7	16
Morocco 1990, 2015	0	17
United Arab Emirates 1990, 2015	0	17.5
Saudi Arabia 2004, 2015	0	19.9
Mauritania 1997, 2015	1.3	25.2
Sudan 1997, 2011	5.3	25.6
Iraq 1990, 2015	10.8	26.5
Tunisia 1990, 2015	4.3	31.3

Source: United Nations Statistics Division, Millennium Development Goals Indicators: country and regional progress snapshots. Available from: http://mdgs.un.org/unsd/mdg/Host.aspx?Content=Data/snapshots.htm.

The region faces problems arising from conflict and related issues on human rights, peace and security. Population growth, the youth bulge, high unemployment, rapid urbanization and crowding in cities, large migrant flows, and shortages of arable land, food and water are all factors that will shape implementation of the SDGs in the Arab region. Gender equality is vital to achieving sustainable development, regardless of the policy priorities any one country may set itself. The SDGs provide all Arab countries with added incentive to tackle gender equality and thus stimulate development.

At elections in the Sudan in 2015, women took 130 seats in parliament, or 30.5 per cent of the total. All but two independents were on electoral lists submitted by parties. The result is attributed in part to the National Electoral Law of the Sudan, which allows political parties whose electoral lists that present more than 4 per cent of women candidates to nominate women for reserved seats.

The United Arab Emirates continue to work on enhancing the political representation of women. However, in the 2015 elections, only 78 women candidates stood for election, compared with 85 in 2011. Nine of the 40 members (22.5 per cent) of the Federal National Council are women, only one of whom was directly elected.[12] Women in the United Arab Emirates hold around 30 per cent of decision-making positions and 10 per cent of the jobs in the diplomatic corps. Women hold four ministerial positions, as well as the position of Secretary-General of the Cabinet.

As a result of elections in 2015 in Egypt, women hold around 15 per cent of seats in parliament. Eight parties included 100 women on their electoral lists, and a further 110 ran as independents in the polls. In all, 8.2 per cent of candidates were women.[13] Recent legislation guarantees a minimum of 5 per cent representation for women (70 seats) in a chamber comprising 568 elected representatives and 28 appointed by the President.

In Saudi Arabia, women voted for the first time in the 2015 municipal elections. Women in Kuwait have been entitled to stand in parliamentary elections since 2006. In Morocco, an article on gender parity has been added to the Constitution.

Not all recent elections in the region have resulted in gains for women. In Oman, only 20 women stood for election in 2015, down from 77 in 2011, and only one was elected. Women comprise only 1.2 per cent of the members of parliament and there are growing calls for electoral quotas.

Only a few countries in the Arab region have quota systems for female representation. In Egypt and Jordan, 10 per cent of seats in parliament are reserved for women, while in Saudi Arabia and the Sudan the figure is 20 per cent and 30 per cent respectively. In Egypt, 25 per cent of seats on local councils are also reserved for women. Djibouti (10 per cent), Morocco (15 per cent), Iraq (25 per cent) and Tunisia (50 per cent) have gender quotas for candidate lists.[14] Quotas have so far proven to be the most effective tool for including more women in elected bodies.[15]

Little information is available in the region on the participation of women at the municipality level.

4. Gender dynamics in the labour market

The considerable progress in education for women has not been matched in the workplace. Women in the Arab region continue to face significant hurdles in accessing decent work. More needs to be done to secure decent jobs and improve social protection for women, and to recognize, reduce and redistribute unpaid care and household work.

According to the World Bank, female participation in the labour force averaged 23.4 per cent in 2014, compared with the 75 per cent participation rate for males.[16] That is the lowest regional rate in the world and compares with a world average participation rate of 50 per cent for females and 76.7 per cent for males. The figures do not mean that Arab women are not working or willing to work. Rather, they tend to be heavily involved in the informal sector and unpaid housework and care work, which does not show in official statistics.[17] The informal sector is characterized by poor working conditions, abuse and violence.

Figure 2.22 Regional male and female unemployment rates, 2002-2013

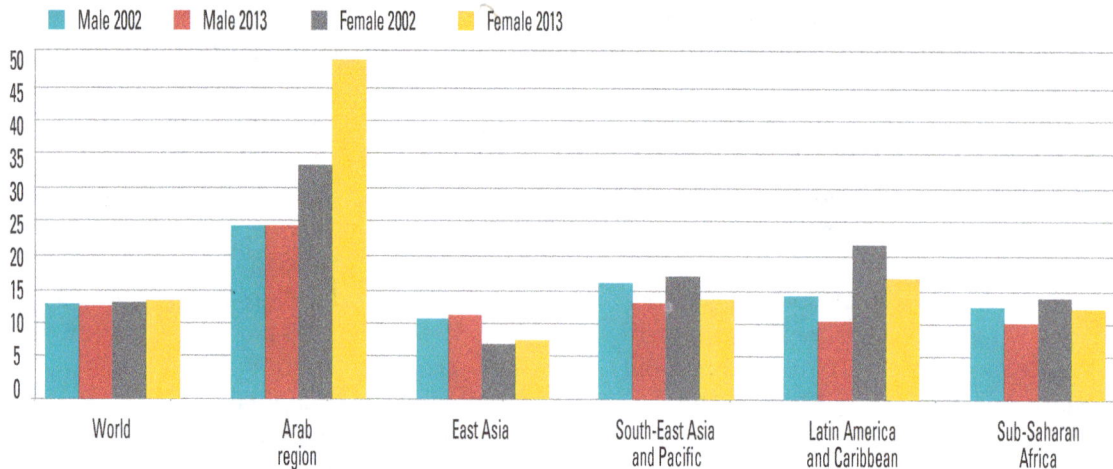

Source: International Labour Organization (ILO), *Key Indicators of the Labour Market (ninth edition)*. Available from http://kilm.ilo.org/2015/install/.

GCC countries score comparatively highly in the region on women's participation in the workforce due to the significant numbers of female migrant workers. In general, the participation of Arab women tails off between the ages 25 of 34 (the most active age group in labour participation for women and men), due to social factors, such as marriage and having children, that lead women to withdraw from the labour market without re-entering afterwards.[18] The Arab region is characterized by a rigid gender-based occupational and sectoral segregation, women tend to concentrate on certain professions that are deemed either convenient or socially acceptable. For example, in GCC countries, women are more represented in the education sector, while in the Maghreb and Mashreq, women are found mostly in agriculture and services. Men on the other hand, are represented in nearly all professions.[19] The public sector is a major employer of women in the Arab region; it offers job stability, relatively good salary and working hours that allow women to balance their work and family responsibilities. In Egypt, three quarters of employees in the public sector are women; in Morocco and Saudi Arabia, nearly half of public sector employees are women.[20]

The Arab region continues to struggle with the highest youth unemployment rates in the world. They reached a peak between 2008 and 2014[21] and rising unemployment was one of the main catalysts for the uprisings in some Arab countries since 2011. An ESCWA study demonstrates the link between unemployment, especially among young people, and the intensity of conflict in the region. As conflict intensity and unemployment grow, the correlation between the two factors intensifies.[22] The region also has one of the highest gender unemployment gaps (figure 2.22). The situation is at its worst for young women. Unemployment for them rose from 31.8 per cent to 46.1 per cent between 2002 and 2013. Large gaps also persist between males and females in other areas, such as pay. Women are still offered lower salaries for the same job. So even for those women who have jobs, employment conditions are poor in terms of wages, social protection, and benefits and entitlements plans, especially in the private sector.

The latest figures from the region confirm that unemployment is rising among women and men throughout the region, with some exceptions such as Qatar and Algeria (figure 2.23). During the past five years, the

Figure 2.23 Unemployment and labour force participation rates (selected countries)

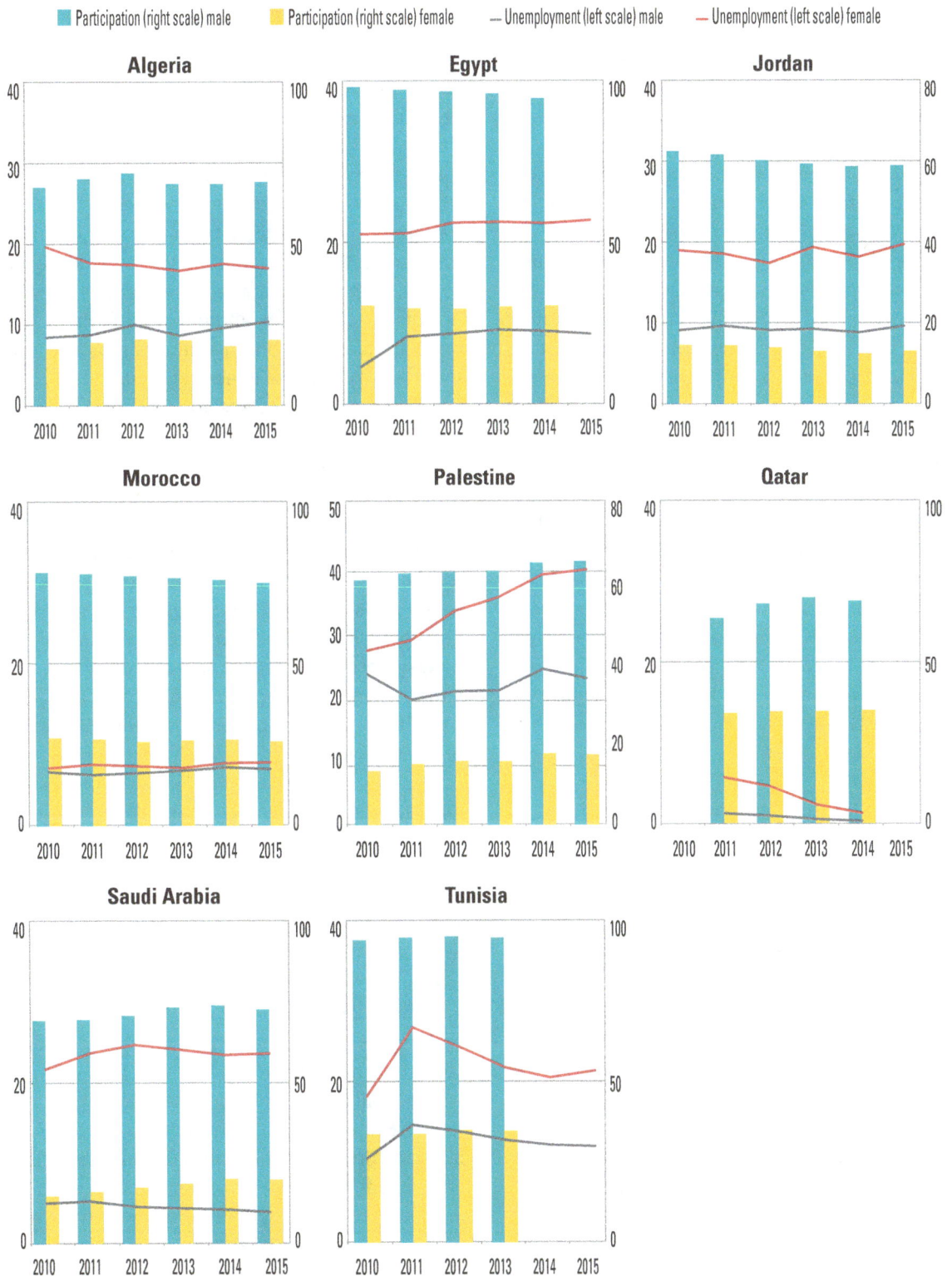

Legend: ■ Participation (right scale) male ■ Participation (right scale) female — Unemployment (left scale) male — Unemployment (left scale) female

Algeria • Egypt • Jordan • Morocco • Palestine • Qatar • Saudi Arabia • Tunisia

Sources: ESCWA staff calculations based on data from national statistical offices (see appendix).

unemployment gap between men and women has also widened in most Arab countries, with exceptions such as Algeria, Morocco and Qatar.

Figures from Qatar are impressive; unemployment is low and the rate for women dropped sharply between 2011 and 2015. Qatar's labour market participation rates averaged 68 per cent for males and 35 per cent for females, with unemployment averaging 1.02 per cent for males and 4.9 per cent for females. Chapter 3 of the Qatari national development strategy addresses the importance of promoting the rights of women as a catalyst for development. The Constitution of Qatar outlaws discrimination based on sex and enshrines the rights to personal freedom, work and education. Under the 2004 Labour Law, women "have the right to equal pay for equal work, equal access to training and promotion opportunities". The 2009 Law of Human Resources Administration defines the rules for appointments to public sector jobs, salaries, allowances, promotions and leave, without distinction between males and females. It grants female workers additional benefits and leave entitlements, including maternity leave and time for breastfeeding newly born babies.[23]

In Palestine, the occupation and regular clashes between Palestinians and the Israeli security forces are straining the economy and driving unemployment higher, particularly among educated youth. The hold over the country's resources by the occupying power and restrictions on movement aggravate the employment situation. They have also impoverished the agricultural sector, which over the past decade formally employed some 13 per cent of the population, and a good deal more informally.[24] While labour force participation for men increased from 66.8 per cent in 2010 to 71.9 per cent in 2015, it remained very low for women, rising from 14.7 per cent in 2010 to 19.1 per cent in 2015. Social, cultural and institutional barriers, Israeli restrictions and the high levels of violence against women, all stop Palestinian women from joining the labour market.

In Saudi Arabia, male unemployment dropped from 7.1 per cent in 2010 to 5.5 per cent in 2015. However, with female unemployment at 33.3 per cent in 2015, the gender gap in unemployment between men and women remains among the highest in the region. Policies aimed at encouraging more Saudi nationals into work have been less successful for women than men. That can be explained in part by the fact that the oil industry tends not to attract women, and the lack of job opportunities for women, who are mostly university graduates in education and the humanities. Nevertheless, the female workforce participation rate rose from 12.9 per cent in 2010 to 17.4 per cent in 2015. The main labour market challenge is the country's heavy reliance on non-Saudis to fill private sector jobs, while Saudis themselves show a growing preference for the public sector, lead to potential skills and salary gaps between Saudis and non-nationals. The country is addressing those issues with its wage protection system, and programmes aimed at encouraging the employment of Saudi nationals and better regulating the status of foreign workers.

Youth and university graduates are the groups most affected in Egypt by unemployment. The situation is expected to worsen in the absence of clear policies to tackle the deteriorating economic and political situation. According to one survey, a staggering 91.1 per cent of young workers in Egypt were in informal employment in 2012.[25] That serves to underscore the problems that young Egyptians face in terms of poor social protection, low wages, lack of health insurance and long working hours. Women continue to have difficulty finding and keeping decent jobs. The gap between men and women remains wide in terms of unemployment and labour market participation. Signs of an upturn in late 2014 provided a glimmer of hope for improvement in the labour market.

In Tunisia, unemployment rose from 14.9 per cent in 2010 to 17.55 per cent in the fourth quarter of 2015. Women have greater difficulty getting work than men. In Jordan, unemployment also rose in the same period, from 10.1 per cent to 11.7 per cent for men and from 20.8 per cent to 23 per cent for women. While 60 per cent of men are active in the labour market, only 13.3 per cent of women participate.

In Morocco, the gap in unemployment between men and women has dropped to around 1 per cent in 2015. The average female participation rate, however, remains low at 24.8 per cent, compared with that of men, at 71.5 per cent.

Conflict and displacement have only made things worse for women, who increasingly find themselves forced to work in the informal sector as the number of households headed by women grows. Egypt, Jordan, Lebanon and Tunisia have been affected by spillover from conflicts in Libya and the Syrian Arab Republic. Chapter 3 of this Survey addresses the effects of conflict on those countries in detail.

There is an oversupply of labour at all levels of education (figure 2.24) and a gap in unemployment rates between men and women, no matter what their level of education (primary, secondary and tertiary). As a rule, the higher the educational attainment, the higher the rate of unemployment, particularly among women. In Saudi Arabia, the unemployment rate for women with only primary education or less was estimated by the International Labour Organization (ILO) at 0.5 per cent in 2009, but at 18 per cent and 31 per cent for women with secondary and tertiary education respectively. Unemployment among people with only primary education or lower is lower in Bahrain, Egypt and the United Arab Emirates than in other countries in the region due to the prevalence of agriculture in their economies.

This situation is typical in countries where education and training systems are not in tune with the skills needs of the economy, including in its most promising growth sectors. Graduates, poorly informed about labour market requirements in their country, end up with educational profiles that are inappropriate for market needs, making their first attempts to

Figure 2.24 Unemployment by level of education (latest available year)

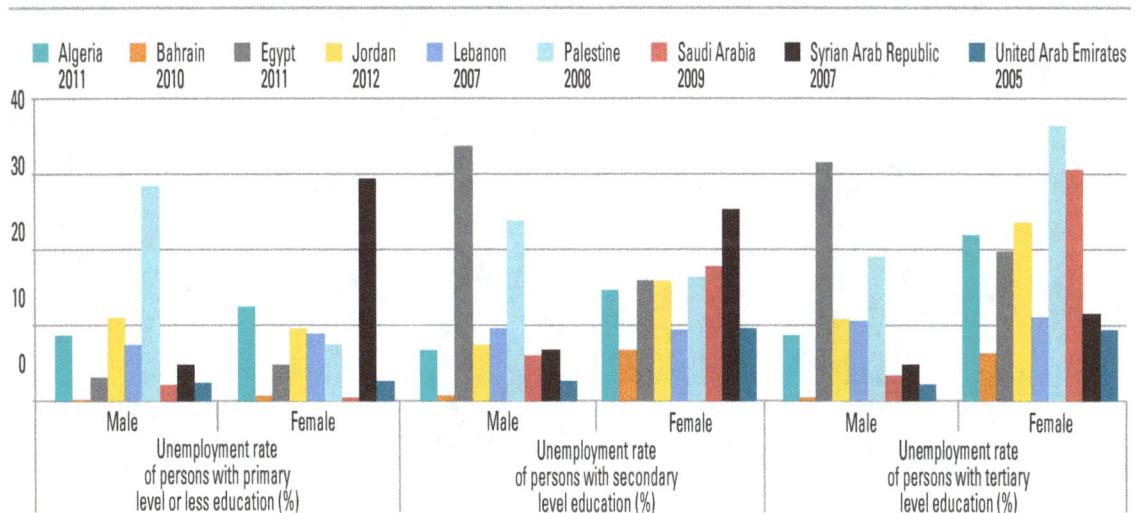

Source: ILO, 2015 KLIM, 9th edition (see figure 2.22).

enter the market difficult. According to one ILO index, this skills mismatch affected 41 per cent of male and 27 per cent of female graduates in Egypt in 2012.[26] The same index indicated a mismatch of 7 per cent for men and 31 per cent for women in Tunisia in 2013. Most women in the Arab region choose academic programmes geared to social sciences, business and law, but there is an oversupply of such graduates.

5. Domestic work

Migration of domestic workers, mainly from Asia and Africa, to the Arab region began in the early 1970s after the oil boom that took place mainly in the GCC subregion.[27] Saudi Arabia and Qatar were the main destinations of Sri Lankan migrant workers between 2009 and 2013.[28] Official Sri Lankan data in 2013 reveal that 22 per cent of male emigrants and 35 per cent of female emigrants went to Saudi Arabia for employment. More than 40 per cent of those migrants were employed as domestic help.

Domestic workers from the Philippines and Nepal tend to be more educated than their counterparts from other countries of origin and normally have a good command of a foreign language such as English or French. As a result, demand for them for household work in Arab countries such as the United Arab Emirates is high.[29] Migrant domestic workers are predominantly female.

In many countries of the Arab region, employment of a domestic worker is a sign of social status. Migrants, particularly women, are attracted to domestic work by wages that are higher than in their home countries. They use the money to provide for their families at home, purchase property or deal with debt.[30]

According to ILO estimates, around 2.1 million people were employed in 2010 in domestic work in the Arab region, twice the number reported in 1995. Domestic work accounts for 5.6 per cent of total employment in the region.[31] It accounts for a much greater share

Table 2.3 Number of domestic workers and their share in employment of migrants, by sex (latest available year)

Country/territory	Year	Number of domestic workers		Domestic workers as percentage of migrant workers	
		Female	Male	Female	Male
Bahrain	2009	4 855	28 000	42.2	5.8
Iraq	2008	3 500	6 200	0.2	0.1
Jordan	2009	4 400	1 700	2.2	0.2
Kuwait	2005	151 100	95 000	53.3	11.3
Oman	2009	69 300	25 300	59.3	2.8
Qatar	2009	48 100	32 200	38.9	2.8
Saudi Arabia	2009	507 900	276 600	47.1	3.9
United Arab Emirates	2008	146 100	90 500	42.4	6.0
West Bank & Gaza	2008	200	300	0.2	0.1
Yemen	2005/2006	8 100	15 200	2.5	0.4

Source: ILO, *Domestic Workers across the World: Global and National Statistics and the Extent of Legal Protection* (Geneva, 2013). Available from www.ilo.org/travail/Whatsnew/WCMS_173363/lang--en/index.htm2013.

in GCC countries: Kuwait (32 per cent), Oman (31.5 per cent), Saudi Arabia (25.5 per cent) and the United Arab Emirates (24.2 per cent). The number of women domestic workers in all those cases far exceeds the number of men. That said, the number of male domestic workers in the region is much higher than in other regions. For instance, 276,600 male domestic workers were employed, commonly as gardeners and drivers, in Saudi Arabia in 2009. It is noteworthy that domestic work accounts for a large share of total female employment in GCC countries: Oman (59 per cent); Kuwait (53 per cent); and Saudi Arabia (47 per cent). Almost one third of all female wage workers in the region are employed as domestic help, which indicates the high demand for those services and the low female employment to population ratio, especially in GCC countries.[32]

In the United Arab Emirates, each household employs an average of three domestic workers.[33] In Kuwait, it is taken for granted that households have at least one domestic worker.[34] In 2013, it was estimated that 296,000 non-nationals were employed in private households in Kuwait.[35] In Saudi Arabia, around 900,000 people, more than half of them women, were engaged in domestic work in 2013.

It is difficult to come by comprehensive and updated employment data by economic sector for nationals and non-nationals. Moreover, female domestic workers are isolated in the homes where they work and might not always be included in official data counts.[36]

In some Arab countries, action has been taken to protect domestic workers, addressing issues such as the timely payment of wages, social security, minimum wages, labour dispute settlement and health insurance.[37] In Jordan, for example, regulations were introduced in 2012 to limit the working day of domestic workers to a maximum of eight hours, and stipulating that workers may leave the home

without permission from their employer outside working hours.[38] In 2015, Kuwait passed Law No. 68, which gives domestic workers enforceable labour rights, including a weekly day off, 30 days of annual paid leave and a 12-hour working day with rest periods.[39]

The Abu Dhabi Dialogue, composed of the 11 Colombo Process countries on the one hand[40] and, on the other, the GCC countries and Yemen, was set up to discuss initiatives to influence practices and policies that benefit countries of origin and destination and improve the well-being of temporary contractual workers, including domestic workers.[41]

Many Arab countries have engaged in bilateral, regional and global cooperation on migration and agreements with countries of origin. Such talks have taken place between the United Arab Emirates and the Philippines (2007) and Ethiopia (2012), Lebanon and the Philippines (2012), Jordan and the Philippines (2012) and between Saudi Arabia and Bangladesh, Indonesia, the Philippines, Sri Lanka and Viet Nam between 2013 and 2015.

Most other countries in the Arab region depend on contractual agreements to regulate the relationship between employers and domestic workers. Such contracts may offer certain protection to the worker, but they are normally standardized and the worker has no negotiation power or legal capacity to enforce his or her rights, effectively giving more control to the employer. This can lead to problems such as domestic violence and abuse.

Labour legislation needs to be reinforced to take into account the needs and rights of domestic workers and apply sanctions in cases of non-compliance. Another challenge is to monitor enforcement of such laws or related bilateral/international agreements. Target 5.4 of SDG 5 on gender equality calls for "recognizing and valuing unpaid care and domestic work through the provision of public services, infrastructure and social protection policies and the promotion of shared responsibility within the household and the family as nationally appropriate".

Initiatives taken thus far, while not always properly enforced, are a step in the right direction. When fully implemented and monitored, they may even encourage unemployed nationals to consider this type of work.

D. Concluding remarks

The Arab region is facing mounting socioeconomic challenges. Reduced oil revenues are likely to weaken the position of GCC countries in fiscal terms and with respect to their balance-of-payments situations. Nevertheless, they are not expected to face fiscal or external constraints in terms of expansion in domestic demand. Business sentiment and consumer confidence remain weak, but steady growth in domestic demand over the next two years is projected for GCC countries, in part as a result of the rapid growth of the Indian economy. GCC countries face challenges regarding how to diversify their economies. A series of measures, including subsidy reforms, highlight the seriousness of policy efforts to cope with lower oil prices. GCC Governments are expected to make progress in fiscal consolidation aimed at coping with the "new normal" of low oil revenues.

Other Arab countries have benefited from lower commodity prices, including for food and energy. However, the margin of benefit was much lower than expected. Slight improvements in trade balances were offset by weaker inflows of foreign capital resulting from the shift in United States monetary policy. As a result, balance-of-payments conditions generally tightened, as it became more difficult to finance current account deficits. Deteriorating balance-of-payments conditions will be a major constraint on economic growth in 2016 in the Mashreq and Maghreb subregions and among Arab LDCs. The conflicts in Iraq, Libya, Palestine, the Syrian Arab Republic and Yemen are an added constraint on growth. Tighter balance-of-payments conditions restrict the expansion of domestic demand and adversely affect living standards unless effective external assistance is provided. The need for such assistance is likely to increase in 2016 in these subregions.

In spite of reforms in some countries, indicators suggest that women in the Arab region are more disadvantaged economically, politically and socially than women in other regions. In spite of rising literacy and educational attainment rates among women, unemployment remains high, especially among young women. Average regional economic growth of 0.9 per cent in 2015 is insufficient to absorb the rapidly growing supply of labour and therefore to prevent a potential unemployment crisis for men and women, and especially among the young. According to the World Bank, gender gaps in entrepreneurship and labour force participation will lead to estimated income losses of around 25 per cent in 2016.[42]

The presence of women in political institutions such as parliament has dropped back since the uprisings of 2011. The enforcement of quota systems remains the most recommended means to increase women's participation and representation in decision-making.

There is a long way to go on gender equality in the region but much has been achieved. Most Arab countries have ratified the Convention on the Elimination of all Forms of Discrimination against Women and adopted the Beijing Declaration and Platform of Action,[43] and are working to implement Security Council resolution 1325 (2000).[44] In 2015, Arab countries agreed to place gender equality at the core of their development in the framework of the SDGs. Most of them have introduced legal reforms to improve the status of women, eliminate discrimination against them and protect them from gender-based violence. In Lebanon, for instance, legislation passed in 2014 allows women recourse to the courts in cases of domestic violence; similar legislation is in place in Morocco and Tunisia. Algeria passed legislation in 2016 punishing acts of sexual harassment and violence against women.[45]

Political will, institutional capacity and meaningful
engagement with civil society are needed
to implement policies, reforms and measures aimed
at preventing conflict.

3. Effects of Five Years of Upheaval on Arab Countries

A. Introduction

In 2011, citizens across the Arab region rose up and demanded more voice in government and accountability from their rulers. This so-called Arab Spring, mainly driven by limited opportunities for political participation and little to no equitable distribution of economic gains, was the latest in a series of political upheavals in the region that have taken place since the 1970s. Some of them have lead to democratization, while others have involved the replacement of one ruling elite by another.

Economic analysts suggest that political regime change has a long-term positive impact on growth, employment and macroeconomic stability. Even when it does not result in democratization, regime change can bring greater growth in the long run. The effect is non-linear and the transition period between two regimes can be fraught with problems. Some analysts have concluded that, for one or two years of transition, growth declines by around 11 percentage points where transition is successful, and 7 percentage points when not.[1]

The process of political transition now underway in the Arab region has not adhered to this pattern. The initial positive momentum has degenerated into chaos and insecurity, and transition in Libya, the Syrian Aran Republic and Yemen has transformed into war. Other countries, such as occupied Palestine, were already affected by conflict to one degree or another before 2011. In addition, many countries are experiencing the spillover effects of conflict. Countries directly and indirectly affected by conflict have lost a cumulative $613.8 billion vis-à-vis pre-conflict projections since 2011. Continued fighting will deter foreign investment, dampen trade opportunities and thereby adversely impact macroeconomic balances.

Little attempt has been made in recent literature on the conflicts to provide a region-wide study of the impact on macroeconomic variables or deep analysis of the affect on neighbouring countries in particular. In this chapter, we aim in the first section to measure the overall socioeconomic impact on the region of events over the five years since the uprisings began Tunisia in 2011, and then to examine the particular cases of Lebanon, the Syrian Arab Republic and Tunisia.

In the second section, we first look at the dire human and economic cost of civil war in the Syrian Arab Republic and its effects on Lebanon. We then turn to Tunisia, which is dealing with the consequences of its own transition and the spillover from the civil war in neighbouring Libya, and conclude by examining the adverse socioeconomic effects of the occupation in Palestine. These observations will draw on data generated through this exercise and estimates from existing conflict analysis. A range of suggested policy options for mitigating the adverse impact of conflict follows.

B. The impact of political change on economic performance

1. The link between conflict and economic development

Economic volatility can lead to and result from political instability and transition. Underdevelopment can be a cause and a consequence of conflict.[2] Conflict can have a dual impact on a country, by knocking it off its growth path and then preventing catch-up with its previous trajectory long after the conflict ends. "Illegitimate" regimes facing sustained opposition expend more State resources on maintaining order, leaving less in the budget for social protection, infrastructure and other expenditure priorities. Even one year of minor conflict can reduce GDP growth by between 1 and 2 per cent.[3]

Civil wars are particularly costly in terms of physical capital destroyed or relocated and human capital displaced. Capital does not immediately return to pre-conflict levels due to the lingering effects of war even after it is over. Conflicts reduce not only the level of GDP, but also the rate of growth. One study suggests that civil wars reduce annual growth rates by 2.2 per cent, due to destruction of capital stock and reduced production during the war. In the years following a short war, growth rates continue to be low (a 2.1 per cent loss due to war overhang and the difficulty in resolving problems that led to the war), but in the years following a long war, during which capital stock had time to adjust to new low levels, growth rates will actually

be higher.[4] There is thus a potentially large dividend to ending long wars, and that has implications for the Syrian conflict. Borrowing to finance wars drives up debt, which burdens countries thereafter.[5] Five sectors are seen as particularly vulnerable to the impact of conflict: construction, manufacturing, transport, distribution and finance. On the other hand, subsistence agriculture can increase as a percentage of GDP as mobile capital flees from conflict areas, leaving the local economy more primary-commodity dependent.[6]

The impact of political change on growth has been observed across time and in a variety of contexts. The growth trajectory of a country at the time of political instability may take the form of a "J-curve".[7] Political transition or conflict brings an immediate dip in economic growth, but in time it rebounds to a new equilibrium above that which preceded the change. An extension of this theory indicates that long periods of economic and social development followed by a reversal of gains or simply by real and perceived inequality of opportunity will lead to revolutionary tendencies. It is thus not simply poverty or poor living conditions that lead to unrest, but rather a feeling of exclusion or the fear

Figure 3.1 Rate of economic growth during political transition in Portugal and Spain (percentage)

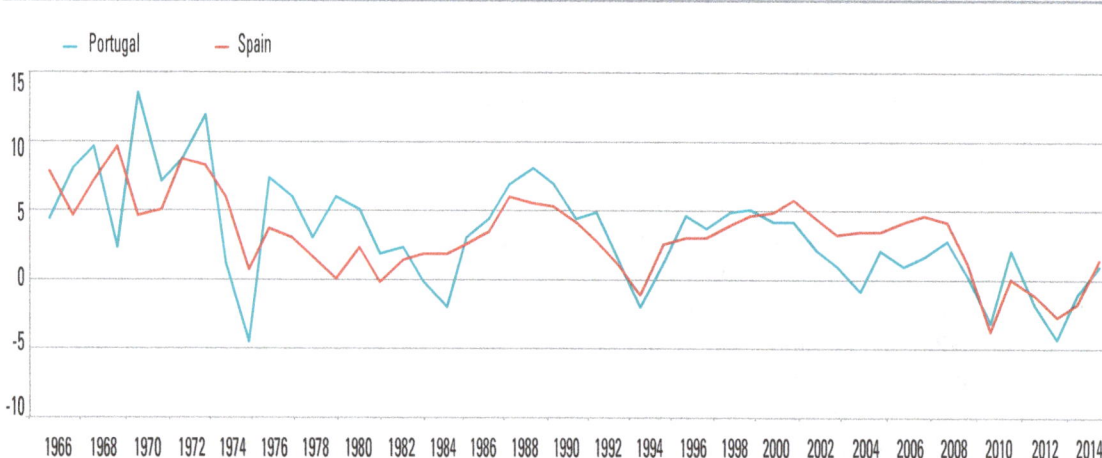

Source: ESCWA staff calculations, based on World Bank, World Development Indicators database. Available from http://data.worldbank.org/products/wdi (accessed 30 March 2016).

of a reversal of fortunes.[8] A country's growth trajectory will dip during this period of instability before returning to and surpassing its previous level, hence resembling a J-curve.

ESCWA analysed the impact of conflict and political instability on economic, social and political development, with regression analysis finding that increasing battle deaths in conflict countries by 1 per cent decreases GDP per capita in the subsequent year by 0.0296 per cent.[9] There are also significant negative correlations concerning years of schooling and governance.

Conflicts and political unrest affect neighbouring countries and regional stability. One study, looking at the impact of conflicts on neighbouring countries through the prisms of human capital, physical capital, labour growth and intercept shift, shows that civil wars between 1961 and 1995 brought about an 85 per cent short-term fall and 31 per cent long-term fall in mean growth in the affected countries, and caused both short and long-term spillover effects in neighbours.[10] The omitted variables that can lead to unrest and conflict (such as inequality, ethnic and religious tensions, lack of voice and accountability) can have a socioeconomic impact too.

2. The conflict-economic development link in other regions

The J-curve hypothesis finds confirmation in many regions that have undergone a political change since the 1970s. In Portugal, the Carnation Revolution of 1974 was followed by negative GDP growth of -4.3 per cent in 1975. With the restoration of democracy in 1976, growth rebounded to 6.9 per cent (figure 3.1). In Spain, growth slumped to near zero in 1975, before a small rebound the following year. The more gradual nature of Spain's transition to democracy is reflected in the time it took to return to higher growth.

The transition from communism in Eastern and Central Europe between 1989 and 1999 was also marked by at times deep and protracted recession with initial economic dislocation and trade disruption, and accompanied by high or hyperinflation as prices moved to market levels and Governments resorted to monetary financing of gaping fiscal deficits.[11] However, those countries brought fiscal deficits and inflation under control. In contrast to the turbulence and divergence of the 1990s, growth patterns in the early and mid-2000s were uniformly strong, due to the impact of

Figure 3.2 GDP growth rate, Eastern European and post-Soviet economies (percentage)

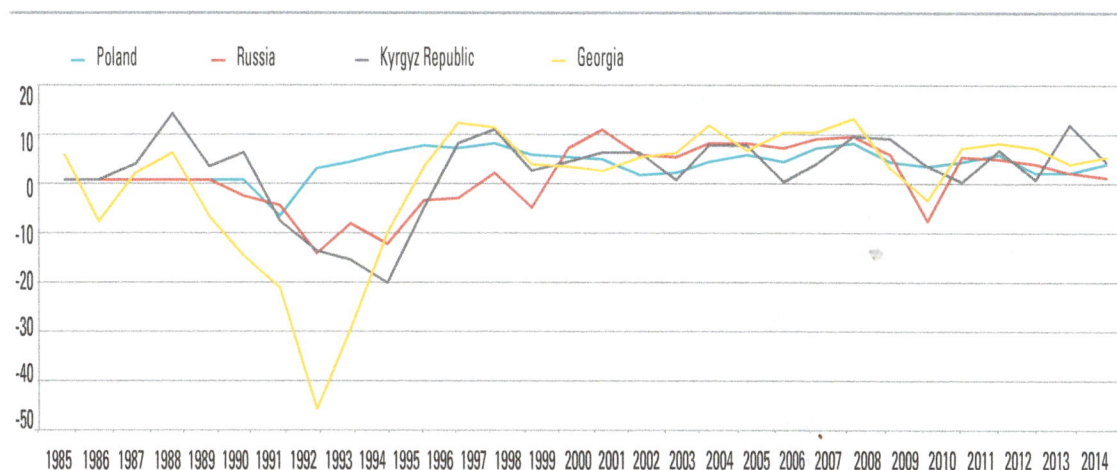

Source: ESCWA staff calculations, based on World Bank, World Development Indicators database. Available from http://data.worldbank.org/products/wdi (accessed 30 March 2016).

macroeconomic stabilization policies, coupled with high prices for energy exports, boosting average growth for the region to 6 per cent.

The growth falls and recoveries for some post-Soviet and Eastern European countries are illustrated in figure 3.2, with countries experiencing, to varying degrees, recessions in the early-to-mid 1990s and subsequent recovery and growth. After a destructive war and independence in the early 1990s, Bosnia and Herzegovina rebounded with 89 and 34 per cent growth in 1996 and 1997 respectively.

Confirming the spillover effects of political uncertainty and conflict, one study on Eastern Europe from 1989 to 1994 found that including a dummy for "regional tension" reduced the average annual growth rate over the five years by 9 per cent.[12]

The cases of Argentina and Chile reveal sporadic rises and falls in GDP growth rates over the past decades, fluctuating between more than 10 per cent growth and more than 10 per cent contraction. Some of those troughs and peaks are due to political transition and crisis and subsequent restoration of order and democracy. The transitions of Chile (1972-1973) and Argentina (1975-1976; 1982) resulted in immediate GDP falls and eventual rebound.

C. An overview of the socioeconomic implications of the "Arab Spring"

One lesson from these findings is that, despite the sharp decline in GDP and other macroeconomic indicators during political upheaval, there are precedents for a growth rebound even to above pre-crisis levels. However, political transitions in the Arab region have by and large not led to this growth rebound. One specificity of the region is that political transitions have not been backed by reforms addressing the issues that led to unrest in the first place.[13] Furthermore,

political upheaval in some countries has spiralled into armed conflict. This places the Arab region at a particular disadvantage when it comes to planning, achieving and monitoring the SDGs.

1. Macroeconomic considerations

We will now compare pre-conflict economic projections with actual performances in the Arab region, in order to identify the economic potential lost through conflict. We will look at: (i) countries that had been in conflict prior to 2011;[14] (ii) countries engaged in ongoing conflict since 2011;[15] and (iii) neighbouring countries affected by post-2011 conflicts.[16] As a counterfactual to the crises, we will compare projections made by the International Monetary Fund (IMF) and national Governments in 2010 with actual performances by the end of 2015.

(a) Growth

Realized growth performances vis-à-vis projections reflect the impacts of various crises, including conflict and political uncertainty in

Figure 3.3 Total GDP, countries in conflict since 2011

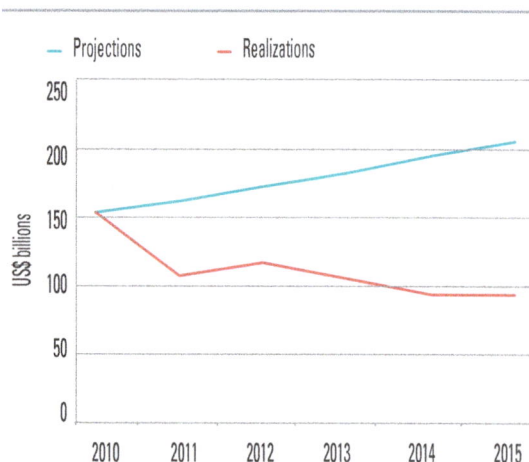

Source: ESCWA staff calculations based on IMF Article IV consultations (2008-2014).
Note: GDP data for the Syrian Arab Republic taken from calculations by the National Agenda for the Future of Syria (NAFS, 2016).

Figure 3.4 Total GDP, countries affected by conflict

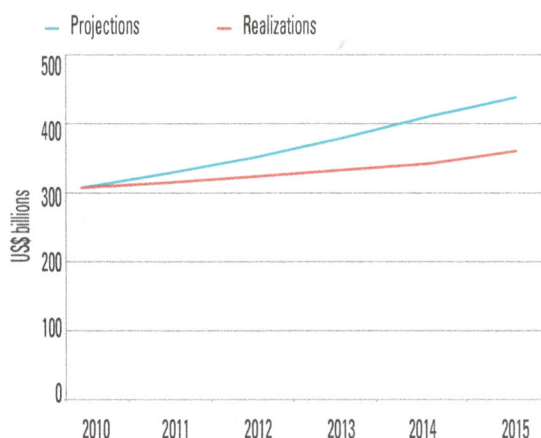

Source: ESCWA staff calculations based on IMF Article IV consultations (2008-2014).

Figure 3.5 Total GDP, countries in conflict prior to 2011

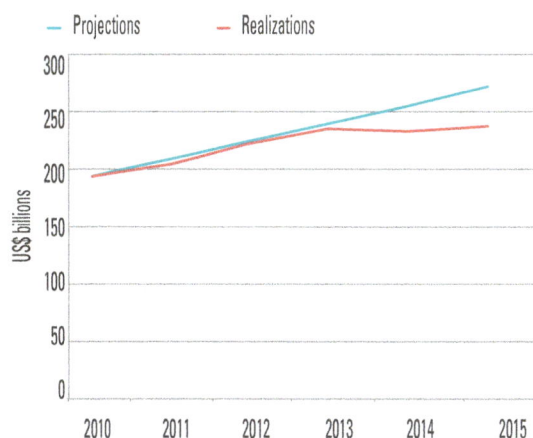

Source: ESCWA staff calculations based on IMF Article IV consultations (2008-2014).

the Arab region, rising and falling oil prices and a global economic slump. The difference between GDP projections and realizations for countries in conflict after 2011 – which by 2011 was already large and continued to grow through 2015 – is illustrated in figure 3.3.

In the case of countries impacted by neighbouring conflict and/or domestic political unrest, a small but growing difference between GDP projections and realizations can be seen over time (figure 3.4). Together, countries in conflict since 2011 and countries affected by conflict through spillover effects have experienced a cumulative net underperformance in GDP of $613.8 billion since 2011, or 6 per cent of the region's total GDP between 2011 and 2015.

In order to compare with other countries to isolate for the effects of the Arab uprisings, we see that for countries experiencing conflict prior to 2011, and for GCC countries, realizations either closely followed or exceeded expectations (figures 3.5 and 3.6).

Overall, Arab countries in conflict are witnessing the first, downward-sloping

Figure 3.6 Total GDP, GCC countries

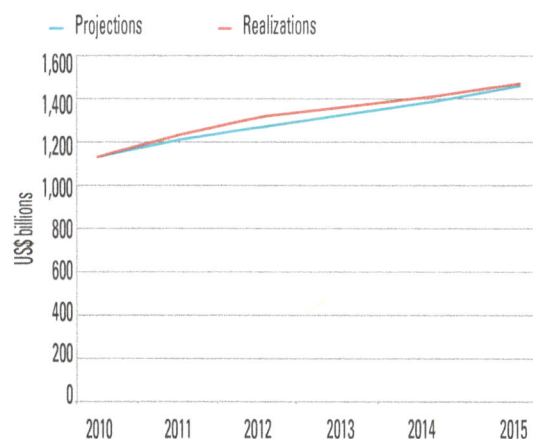

Source: ESCWA staff calculations based on IMF Article IV consultations (2008-2014).
Note: Data for Bahrain and Oman taken from the Economist Intelligence Unit (EIU).

segment of the J-curve in the response of GDP to crisis. Of note are the concentration of conflict-impacted countries among under-performers, and oil producers among the over-performers, despite the plateau and fall of global oil prices over the past two years.

Figure 3.7 Cumulative GDP gains (losses) by country

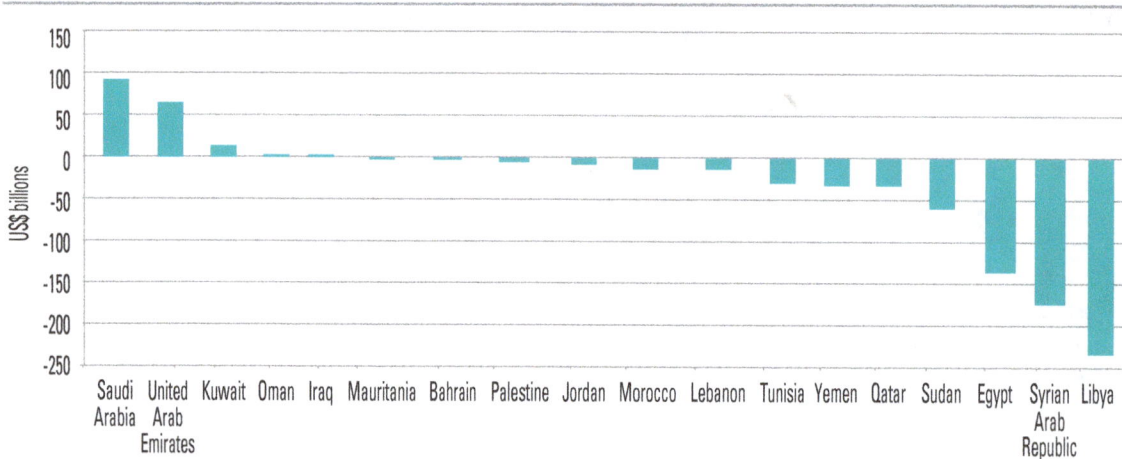

Source: ESCWA staff estimations.

Figure 3.8 Fiscal balance, countries in conflict since 2011

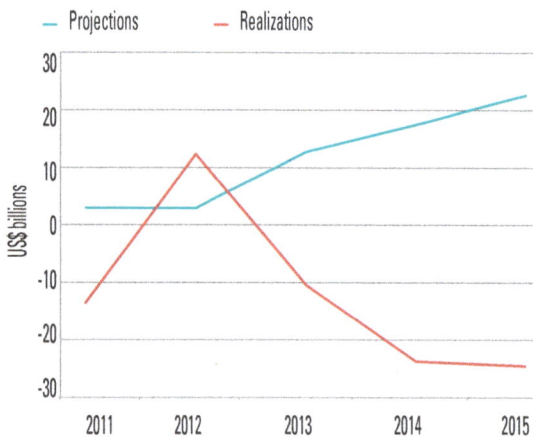

Source: ESCWA staff calculations based on IMF Article IV consultations (2008-2014).
Note: Data for the Syrian Arab Republic based on EIU (2011) projections.

Figure 3.9 Fiscal balance, countries affected by conflict

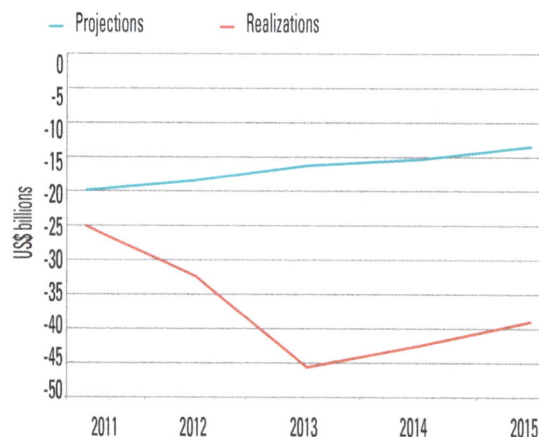

Source: ESCWA staff calculations based on IMF Article IV consultations (2008-2014).

(b) Fiscal balance

Greater than expected expenditure needs during conflicts, coupled with reduced revenues due to dampened economic activity, have worsened the fiscal balances of countries in conflict since 2011 (figure 3.8). The spike in realized fiscal balance in 2012 is driven by Libya returning to oil production following fighting in 2011.

The fiscal balance in countries affected by conflict has also deteriorated due to the need to address spillover from crises (figure 3.9). Overall, countries in conflict since 2011 and countries experiencing spillover together have had a fiscal balance shortfall of $243.1 billion, $217.9 billion more than had been projected.

Countries that were experiencing conflicts prior to 2011 also suffered large budget shortfalls, with a cumulative deficit of $43.7 billion since 2011. Prior to 2011 they had anticipated budget surpluses.

Lastly, plunging oil prices have decimated the fiscal balance of GCC countries (figure 3.10).

Figure 3.10 Fiscal balance, GCC countries

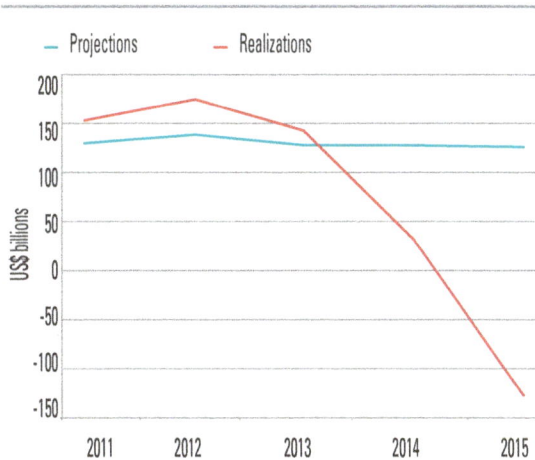

Source: ESCWA staff calculations based on IMF Article IV consultations (2008-2014).

(c) Debt

A final macroeconomic trend to note is rising debt, in particular in some countries in conflict. The use of different methodologies for debt data collection across the Arab region necessitates a country-by-country analysis. National figures – whether from Article IV or EIU data – differ in terms of net or gross, and domestic, external or total. Although debt figures are difficult to compare between countries, trends in different forms of debt in countries in and affected by conflict can be seen.

In Iraq and Libya, high oil prices helped reduce debt from conflict-affected levels in 2011 to stand on par with or even exceed earlier projections by 2013 (figure 3.11). However, falling global prices and the return of uncertainty in both countries caused debt to increase again from 2014 onwards. Falling oil rents had a similar impact in Saudi Arabia.

Other countries in conflict or affected by conflict have mixed results (figure 3.12). Lebanon did better than anticipated in terms of total government (or public) debt, but this

Figure 3.11 Debt levels, by country

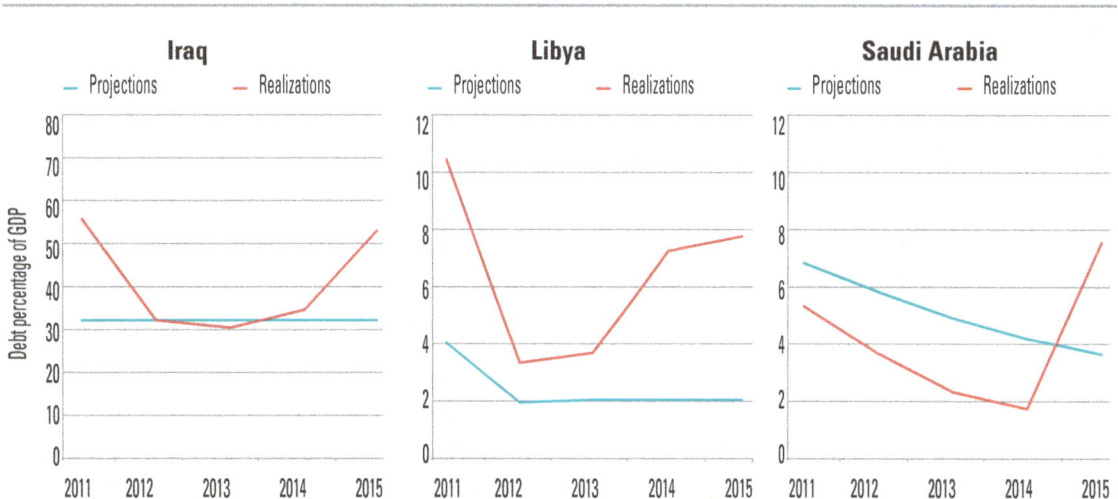

Source: ESCWA staff calculations based on IMF Article IV consultations (2008-2014).
Note: Debt figures are in net public debt for Libya, total government debt for Iraq, and gross domestic debt for Saudi Arabia.

Figure 3.12 Debt levels, by country

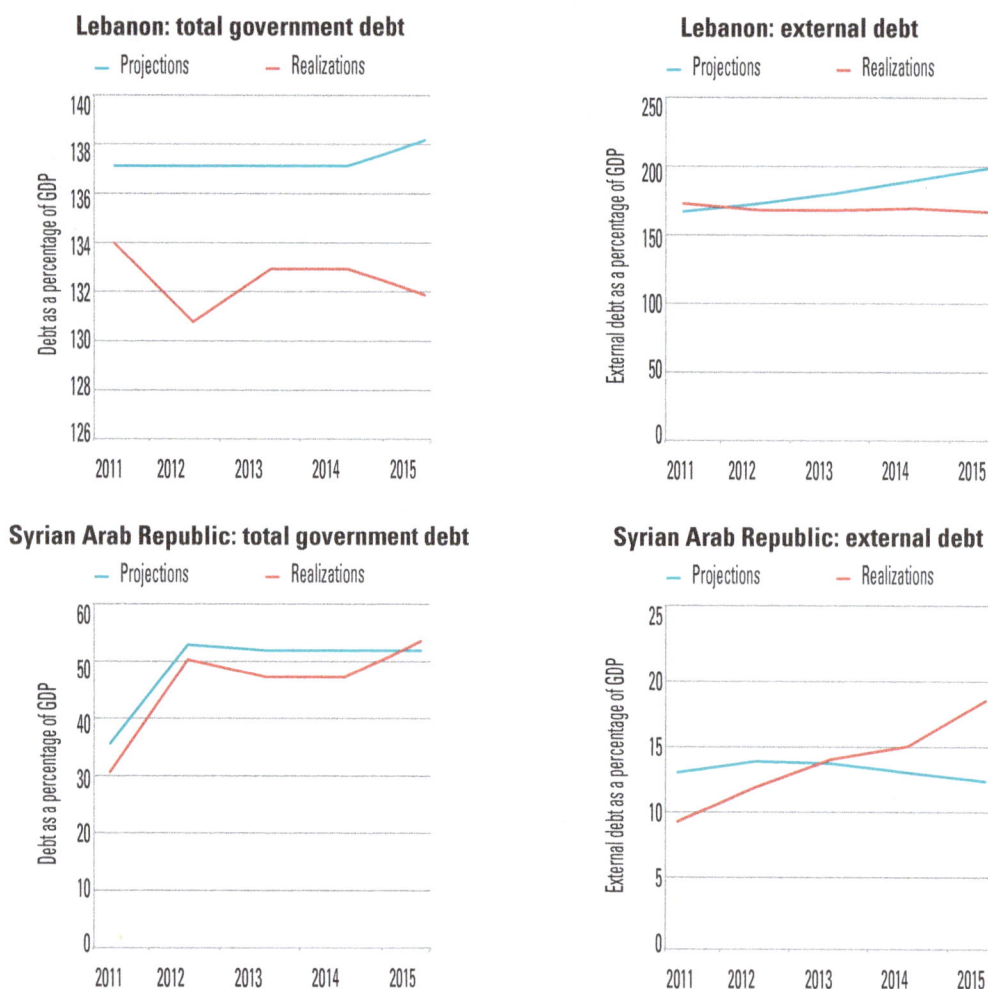

Lebanon: total government debt
— Projections — Realizations

Lebanon: external debt
— Projections — Realizations

Syrian Arab Republic: total government debt
— Projections — Realizations

Syrian Arab Republic: external debt
— Projections — Realizations

Source: ESCWA staff calculations based on IMF Article IV consultations (2008-2014).
Note: The term "total government debt" is used in IMF data, while the term "public debt" is used in EIU data.

was outweighed by external debt, reflecting a dependence on external financing. In the Syrian case, government debt closely reflected projections, perhaps due to, among other reasons, the difficulties in borrowing further in times of conflict. External debt, however, was considerably higher than projected.

The state of revenue collection during conflict, as well as the proportion of external assistance provided as grants or loans, will heavily influence policy recommendations on how to finance post-conflict reconstruction.

(d) Regional integration, trade and conflict

In spite of initiatives to promote regional integration, such as the subregional GCC, the Greater Arab Free Trade Agreement (GAFTA) and Arab customs union (ACU), the region remains much less integrated than comparable regions, such as the Association of Southeast Asian Nations (ASEAN), the African Union and the MERCOSUR common market area in Latin America. In general, trade, investment and migration ties link Arab North Africa with the EU and sub-Saharan Africa, and the Mashreq

Figure 3.13 Regional exports as percentage of total exports, by country

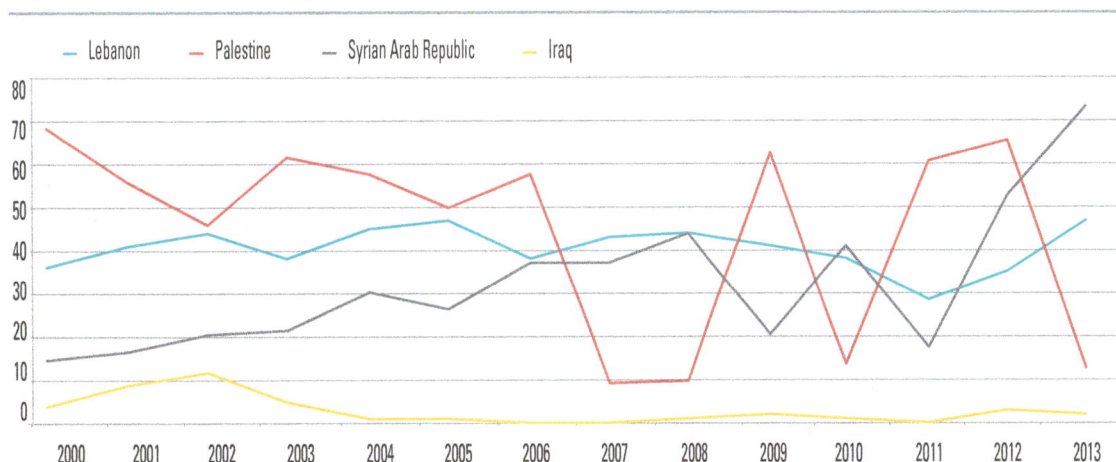

Source: ESCWA staff calculations, based on ESCWA, *Assessing Arab Economic Integration – Towards the Arab Customs Union* (Beirut, 2015, E/ESCWA/EDID/2015/4). Available from https://www.unescwa.org/sites/www.unescwa.org/files/publications/files/assessing-arab-economic-integration.pdf.

with the EU and Turkey. Other external partners such as the United States and China present more opportunities for Arab countries than do their neighbours.

Conflicts are preventing further integration and in fact unravelling progress made in the past, leading to the disintegration of trade and economic links within and between countries. Drops in exports during periods of instability are notable in, for instance, Libya (2011 and 2013), the Sudan (2011-2012) and Yemen (2011 and 2015).[17] Fully implementing GAFTA and advancing towards the ACU is near impossible when several countries across the region are mired in conflict. The situation is made worse by political divisions across the region that perpetuate the conflicts and crises. Arab regional trade represents only a small fraction of total trade (including oil).[18] However, regional trade between neighbours is increasingly important for countries in conflict, such as the Syrian Arab Republic (figure 3.13). Leaving aside petroleum industries, we see that, among countries directly and indirectly affected by conflict, exports to other Arab countries account for a significant portion of total trade, but that imports from within the region remain limited (figure 3.14).

Figure 3.14 Regional non-oil trade as a percentage of total trade, 2014

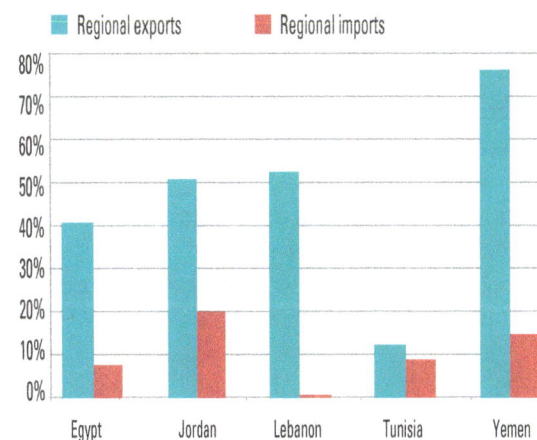

Source: ESCWA staff calculations based on World Bank, World Integrated Trade Solution database. Available from http://wits.worldbank.org/ (accessed 21 March 2016).

Conflicts have further disrupted regional infrastructure projects. Many gas pipelines and electricity grids run through the Syrian Arab Republic to Lebanon, and to Turkey for export. Tourism has also been hit, with tourist arrivals dropping not only in countries at war, but in their neighbours as well. Between 2012 and 2013, tourism fell in Egypt, Jordan, Lebanon and Saudi Arabia.[19] Arab remittance-sending workforces in countries such as Libya and Iraq have also been hurt. For example, 100,000 Egyptians were forced to return to Egypt due to the conflict in Libya.[20]

2. Social implications

(a) Population displacement

Not since the Second World War have we witnessed forced displacement on such a scale resulting from conflict and persecution, with the number exceeding 65.3 million by the end of 2015, according to the United Nations Office of the High Commissioner for Refugees (UNHCR).[21] The Syrian Arab Republic accounts for many: 6.6 million people displaced internally and 4.8 million externally.[22]

The global refugee population increased by 12.2 per cent between the end of 2014 and the end of 2015, according to UNHCR. Arab countries accounted for a considerable share (table 3.1). Adding 5.2 million refugees registered by the United Nations Relief and Works Agency for Palestine Refugees in the Near East (UNRWA),[23] the Arab region remained the largest source of refugees. In terms of destination, Europe witnessed the greatest rise in the numbers of incoming refugees, which grew by 43 per cent over the same period.[24] The figure may be higher, as many people continue to cross the Mediterranean Sea to Europe and may not be reflected in UNHCR records.

Turkey hosts more refugees – 2.7 million Syrians – than any other country in the world. Lebanon hosts more per capita than any other country, with refugees accounting for roughly a quarter of the total population. Germany was the world's biggest recipient of new asylum claims (159,000) in the first half of 2015. Between April 2011 and December 2015, 897,645 Syrian applications for asylum were registered in Europe, with Serbia and Germany being the top destinations and together accounting for 59 per cent of all applications. Austria, Denmark, Hungary, the Netherlands and Sweden together accounted for 29 per cent, and the remaining countries 12 per cent.[25]

Figures for Arab refugees by country of origin and asylum can be found in table 3.2, with staggering numbers across the region and in Syria in particular. In Yemen, there were estimated to be 2.5 million IDPs by the end of December 2015. In Libya, the number of IDPs almost doubled from 230,000 to more than 434,000 in 2015.[26] According to statistics from ESCWA and the International Organization for Migration (IOM), 137,631 refugees and migrants reached Europe by sea from Libya in 2014, and 1,700 persons are estimated to

Table 3.1 Refugee population by region, 2015

Region	Total refugees (end 2014)	Total refugees (end 2015)	Percentage change
Africa	4 445 977	5 211 282	17.2 per cent
Americas	467 883	453 214	-3.1 per cent
Asia and the Pacific	4 257 839	4 262 995	0.1 per cent
Europe	540 185	594 370	10.1 per cent
Middle East and North Africa	4 539 626	5 441 985	19.0 per cent
Total	14 380 094	16 121 427	12.2 per cent

Sources: UNHCR, "World at war - global trends: forced displacement in 2014" (Geneva, June 2015), p. 53; and UNHCR, "Global trends: forced displacement in 2015" (Geneva, June 2016), p. 65, annex table 2.
Note: The figures for Africa exclude North Africa.

Table 3.2 Refugees in the Arab region by country of origin and asylum

Country	Total refugees and people in refugee-like situations		IDPs, including protected/assisted by UNHCR and people in IDP-like situations
	By country of origin	By country of asylum	Number
Egypt	16 105	226 344	
Iraq	377 747	288 035	3 962 142
Jordan	1 767	664 102	
Lebanon	4 329	1 172 388	
Morocco	1 559	2 144	
State of Palestine	97 241		
Sudan	640 919	356 191	2 342 979
Syrian Arab Republic	4 837 134	149 200	7 632 500
Tunisia	1 484	824	
Yemen	5 832	263 047	2 500 000
Libya	4 317	27 948	434 869

Sources: UNHCR, Syria regional refugee response, available from http://data.unhcr.org/syrianrefugees/regional.php (accessed 29 March 2016); UNHCR, *Mid-Year Trends 2015* (Geneva, 2015); and Internal Displacement Monitoring Centre data, available from www.internal-displacement.org/middle-east-and-north-africa/yemen/figures-analysis (accessed 29 March 2016).

have lost their lives in the attempt in the first quarter of 2015.[27]

Displacement affects the country of origin, the country of destination and the displaced persons. Many countries in the region are both the point of origin and destination for refugees, and migration is mixed due to the range of reasons motivating different groups of migrants.[28]

i. *Effect on destination countries*

Destination countries for refugees and displaced persons face challenges and opportunities, depending on how the country's characteristics, such as population size, wealth, demography and the availability of support services, match with the socioeconomic status and needs of refugees. Most host countries in the region are developing countries with scarce resources, implying considerable burdens on Governments, donors and communities.

For example, the provision of utilities, housing and other amenities to citizens and refugees is made more difficult by the population influx. Temporary housing or camps for refugees can also have adverse effects on the local ecosystem and environment.

Refugees bring competition to the local labour market, which can lower wages, particularly in the informal economy, and fuel local unemployment, thereby feeding tension between local and refugee populations. However, new workers bring new skills and ideas with them, which can help spur innovation and entrepreneurship while filling gaps in the local labour market. Policymakers in destination countries should make a priority of absorbing new workers while providing for nationals. International migration needs to be managed well in order to obtain the best possible results from the global migration and refugee flows.[29]

ii. Effect on countries of origin

The exodus of business people, highly skilled professionals and family members has a negative effect on the economy and institutional memory of countries of origin, and can exacerbate the crisis that triggered the outward migration in the first place. After prolonged war, refugees find it hard to return to their country, where basic needs such as water and sanitation may not be available, let alone decent jobs. Countries that depend heavily on remittances have difficulty accommodating returnees. The return of thousands of Egyptians who had been working in Libya aggravated socioeconomic problems in Egypt and hit the communities that had depended on their remittances hard. Countries find it challenging to obtain humanitarian assistance for IDPs, and to find new sources of economic activity in the absence of a significant proportion of the population.

iii. Effect on the refugees or IDPs

Relocation to refugee camps poses potential health hazards, including malnutrition and exposure to infectious diseases, in addition to the trauma of displacement. The health of migrants in the region – other than meeting the most basic needs for survival – has not been viewed as a priority, and health-care services and sanitation are generally poor. Refugees frequently face discrimination, exploitation, sexual abuse and forced marriage, while being restricted in movement and prohibited from seeking formal employment. The rare work opportunities available are often in hazardous sectors such as construction.[30] Nevertheless, job opportunities can arise for refugees to bring their skills to a new setting.

The long-term impact on displaced people can be more profound in the case of protracted conflict, with the emergence of a "lost generation".[31] Access to quality education and health services for the displaced is therefore essential to cushion the long-term impact of conflict and displacement on whole generations of Arab youth. Policymakers must also tackle the question of residency and citizenship, not only of displaced persons but also of those born abroad, in order to prevent the emergence of a generation of stateless people.

(b) Impact of political change on employment and poverty

Unemployment has worsened in countries that underwent political transition, such as Egypt and Tunisia, and in those affected by major inflows of refugees from neighbouring conflict-affected countries, such as Jordan. Unemployment among women, already higher than the rate for men in 2010, has increased at a more rapid rate with unrest and conflict. Rising unemployment only serves to deepen the frustration of young people, for whom lack of work was a key cause of the uprisings in 2011. Disenfranchised youth are also ripe for recruitment campaigns by radical groups.

Only 4 per cent of the region's population lives below the global extreme poverty line of $1.25, the rate increases markedly if the poverty line is set at $2 (19 per cent) or $2.75 (40 per cent).[32] Available data indicate that the rate of poverty in the Syrian Arab Republic, as defined using the national lower poverty line, rose from 12.3 per cent in 2007 to 43 per cent in 2013.[33] The Regional Refugee and Resilience Plan estimates that the percentage of Syrian refugee households in Lebanon living below the poverty line rose from 50 per cent in 2014 to 70 per cent in the first quarter of 2016.[34]

Conflict stymied efforts to reach many MDG targets in the Arab region, particularly those on life expectancy, primary school enrolment gender ratios, infant mortality and access to water. Five years of conflict can, even without many direct casualties of fighting, "push 3-4 per cent of the population into undernourishment".[35] Conflict can further increase infant mortality by 1 per cent through the destruction of medical infrastructure and the diversion of funding away from health care.

(c) Women and armed conflict

The conflicts in the Arab region have caused many, mostly civilian causalities due to the targeting of populated areas, more than a quarter of them women and children. According to the United Nations Office for the Coordination of Humanitarian Affairs (OCHA), 2,220 Palestinians were killed in the Gaza

Figure 3.15 Registered Syrian refugees

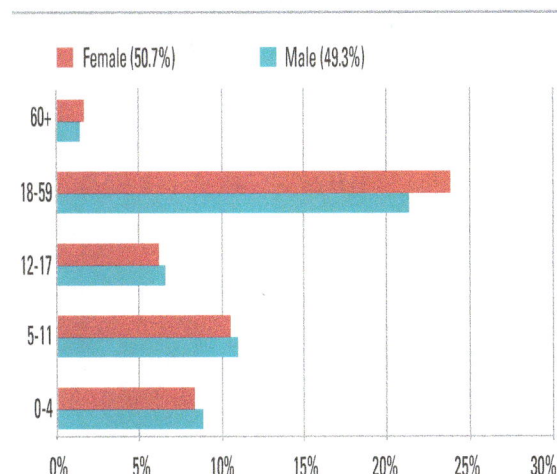

Source: UNHCR, Syria regional refugee response. Available from http://data.unhcr.org/syrianrefugees/regional.php (accessed 29 March 2016).

Box 3.1 Gender-based violence in areas of conflict in the Arab region

Data on gender-based violence is scarce and gender-based violence is under-reported for many reasons: the fear of social stigma and dishonour, the lack of psychological support and access to education, widespread illiteracy among women, and the perceived futility of reporting as a result of weak administration of justice, apathy and political pressure.[a] In spite of the prominent public role of women in the uprisings in Egypt, Tunisia and elsewhere in 2011, attitudes in the region to violence against women remain ambivalent. The post-uprising reality has largely dashed women's expectations.

The apparent rise in the incidence of gender-based violence in past years in many countries in the region may be due in part to heightened awareness of the issue and more proactive initiatives on the part of the authorities, media, research institutions, human rights activists, non-governmental organizations (NGOs) and other stakeholders to identify, report and end such violence. In countries such as Algeria, Iraq, Jordan, Lebanon, Morocco and Tunisia, Governments have released ministerial declarations on gender-based violence or pledged to pass legislation and take other measures to combat it.

However, in 2013, the United Nations Entity for Gender Equality and the Empowerment of Women (UN-Women) issued a report voicing concern at the failure of many Arab countries to take steps to implement Security Council resolution 1325 (2000). That same year, the Ministerial Council of the League of Arab States adopted a regional strategy on women, peace and security in the region. In 2015, ESCWA noted that five Arab countries were designing and implementing national plans of action regarding the resolution, while the majority were incorporating elements of it in to national policy on gender equality and combatting violence against women.

In 2015, the global study by UN-Women on implementation of the resolution indicated that uniformed female personnel were critical for winning trust in communities and shaping peace operations to better respond to their protection needs. It also shows that peace negotiations influenced by women are more likely to end in agreement and endure, and that women are best placed to detect early signs of radicalization in their families and communities, and to act to prevent them.

[a] UN-Women, 2013.

conflict of 2014, including 1,492 civilians, of whom 551 were children and 299 women.[36] In Yemen, around two million women and children are acutely malnourished due to the lack of food and drug supplies in besieged areas and the destruction of health care facilities.[37] Half of all registered Syrian refugees are female, mostly aged between 18 and 59 (figure 3.15).

The Beijing Declaration and Platform for Action clearly sets out the consequences of armed conflict on societies in general and on women and children in particular (box 3.1). In situations of war and chaos, women are often subjected to different forms of gender-based violence, including sexual abuse, rape, torture and slavery. The extreme abuses committed by the so-called "Islamic State" have received particular attention from the international community. Even those who escape the fighting often end up suffering from displacement, poverty, loss of home and family. Nonetheless, women play a paramount role in maintaining family livelihoods amid the chaos of war, and in promoting peace in communities during negotiation processes.

3. Institutional implications

While post-war reconstruction projects may restore a country's capital stock and return growth rates to their pre-crisis levels within a measurable amount of time, the effect of conflict on administrative capacity, relations between political factions, and the relationship between the State and its citizens may be altered in incalculable and indefinite ways.

(a) Economic governance and political aspects

Until the 2011 uprisings, the lack of representative government in the Arab region often came, especially when oil rents fuelled the economy, with a measure of stability. That state of affairs no longer seems sustainable since the uprisings and in an era of low commodity prices. Past conflicts in the Arab region have, rather than leading to change in the political system, tended to entrench the ruling establishment, leading to a "political conflict trap".[38]

Moreover, conflict can exacerbate already existing social fragility. Gates and others find that, "on average a conflict increases the odds of a riot occurring the next year by more than 250 per cent".[39] Even after the fighting ends, society is marked by lasting scars and divisions. That has an impact on surviving institutions, post-war policymaking, and the protection of human rights and civil liberties. The potential for renewed conflict remains tangible.

(b) Corruption

Along with the growth-conflict trap, corruption is an endemic problem that drives societies to unrest, and can become still worse during and following a conflict. Corruption is a feature of States with poor capacity that are also susceptible to conflict.[40] If corruption is perceived to be consistently high, and particularly if it seems to privilege one group over another, conflict may ensue. The U4 Anti-Corruption Resource Centre divides corruption in the political economy into two potential forms: *official mogul corruption,* with a small ruling elite that captures the State, and an *oligarch-clan* system, with fragmented and competing elites, which can emerge under power-sharing arrangements.[41]

During a civil or cross-border conflict, illicit activities such as smuggling, bribery, extortion, price gouging and organized crime, flourish. Bribery becomes the main means of obtaining life necessities. Experience in Afghanistan and elsewhere shows that groups engaged in such activities are often connected politically and to the military, and have a vested interest in preventing conflict resolution. In African countries, corruption has kept countries in vicious

Box 3.2 Lessons from Lebanon

Civil war ravaged Lebanon from 1975 to 1990, when a new power-sharing arrangement was put in place under the Ta'if Agreement. By then, the Lebanese economy had hit rock bottom, with $25 billion of physical assets destroyed, and real GDP per capita at one third that of 1974.

The new Government, represented by the Council of Development and Reconstruction (CDR), presented a national reconstruction and development plan, Horizon 2000. Three major sources of finance were identified: national budget surplus (expected by the beginning of 1996); internal borrowing through treasury bills; and foreign financing in the form of grants, loans or a mixture of both. The 10-year reconstruction programme proposed three phases: rehabilitation (1993-1995), reconstruction (1996-1998) and redevelopment (1999-2003). The first phase relied completely on borrowing, mainly external loans and grants (66 per cent and 21 per cent respectively); the second and third period would increasingly depend on budget surpluses (38 per cent and 65 per cent respectively), with dependence on loans and grants set to decrease considerably (to 10 per cent and 4 per cent respectively). The initial $11 billion cost estimate was soon revised upwards to $17.7 billion.

By the late 1990s, however, the Lebanese economy was beset by difficulties as GDP growth fell short of expectations. The fiscal deficit reached 25 per cent of GDP in 2000.[a] To prevent what seemed to be a major incipient recession, the Government resorted to borrowing to help finance essential activities. Through the Paris I, II and III meetings (2001, 2002 and 2007), it sought the help of the international community to complement its efforts in bringing about a virtuous cycle of lower fiscal deficits, declining debt ratios and lower interest rates, which could unleash the potential of Lebanon's private sector.

Those efforts did not bring about the desired results and, in 2011, the Government spent $5.2 billion on foreign debt payments. At 55 per cent of revenue, it was the highest level of debt payment of any country in the world. The reliance on loans for reconstruction, overly optimistic growth projections, and an ill-equipped post-war bureaucracy contributed to this. Kisirwani noted that, "while the Ta'if Agreement put an end to the war, it failed to end political conflicts and meet the aspirations of all communal groups".[b]

A lesson for the Syrian Arab Republic and Libya is that, although a quota-based power-sharing political arrangement may be necessary to end an armed conflict, it needs to be phased out over time in order to enable the Government to take effective decisions. Political deadlock plagues Lebanon, which has been without a president since May 2014, 26 years after peace was achieved in 1990. It will be difficult for Lebanon to realize its reconstruction objectives without a more inclusive political consensus.[c]

[a] Sherry, 2014
[b] Kisirwani, 1997.
[c] Ibid.

cycles of conflict, with funds diverted from development and reconstruction, and trust in the State minimal.[42]

Corruption is also a threat in the post-conflict period, due to massive inflows of aid and investment, low dependence on domestic resources and the resulting lack of accountability, and the re-concentration of political power in the hands of the victors. Other States and multinational corporations often engage in bribery to win contracts or do business with subversive non-State actors. The level of corruption can follow a J-curve rebound following unrest. For example, in the case of Tunisia, highly centralized corruption before the political transition has given way to diluted bribery and corruption that is in fact higher on aggregate than before, as per the *oligarch-clan* system.

Following a crisis, political power and civil society groups often remain aligned according to pre-crisis divisions, and combating corruption takes a back seat to efforts to end hostilities, repatriate the displaced and rebuild. It is also true that corruption can contribute to a degree of stability initially by creating networks in post-conflict situations. However, to prevent such "beneficial" corruption from becoming entrenched, anti-corruption institutions need to be set up early in the post-conflict period. The failure to tackle corruption

allows wartime rent-seeking to continue after the fighting has ended.

According to the Transparency International Corruption Perception Index, Arab countries feature among those perceived as most corrupt across the globe, with four Arab countries ranking in the top 10 in 2015. The performance of many Arab countries on corruption has worsened since 2011 (table 3.3).

Country case studies highlight the link between corruption and the uprisings of 2011. In Libya, corruption and favouritism in government and business were rife and

Table 3.3 Corruption Perception Index for Arab countries

	2012	2013	2014	2015
Countries in conflict since 2011				
Libya	21	15	18	16
Syrian Arab Republic	26	17	20	18
Yemen	23	18	19	18
Countries affected by conflict				
Egypt	32	32	37	36
Jordan	48	45	49	53
Lebanon	30	28	27	28
Tunisia	41	41	40	38
Countries in conflict before 2011				
Iraq	18	16	16	16
Sudan	13	11	11	12
Other Arab countries				
Algeria	34	36	36	36
Bahrain	51	48	49	51
Kuwait	44	43	44	49
Mauritania	31	30	30	31
Morocco	37	37	39	36
Oman	47	47	45	45
Qatar	68	68	69	71
Saudi Arabia	44	46	49	52
United Arab Emirates	68	69	70	70

Source: Transparency International, *Corruption Perceptions Index 2015.* Available from www.transparency.org/cpi2015.
Note: Scoring: 0 = highly corrupt, 100 = very clean.

helped to fuel discontent. Since the change of Government in 2011, corruption has continued unabated and has eroded public confidence in the rival groups vying for power. They have been accused of illicit dealings regarding oil sales and weapons purchases, undue exertion of influence, poor financial management and failure to pay civil servants' salaries.[43] Other States and foreign firms have been complicit and several high-profile cases of bribery have come to light involving businesses from Europe, the United States and elsewhere.

In the Syrian Arab Republic, a difficult period of economic transformation prior to 2011 coincided with prolonged drought, fuelling discontent in rural communities.[44] While ordinary citizens needed to bribe their way to access to malfunctioning State institutions, a small inner circle of party members revelled in State largesse. Little has come of corruption investigations announced by the Government as late as 2015.[45] The war has further fractured the relationship between the State and the people: a new social contract will be needed when the war is over.

In Yemen, corruption played a key role in prompting the removal of the unity Government in 2011. Little changed thereafter and corruption helped to fuel the discontent that led to hostilities in 2015.[46]

D. Countries in conflict – the Syrian civil war

Now in its sixth year, the Syrian civil war has led to one of the most severe humanitarian crises of the new millennium. The international community has failed to end the conflict or provide adequate aid. Recent estimates put the total death toll at 470,000.[47] The country's population has decreased by one fifth, due to casualties and emigration. The war has been accompanied by atrocities, the rise of the so-called "Islamic State", a regional and global

Figure 3.16 Anticipated GDP level and growth, Eleventh Five-year Plan

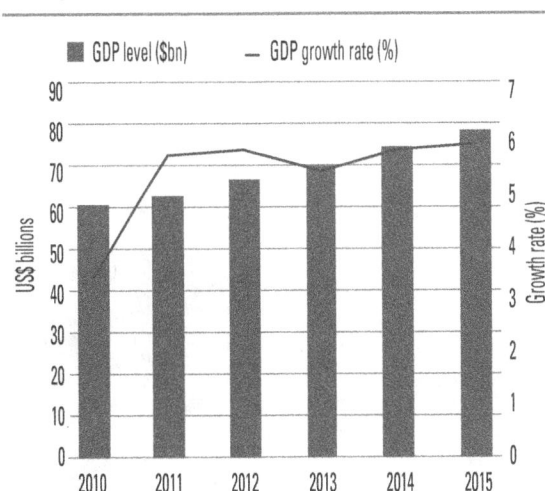

Source: ESCWA calculations based on NAFS, 2016.

refugee crisis, and external intervention that has only fuelled hostilities.

The conflict has left a once middle-income economy in ruins. Various studies have been conducted on the impact of the war on the economy. However, official data have been scant since the war began and account only for activities in areas controlled by the Government. Data on other regions are more difficult to gather.

In this study, we make use of the most recent estimates of economic losses and look at potential post-war projections.

1. Pre-conflict situation and trajectory

According to the Government's Eleventh Five-year Plan, GDP stood at $60.2 billion in 2010 and was set to grow steadily in the years to 2015 (figure 3.16). Under the plan, public investment was to rise from SYP 309 billion to SYP 514 billion between 2011 and 2015, with major investments in public administration, transportation, water and electricity. In practice, those plans have been stripped back and funds have been diverted to military expenditure.

Figure 3.17 Sectoral distribution of physical capital loss

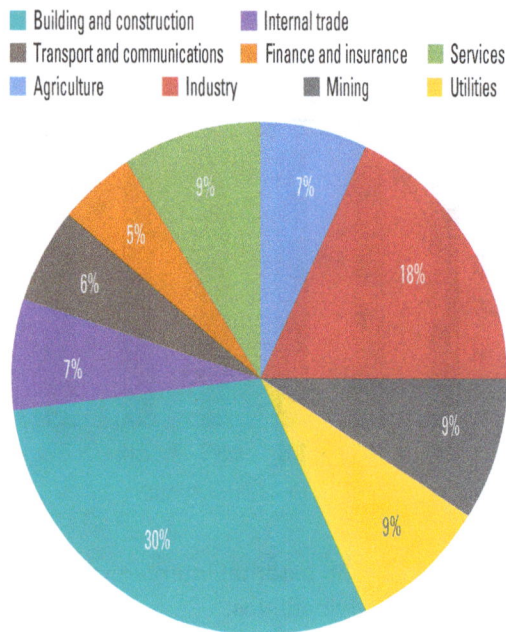

Source: NAFS, 2016.

2. Impact of the conflict

According to National Agenda for the Future of Syria (NAFS) estimations, the Syrian conflict has caused losses of $259 billion since 2011, including $169 billion from lost GDP as compared with pre-conflict projections, and $89.9 billion from accumulated physical capital loss. The Syrian Centre for Policy Research (SCPR) says that overall GDP loss has been three times the size of the country's GDP in 2010.[48] The degree of destruction has increased over time, and ramped-up bombing campaigns since late 2015 have begun targeting infrastructure and economically vital sectors such as energy, which had previously been largely immune. This will further diminish the productive capital stock left at the end of the war.

Building and industry have borne the brunt of destruction (figure 3.17). Output of manufacturing, a key subsector for job and income creation and an indicator of economic transformation, now stands at one third of its 2010 level.

Despite farming losses, favourable weather and the shift to smallholder agriculture during the conflict lifted agriculture's share of GDP from 17.4 per cent before the crisis to 28.7 per cent in 2015. That has been matched by a fall in the GDP share of other sectors, particularly mining (an 11.6 percentage point drop) and internal trade (a 4.5 percentage point drop).[49] Other subsectors, including tourism and utilities, have also been adversely affected.

Public and private sector consumption and investment continue to slide. Public consumption dropped by nearly one third from 2014 to 2015, and household consumption has fallen as consumer price index (CPI) inflation has risen.[50] "Semi-public" consumption (that is, consumption in areas beyond the Government's control) represented 13.2 per cent of GDP in 2015. For example, the so-called "Islamic State" controls three quarters of oil production.

Unemployment rose from 15 per cent in 2011 to 48 per cent in 2014. Some three million Syrians,[51] responsible for 12.2 million dependent family members, have lost their jobs during the course of the conflict.[52] More than 80 per cent of the Syrian population were living below the poverty line at the end of 2015, as opposed to 28 per cent in 2010.[53] Areas with the highest poverty rates include Al-Raqqa, Idlib, Deir El Zor, Homs and the rural area around Damascus, all of which have witnessed some of the most brutal and prolonged battles of the conflict so far. The deep descent into poverty has been fuelled by rising unemployment, the loss of property and assets by large numbers of IDPs and sharp cuts in food and fuel subsidies.

The continuing economic destruction will translate into a new lower level and trajectory for the Syrian economy, with greater dependence on imports and aid. Debt,

Box 3.3 Rwanda – a success story

In the years since a bloody and divisive ethnic civil war ended in 1994, Rwanda has built national unity while diversifying and transforming its economy.

Following the assassination of President Habyarimana in April 1994, Rwanda's majority Hutu population carried out a genocide of the minority Tutsi population. In just 100 days, 800,000 Tutsi and moderate Hutus were killed, and many were displaced internally and externally. The damage to the economy was severe, with economic infrastructure crippled, and power plants, factories and hospitals destroyed.[a]

The immediate response of the new political leadership under Paul Kagame, with belated support from the international community, helped put Rwanda on a path to rapid reconstruction. The United Nations International Criminal Tribunal for Rwanda prosecuted only the principle perpetrators of the violence, while community tribunals operated at the local level.[b] New policies were aimed at downplaying ethnic differences and promoting a unified Rwandan identity. The country thus largely avoided the kind of severe reprisals that could have come after a conflict and genocide on that scale.

Figure A Net ODA received per capita, current US dollars

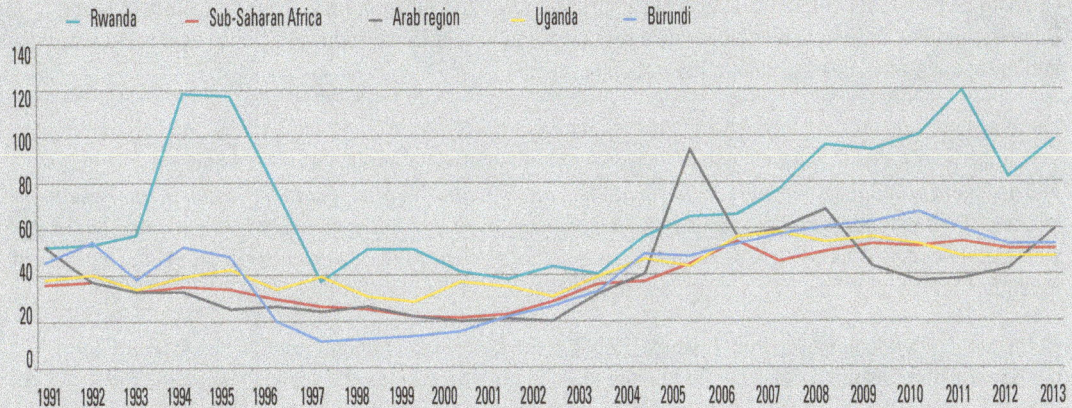

Figure B GDP growth

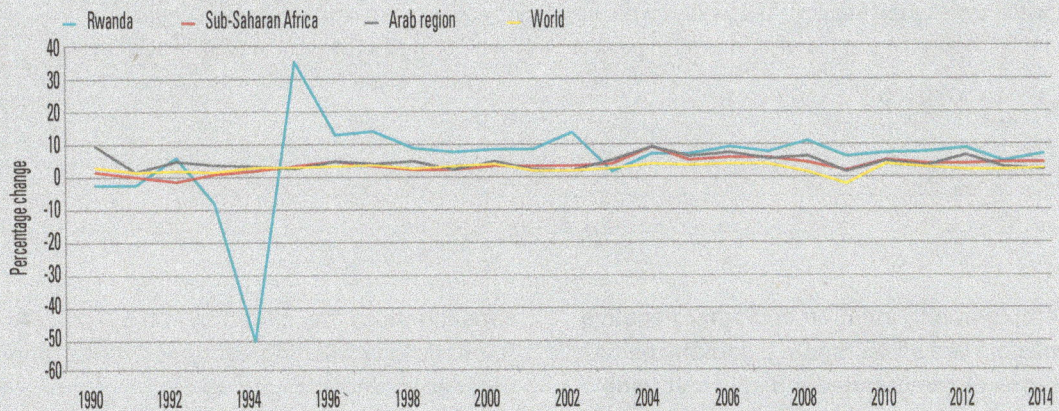

Source: World Bank, World Development Indicators database. Available from http://data.worldbank.org/products/wdi (accessed 30 March 2016).

Good governance, economic reforms and accountability transformed the landlocked and resource-poor country into a regional economic leader. Focus was placed on education and agricultural transformation, with support going to smallholders in traditional crops and the promotion of a move towards higher income coffee and tea niche-products. Official development assistance (ODA) played a key role in new infrastructure investments, with receipts increasing tremendously after 1994 and standing at a higher level per capita than comparable countries and regions (figure A).

Later stages of economic reform involved a shift towards services, promoting the country as a regional and global hub for services, particularly in information and communications technology and tourism. Services drove over half of the GDP growth between 2007 and 2013, and the Government envisages services to account for nearly half of GDP by 2020.[c] Those reforms have had a noticeable impact. Since 1994, the growth rate of Rwanda has largely remained above the averages for sub-Saharan Africa, the Arab region and the world (figure B).

According to the Transparency International Corruption Perception Index, Rwanda had the fourth lowest level of perceived corruption in Africa (44th lowest globally) in 2015. The country's inclusive gender policies are well known. Under the 2008 Constitution, women are to hold at least 30 per cent of decision-making posts, and more than half the seats in parliament are held by women.[d]

Opening up to investment and business has improved Rwanda's performance across a variety of Doing Business indicators, where it notably ranks second globally in getting credit, twelfth in registering property, and thirty-seventh in dealing with construction permits.[e]

There are positive lessons from Rwanda for the future of the Syrian Arab Republic. The conflict in Rwanda was brief, but the death toll was high and divisions seemed insurmountable. Directed economic policies and a vision of reconciliation and unity helped the country to lay the groundwork for much of its present success. Diversification based on primary commodities can help to boost incomes and lead to an eventual shift to services. In the Syrian Arab Republic, new sectors will have to be linked to job creation. The case of Rwanda shows that providing a strong message of reconciliation can attract donors.

Notes of caution also emerge from Rwanda. Political will has helped the country to move forward, but the Government has been criticized for banning dissent and the President is seeking to amend the Constitution in order to run for yet another term. Rwanda also stands accused of contributing to instability in neighbouring Democratic Republic of Congo.

In the Syrian Arab Republic, progress and reconstruction cannot come at the expense of equal participation and good relations between political and ethnic groups at home, and with its neighbours.

[a] The Economist, 2016a
[b] AfDB, 2011
[c] ECA, 2015.
[d] ECA, 2016.
[e] World Bank, 2016d, p.229.

unemployment, inflation and other negative indicators are all worsening, and any gains in terms of remittances and informal trade are vastly offset by the physical losses and opportunity costs of the war. So, although theory posits that countries in long-term conflict may adjust to the economic consequences, the situation in the Syrian Arab Republic is worsening every year according to most economic indicators.

The conflict has triggered an unprecedented refugee crisis. The plight of refugees has been documented but global humanitarian

Table 3.4 Projected and actual GDP growth rate, Lebanon (percentage)

	2012	2013	2014 baseline influx	2014 high influx
Pre-crisis projected GDP growth rate	4.3	4.4	4.4	4.4
Current (with crisis) estimated and projected growth rate	1.4	1.5	1.5	1.9
Change in real GDP growth rate	-2.9	-2.9	-2.9	-2.5

Source: United Nations and World Bank, Lebanon: economic and social impact assessment of the Syrian conflict. Report No. 81098-LB (Washington D.C., 20 September 2013). Available from http://documents.worldbank.org/curated/en/925271468089385165/pdf/810980LB0box379831B00P14754500PUBLIC0.pdf.

assistance and legal allowances for displaced persons remain inadequate. Under an agreement reached in London between European and Arab partners in February 2016, it was decided to open markets for manufactured goods, such as textiles, from Jordan because of the refugee burden that country is bearing.[54] According to the ILO, 28 per cent of Syrian refugees in Jordan had work in early 2014. Unemployment in that country had, however, soared from 14.5 per cent in March 2011 to 22 per cent in 2014.

3. Reconstruction

NAFS has developed a road map for recovery and reconstruction to be implemented from day one of a peace agreement in the Syrian Arab Republic. The length of the conflict has provided time to formulate a thorough plan. There are also lessons to be learned from post-conflict success stories in other regions, such as the case of Rwanda (box 3.3). Options for reconstruction will be discussed in the policy recommendations section below.

E. Conflict spillover in neighbouring countries

1. Lebanon

The Syrian civil war has had a profound impact on Lebanon. The two countries historically

have close economic and cultural ties, and all Lebanon's viable land routes for trade and movement of people pass through Syrian territory. In addition to the massive influx of refugees and disruption of trade, falling production and a growing dependence on imports in the Syrian Arab Republic have also altered the trade portfolio of Lebanon. The conflict has placed strain on public services and macroeconomic performance. However, it has also opened up new export and production opportunities for Lebanese firms.

(a) The immediate impact – in numbers

By the end of 2015, 1.5 million Syrian refugees were living in Lebanon, accounting for a quarter of the country's total population.[55] According to a joint report by the United Nations and the World Bank,[56] the initial years of the war (2012-2014) cut real GDP growth in Lebanon by roughly 2.9 percentage points per year (table 3.4). Demand for Lebanese goods in its war-torn neighbour, which was its fifth largest trading partner and the transit route for one fifth of its exports, has fallen. Lebanese manufacturers, especially those that exported to Damascus, have been the hardest hit.[57] Trade costs have also risen. Total losses in Lebanon due to the war have been estimated at $13.1 billion, $5.6 billion of it in 2015 alone.[58]

Tourism arrivals and expenditures have dropped since the start of the crisis, due to

Figure 3.18 International tourist arrivals and expenditures in Lebanon

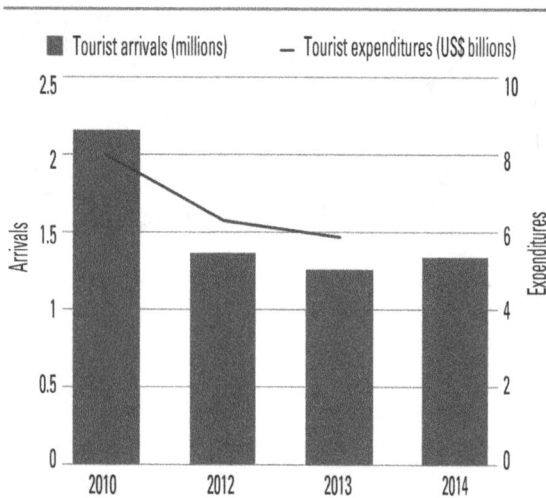

■ Tourist arrivals (millions) — Tourist expenditures (US$ billions)

Source: ESCWA staff calculations based on World Tourism Organization, *UNWTO Tourism Highlights 2015 Edition* (Madrid, 2015).

fears regarding possible spillover of the Syrian conflict and, more generally, political unrest across the region (figure 3.18).

(b) Indirect negative impacts

Refugee and migrant flows to Lebanon have swelled the ranks of the labour force by 50 per cent.[59] It has been estimated that the influx, coupled with stalled job creation, could have left between 220,000 and 340,000 Lebanese, particularly women, the young and the unskilled, out of work, doubling unemployment to 20 per cent.[60] Most Syrian refugees who are working are doing so informally, potentially pushing Lebanese out of such work. Access for refugees to formal work is difficult.

Syrian refugees are present in rural and poor areas of the North, South and Beqaa districts. In 2013, the ILO calculated poverty rates of 53 per cent in the North, 42 per cent in the South and 30 per cent in the Beqaa, compared with the 28 per cent national rate. A 2014 assessment indicated that "the net impact on Lebanon has been the addition of 170,000 to the one million living in poverty".[61]

The situation, it was predicted in 2013, would lead to a budget deficit aggravated by falling tax revenues of $2.6 billion between 2012 and 2014 alone.[62] Recent estimates suggest that the number of vulnerable Lebanese matches that of Syrian refugees (1.5 million). Including 300,000 Palestinian refugees and 42,000 Palestinian refugees displaced from their Syrian homes, that means more than 3.3 million people in need out of a total population of 5.9 million.[63] Further, 52 per cent of displaced Syrians and 10 per cent of Lebanese are classified as "extremely poor" (earning less than $2.40/day). Demand for utilities and other services has risen: by 28 per cent in the case of water since 2011.[64] All this in a country where the State was already weakened by political divisions and strained public finances.

In spite of a glut in food supply on Lebanese markets due to good crop yields and the closing of land export routes, the dropping of subsidies formerly applied by the Syrian Government, which benefited people on both sides of the border, has pushed prices up.[65]

Uncertainty about how long the war will last and continue to affect Lebanon only serves to exacerbate the situation.

(c) Other mixed results

Any potential impact on the import of goods has been cushioned in part by consumption on the part of refugees in Lebanon. Their presence has also contributed to the resilience of the country's diverse export activity. The port of Beirut has been busier since overland trade routes through Syria closed, although the latter began to open again in 2015. Some attribute falls in exports between 2011 and 2013 almost entirely to "the drop in exports of precious stones to South Africa and Switzerland". Although some Lebanese exporters had lost trade by 2012, others were stepping into the breach and replacing lost domestic production in

Figure 3.19 Sources of declining growth in Tunisia (percentage points)

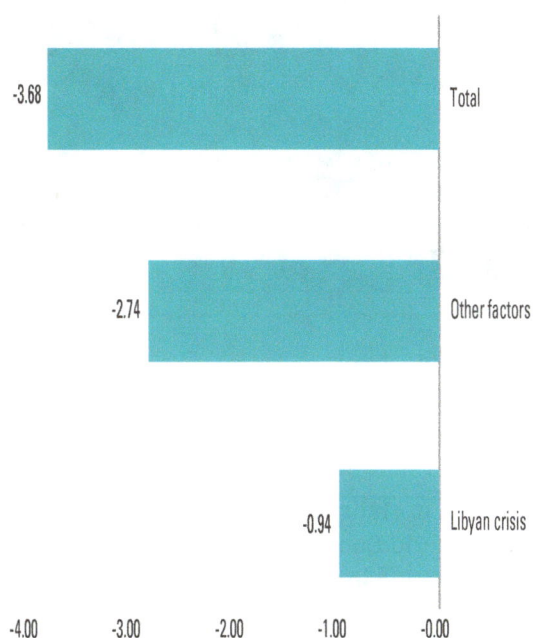

Figure 3.20 Transmission channels (percentage points)

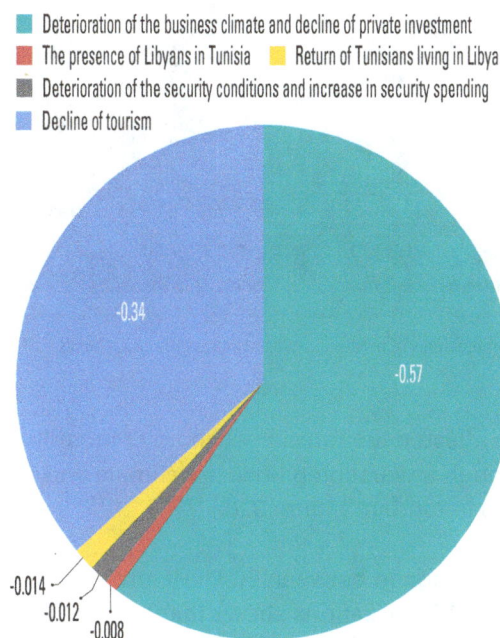

- Deterioration of the business climate and decline of private investment
- The presence of Libyans in Tunisia
- Return of Tunisians living in Libya
- Deterioration of the security conditions and increase in security spending
- Decline of tourism

Source: ESCWA and World Bank, *Impact of Internal Conflicts on Neighbouring Countries: Case of the Libyan Crisis and the Tunisian Economy* (forthcoming).

the Syrian Arab Republic. The disruption of exports caused by the war has been greater in Jordan and Turkey than in Lebanon.[66]

2. The crisis in Libya and the Tunisian economy

Political transition at home and the crisis next door in Libya have buffeted Tunisia's economy. Although the uprising of 2011 led to a change of Government and free elections in 2014, continuing instability and security concerns are having an adverse effect on the economy. In Libya, civil war, the struggle for power and legitimacy between two main rival groups, continued intermittent fighting between various groups and militias even after the signing of peace deals, crippled oil output and falling commodity prices have dealt a major blow to the country's finances. Efforts to restore peace and political unity have to date failed, and the continued uncertainty affects neighbouring countries adversely.

(a) General equilibrium analysis

We use a general equilibrium model to assess the impact of the crisis in Libya on the Tunisian economy. The study is based on Tunisian data from before 2010 and household surveys of Libyans in Tunisia, conducted by the National Statistical Institute.[67]

Tunisia lost an average of 3.86 percentage points of growth per year between 2011 and 2015, when comparing actual growth with IMF projections in 2010. The model demonstrates that 0.94 points of this loss – or nearly nine billion Tunisian dinars (TND) at current prices – may be attributed to the crisis in Libya. The remaining 2.74 basis point loss is attributable to other internal and external factors (figure 3.19).

(b) Worsening business climate and declining private investment

The model demonstrates that the Libyan crisis

Table 3.5 Number of Libyans present in Tunisia and their income

	2010	2011	2012	2013	2014	2015
Number of Libyans in Tunisia (thousands)	32.2	123.5	59.3	63.7	53.3	18.2
Formal income (thousands of dinars)	75.18	71.03	106.82	87.96	108.07	36.88
Informal income (thousands of dinars)	2725	2441	2345	2416	1868	814
Total income (thousands of dinars)	2800.18	2512.03	2451.82	2503.96	1976.07	850.88

Source: Survey of border customs agents and Tunisian banks.

has affected the Tunisian economy primarily through a worsening business climate and a drop in tourism (figure 3.20).

A comparison between 2010 IMF projections and 2015 realizations shows that the volume of private investments in Tunisia stands 25 per cent lower than anticipated. Insecurity was the main reason and 47 per cent of surveyed investors responded that the situation in Libya was a major problem for their operations in Tunisia.[68] ESCWA and the World Bank concluded that one fifth of the 25 per cent drop in private investment in Tunisia could be attributed to the Libyan crisis.

(c) The impact of Libyan nationals in Tunisia

Libyans who have moved to Tunisia due to instability in their own country thus far have not been classed as refugees. They have relocated mainly to access health care, entertainment and other amenities. Typically, they have formal income transferred through bank accounts and informal income valued by customs agents at the border. As of yet, Libyan incomes are transfers and have not been subject to income tax in Tunisia.

Libyan arrivals and the average income they injected in to the local economy peaked in 2010-2011, and tapered off considerably in 2015 (table 3.5).

(d) The return of Tunisians living in Libya

According to statistics gathered for the joint ESCWA-World Bank study, the number of Tunisians living in Libya fell from 85,000 in 2010 to only 25,000 in 2015. Their return home has generated a revenue shortfall, due to declining remittances and increased pressure on the Tunisian labour market. Formal remittances are estimated at around TND 600 per month per worker but reach 2.5 times that amount when informal channels and cash transactions are taken into account. General equilibrium analysis shows that the return of workers to Tunisia pushed unemployment up from 13 to 14.68 per cent.

(e) Security

Many of the attacks that have undermined security in Tunisia in recent years have been in some way connected to the crisis in Libya, which has become a gateway for Tunisian terrorists to and from the Syrian Arab Republic, a transit point for weapons being shipped into Tunisia and a training ground or shelter for terrorists.

Chaos in Libya has hampered coordination between the two countries and made border control expensive. The spate of terrorist attacks since 2011 has obliged the Tunisian Government to increase spending on security and defence. Budget allocations to the Ministry

Figure 3.21 Annual growth rate of the hotels and restaurant services sector

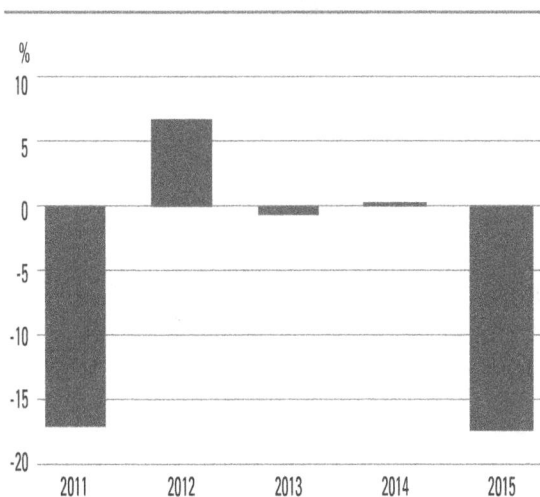

Source: Quarterly Tunisian National Institute of Statistics bulletins.

of Security have risen from less than TND 4 billion in 2010 to TND 9 billion in 2016, an average annual increase of 16 per cent. That means less money for development projects or social spending. Overall, it is estimated that half the increase in Tunisia's security and defence budget can be attributed to the situation in Libya.

(f) Decline in tourism

Tourism, which is an important source of economic activity and foreign exchange in Tunisia, has been set back by the conflict in Libya and attacks directly targeting tourism at Bardo and Sousse in 2015 (figure 3.21). We estimate that half the fall in tourism in 2015 can be attributed to the Libyan crisis.

(g) Macro-level effects

Although the situation in Libya is not the only reason for the poor performance of Tunisia since 2011, it has played a significant part, mainly due to the deteriorating business climate and security situation.

The impact of the Libyan crisis on the Tunisian economy involves a final demand effect,

whereby Tunisian and Libyan households lose part of their revenue and therefore cut consumption, by 26 per cent in Libya and 3.4 per cent in Tunisia. The Tunisian Government has also been obliged to lift current expenditures by 2.2 per cent in order to tackle rising insecurity, and has raised the tax burden on Tunisian households by 41 per cent, further reducing their final consumption. Further damage has come from lost private investments.

With the exception of taxes on household income, all tax revenues – including from corporate tax, VAT and customs duties – have fallen.

The cumulative spillover effects of the Libyan crisis have led to a 3.8 per cent drop in imports, while the decline in production has reduced the volume of exports by 1.7 per cent.[69] The decline in production affects nearly all sectors, particularly hospitality, industry and final consumption sectors such as food and tobacco.

Successful democratic transition in Tunisia may mean that a downward shift in growth could be followed by a positive J-curve rebound in the future.

F. Conflict prior to 2011 – the Israeli occupation of Palestine

After almost 50 years of occupation, peppered with recurrent military offensives and a broad array of long-term policies and practices detrimental to social and economic development, the situation in Palestine is unique.

Those policies and practices include restrictions on movement, trade and private sector activity and have been felt most acutely in Gaza (box 3.4). It has been estimated that one in two Palestinians in the occupied

Palestinian territory, or roughly 2.3 million people, would be in need of some form of humanitarian assistance in 2016.[70]

Economic development in Palestine in the current circumstances is untenable. The deliberate destruction of infrastructure and services, confiscation of land, expansion of illegal settlements and prolonged restrictions on movement and trade are significant obstacles to development.

Due to the devastating 51-day offensive on Gaza in 2014, the Palestinian economy contracted by 0.2 per cent in 2014. Growth declined by 2.1 per cent year-on-year in the first quarter of 2015. It then registered a year-on-year increase of 8 per cent in the first quarter of 2016. That increase, broken down to 4.2 per cent in the West Bank and 21.1 per cent in the Gaza Strip,[71] is largely explained by the very low base in Gaza in the aftermath of the 2014 offensive.

The consequences of the 2014 offensive on Gaza linger: real GDP per capita in the first three quarters of 2015 was less than half of GDP per capita in the West Bank and below the level observed in the same period in 2010.[72]

In the West Bank, growth slowed from 5 per cent year-on-year in the fourth quarter of 2014 to 1.7 per cent in the first quarter of 2015, due to a four-month suspension in clearance revenue transfers by Israel at the beginning of 2015.

Severe import and export trade restrictions on Gaza have been a major disincentive to private sector investment, forcing the economy to restructure inwards towards non-tradable goods and the service sector. Public administration and services together account for more than half of Gaza's GDP (28.2 per cent and 24.3 per cent respectively).[73] Some commercial transfers to the West Bank resumed in November 2014 and export restrictions to Israel were partially lifted in

March 2015, for the first time since 2007. Those moves had little tangible impact on the local economy. Meanwhile, aid flows have continued to be sporadic.

Unemployment in Palestine stood at 26.6 per cent in the first quarter of 2016. In Gaza, the rate skyrocketed during the 2014 offensive and stood at 41.2 per cent in the first quarter of 2016. Unemployment among vulnerable groups, such as refugees (42.1 per cent) and women (62.6 per cent), has remained high.[74] In the West Bank the jobless rate stood at 18 per cent in the first quarter of 2016. Rates were higher for refugees (19.9 per cent compared with 17.3 per cent for non-refugees) and women (28.4 per cent compared with 15.5 per cent for men).[75]

The discriminatory Israeli zoning and planning regime in the West Bank, including East Jerusalem, favours Israeli settlements. It is practically impossible for Palestinians living in Area C[76] to obtain building permits. The combined area in which the Israeli authorities have permitted construction by Palestinians amounts to approximately 0.4 per cent of Area C, compared with 20 per cent with approved plans for Israeli settlements.

The occupation also impedes socioeconomic development in other respects, such as food security. Half of the Palestinian population suffers from more than one micronutrient deficiency. The situation is particularly alarming for female adolescents in Gaza, 72 per cent of whom suffer from Vitamin D deficiencies and 64 per cent from Vitamin A deficiencies.[77]

The quality of health care has declined markedly over the years, and became still worse with the closure of the Rafah crossing into Gaza in July 2013. In the West Bank, Israeli restrictions on movement, in addition to discriminatory zoning and planning polices, impede access by Palestinians to health-care services.

There is a shortage of schools in Gaza and the West Bank. In Gaza, 86 per cent of UNRWA schools operate in double shifts because the blockade and restrictions on the import of building materials has made it impossible to build schools. Restrictions on construction in the West Bank, settler violence and intimidation, and other measures by

---

Box 3.4 Collective suffering in Gaza

Under Israeli military occupation since 1967, the Gaza Strip has been subjected to a near-total blockade since 2007 and to major offensives by the Israeli military, the most intense of which took place in 2006, 2008, 2012 and 2014. Infrastructure has been all but destroyed, the economy is in tatters and people's lives are under constant threat. With more than two thirds born since the Oslo Accords of 1993, most of the population in the Gaza Strip has grown up and lived knowing only the hardships caused by the blockade and the frequent military assaults.

In 2010, the then Commissioner-General of UNRWA referred to the situation in Gaza as "far beyond a humanitarian [crisis]".[a] That was after only three years of blockade and before the most devastating military offensive, which unfolded in July and August 2014. Conditions in Gaza by 2016 are far worse, and more than four fifths of the population depend on aid.[b]

A study done 2016 by ESCWA and Birzeit University on how prolonged exposure to Israeli military violence affects the health of people living in the Gaza Strip and collective trauma concluded that such collective suffering cannot be adequately addressed through individual treatment alone.[c] Real remedies would include lifting the blockade and reconstruction of the Gaza Strip. The study found that, among those surveyed:

- One third reported less than good health.

- One third reported mental health problems and a lack of well-being.

- More than one quarter suffered from moderate to high levels of distress (one third in northern Gaza).

- 84 per cent considered that suffering was part of their lives.

- 78 per cent blamed the blockade for their suffering.

- 17 per cent suffered from hypertension.

- 56 per cent reported that they felt deprived.

- 51 per cent reported moderate to severe human insecurity.

- 45 per cent reported a decrease of family income since the 2014 offensive.

- 4 in 5 families suffered from different degrees of food insecurity.

- 51.5 per cent of households reported that they had to eat less food than needed because of unavailability, 40.2 per cent that they had fewer meals because of insufficient food, and 64.5 per cent that they had to purchase food products on credit.

- During the 2014 offensive, 95 per cent of rural dwellers had to leave their homes.

- During the offensive, 40 per cent of households hosted another family.

[a] IRIN, 2010.
[b] UNRWA, 2014.
[c] ESCWA, 2016b.

---

the Israeli army mean that 50,000 children enrolled in 183 schools in Area C face risks on their way to school, and 10,000 children attend makeshift schools in tents, caravans and tin shacks.[78]

G. Policy recommendations

Policy recommendations focus on three key areas.

First, it is essential for any post-war State to bring about quick wins in the period immediately following the cessation of hostilities, whether in terms of job creation, reconstruction, resettlement of displaced persons, the formation of an inclusive unity government or other steps to build harmony and cement peace.

Secondly, the State needs to address youth unemployment as a matter of priority following transition. Joblessness among young people was one of the key reasons behind the 2011 uprisings. Tunisia, which emerged from the uprisings with a new Constitution and democratic Government, remains unstable with rising overall and youth unemployment. In Tunisia as elsewhere, the failure of State economic planners, civil society, the private sector and labour groups to address chronic unemployment will spell trouble farther down the line.

Thirdly, the availability and sources of finance, domestic or foreign, has implications for the pace and ownership of reconstruction efforts.

Specific recommendations follow hereafter.

1. Financing reconstruction: domestic resources and foreign assistance

Of key importance is the degree to which reconstruction can be financed from within the Arab region in a framework of regional cooperation. That depends on whether available funds are under the control of regional actors, or can be mobilized by them. In order to assess those criteria, ESCWA has made estimates of the net cumulative current account surpluses and total fiscal surpluses of Arab countries between 2000 and 2017 (2015 to 2017 are forecasts).[79]

As of 2015, cumulative external surpluses stood at $2.7 trillion, forecast to decline to $2.4 trillion by 2017. Cumulative fiscal

Figure 3.22 ODA to Latin American countries (millions of US dollars)

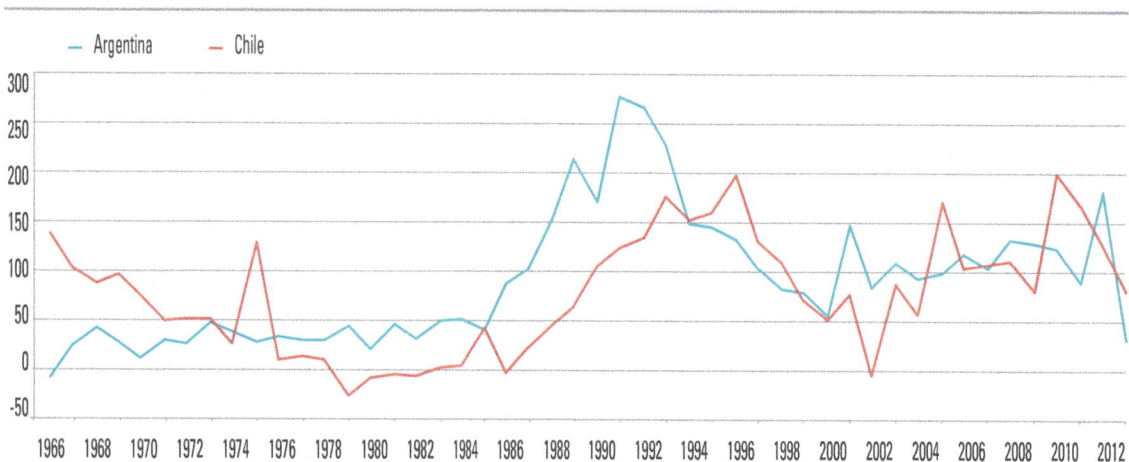

Source: World Bank, World Development Indicators database. Available from http://data.worldbank.org/products/wdi (accessed 30 March 2016).

surpluses stood at $1.1 trillion in 2015 but will drop to $591 billion by 2017. These estimates imply that funds are available in the region to finance future reconstruction. However, the amount is set to shrink due to expected lower energy export revenues and government revenues in the coming years. Most of the funds are beyond the control of Governments, either in the private sector or locked in quasi-government entities such as sovereign wealth funds. A mobilization strategy, requiring cooperation from the private sector and public-private partnerships, could be crucial.

Even if the Governments concerned could harness those funds, nothing guarantees that they would be willing to make the money available, through grants or loans, to their Arab partners for reconstruction.

The flow of ODA and other assistance can increase to post-conflict countries for a number of reasons, for example due to more favourable relations between new Governments and donors, and the ending of sanctions against former regimes. ODA and debt relief are needed immediately for infrastructure projects, humanitarian assistance, State-building and security.[80]

Figure 3.22 and figure 3.23 illustrate aid flows prior to, during and following transitions in Latin America and Eastern Europe. ODA to Argentina rose significantly after its return to democracy in the 1980s. In Chile, ODA increased significantly following both its coup and the return to democracy.

ODA to Poland, the Russian Federation and others swelled in the wake of the fall of communism across Eastern Europe and the collapse of the Soviet Union, and as those countries emerged as new global partners, opening up previously closed markets.

ODA to Georgia spiked following its brief war with the Russian Federation in 2008 due to Western support. The Kyrgyz Republic receives considerable assistance from the Russian Federation and Western donors, a sign to Arab countries that assistance packages can be secured from different sources. Financial assistance and relief, including hefty loans, has flowed into Ukraine since the change of government in 2013 and in view of ongoing conflict. Flows also increased significantly into post-conflict Balkan countries, albeit with different time frames.

Figure 3.23 ODA to post-Soviet republics (millions of US dollars)

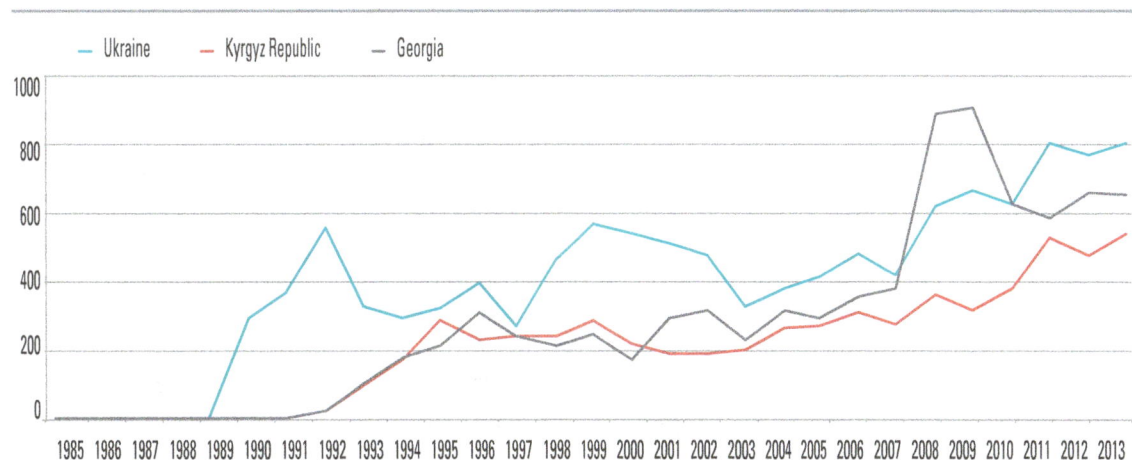

Source: World Bank, World Development Indicators database. Available from http://data.worldbank.org/products/wdi (accessed 30 March 2016).

Figure 3.24 ODA inflows to countries receiving additional post-crisis assistance (billions of US dollars)

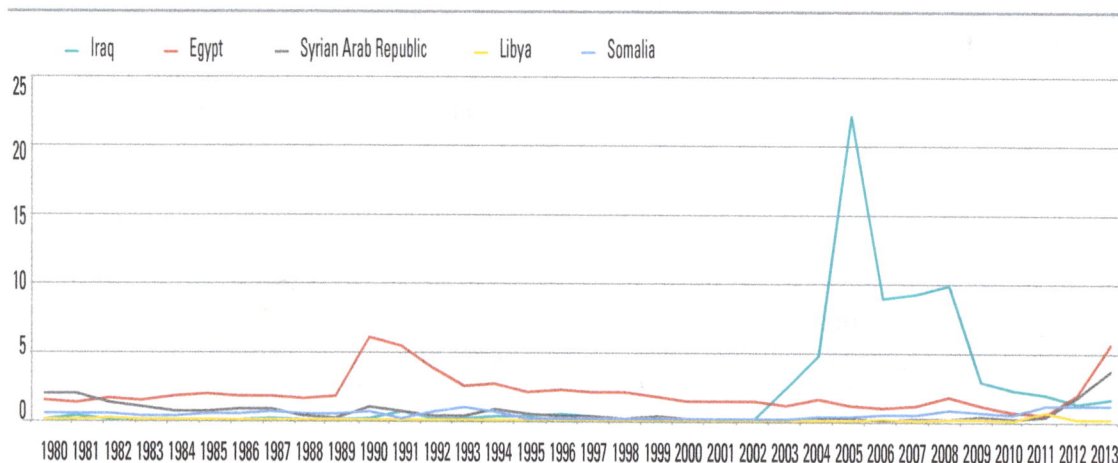

Source: World Bank, World Development Indicators database. Available from http://data.worldbank.org/products/wdi (accessed 30 March 2016).

ODA can be used for post-crisis reconstruction and State-building. International assistance to some Arab countries rose significantly in the wake of various crises, including: Iraq (funds for rebuilding and reconstruction following the US invasion in 2003), Libya (after the 2011 conflict), Somalia (as the security situation has improved somewhat in recent years) and Egypt (during the political transition of 2011) (figure 3.24).

However, others received no significant boost. Neither Algeria nor Lebanon received noticeable additional assistance after their civil wars. Lebanon, however, did receive an extra injection after the Israeli invasion of 2006 (figure 3.25).

Countries emerging from war need to make the most efficient use of possible short-term spikes in aid that tend to occur in the immediate post-conflict period. In the longer run, they need to improve institutions and governance in order to ensure continued donor support.

It is imperative that Arab countries and the rest of the international community provide sufficient assistance during and following the present conflicts, ensuring that it is directed to State-building, social protection and rebuilding infrastructure.

The extent to which assistance is provided in the form of grants or loans, or involves Arab and multinational corporations in rebuilding programmes, will affect the level and sustainability of the region's rebound. Dwindling funds for Syrian refugees, for instance, points to a worrying decline in assistance to regions racked by conflict. That trend should be reversed and regional and international donors should refocus their attention on such war-affected areas.

2. Syrian reconstruction

The NAFS scenario for rebuilding the economy of the Syrian Arab Republic, supposing that hostilities will end in 2016, uses a financial programming model to calculate what will be needed to return the country's GDP to its 2010 level by 2025.

Calculations are based on an incremental capital-output ratio using a simplified Harrod-Domar model, which reflects the halving of investment efficiency due to the conflict,

Figure 3.25 ODA inflows to Arab countries not receiving additional post-crisis assistance (millions of US dollars)

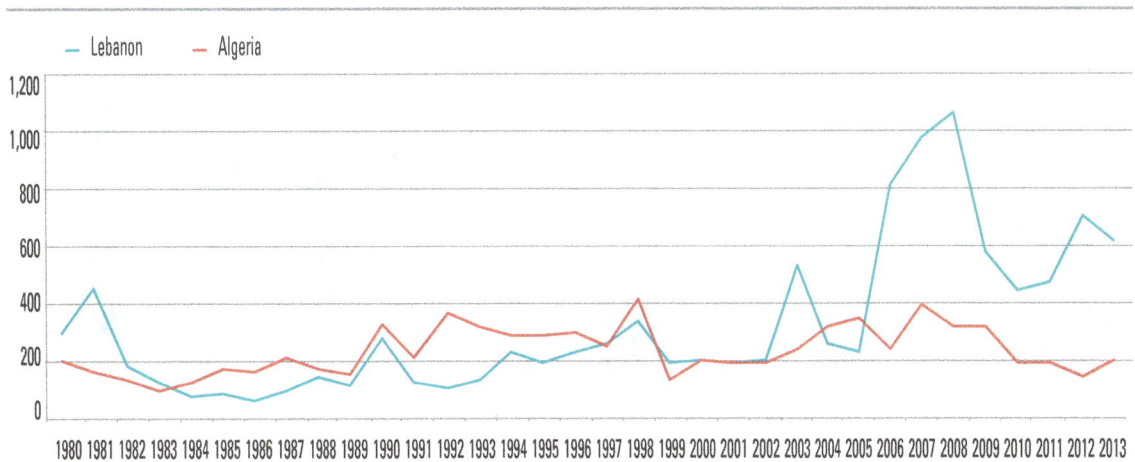

Source: World Bank, World Development Indicators database. Available from http://data.worldbank.org/products/wdi (accessed 30 March 2016).

but anticipates a rebound in that efficiency and capacity to mobilize resources after the conflict. Under the scenario, a minimum public investment of $183.5 billion will be needed to rebuild the country. This equals the sum of cumulative capital loss during the conflict and the investments intended under the 2011 five-year plan, and will boost growth through multiplier effects and stimulate private investment.

Figure 3.26 illustrates projections for the rebound in growth and investment, with an immediate return to positive growth spurred by large investments coinciding with an end to hostilities. Reconstruction could be divided into two phases (figure 3.27): a peacebuilding phase (2016-2018), with a focus on basic needs, ending violence and initiating economic recovery, and a State-building phase (2019-2025), expanding investments to productive sectors and activities, with sectoral allocations presumably based on the five-year plan. The process will require major and expanding investment, particularly from the private sector. Success will depend greatly on the sources and reliability of, and conditions attached to, the available financing options.

An alternative exercise utilizes a computable general equilibrium (CGE) model, based on the assumption that hostilities end in 2016 and implementation of Eleventh National Development Plan, with a focus on rebuilding destroyed capital and restoring public investment.[81]

This yields interesting projections, including a steady increase in GDP similar to the NAFS calculations, but with a spike of 40.6 per cent GDP growth in 2016 due to the immediate infusion of capital and assistance, before it levels off to an average of between 11 and 15 per cent. Capital stock would grow at its pre-crisis rate to reach 2011 levels by 2017 in an optimistic projection. Public investment would spike in 2016 and continue to grow as well, triggering private sector investment. Exports would increase slowly, reaching a value of 20 per cent of GDP by 2020, while imports would boom at 57 per cent of GDP in 2016, later stabilizing at 43 per cent. In the absence of grants, the public deficit and debt would increase to 50 and 200 per cent of GDP respectively. This highlights the importance of tapping into a broad range of alternative financing options. With so many Syrians displaced externally, remittances will play

Figure 3.26 Projected post-conflict GDP and investment growth (billions of US dollars)

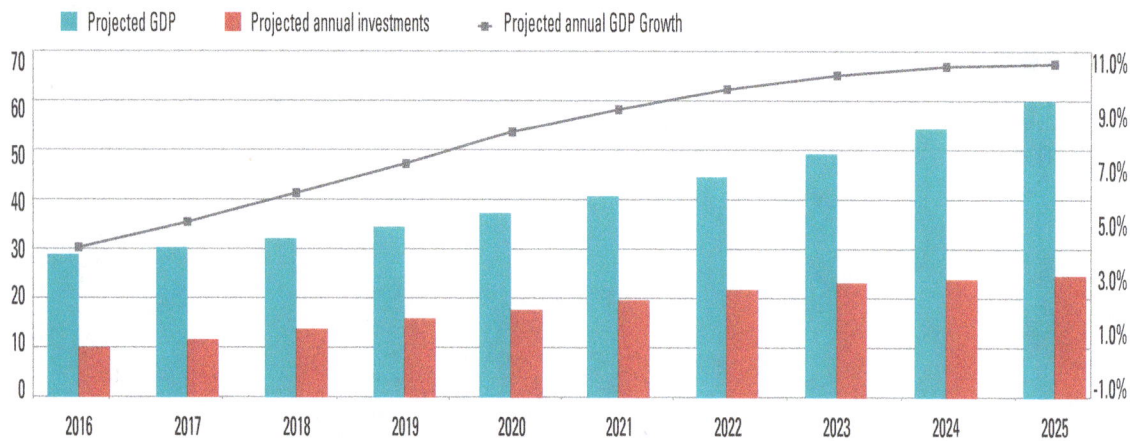

Source: NAFS, 2016.

an important role in rebuilding as many of those who find work will remain abroad and continue to work and send money home.

Post-conflict macroeconomic policy will have to go beyond stabilization and tackle problems resulting from the loss of physical and human capital, brain drain, deep political and geographical divisions, as well as factoring in peacebuilding. The approach to post-war reconstruction in Lebanon offers some cautionary lessons. The economic policies and political arrangements arrived at, although they helped the country to emerge from conflict, did not prove sustainable in the longer term.

At the meeting held in London in February 2016 on supporting the Syrian Arab Republic and the region, European and Arab Governments pledged $11.2 billion to deal with the crisis between 2016 and 2020. That would help make up for past shortfalls in aid to meet the basic needs of refugees (access to shelter, health and water), and create opportunities for them through education and employment. The 2016 Humanitarian Response Plan alone requires $3.18 billion. Signatories must honour their pledges and ensure that the plan is implemented. The inclusion of refugees into workforces will help

to prevent them becoming a "lost generation" and could prove to be an opportunity for the Arab countries in which they have sought refuge if accompanied by job-creating economic policies fostering industrialization and diversification.

3. Lebanon – coping with spillover effects

The United Nations and World Bank estimate that annual spending of $2.5 billion is needed to return public service provision to its pre-2011 level in Lebanon.[82] That includes health, education, social programming and poverty safety nets, infrastructure, water supply and sanitation, electricity, transport and solid waste management. The ongoing garbage crisis in the country highlights the dangerous problem of surplus demand for government utilities coupled with poor institutional frameworks and political deadlock.

The Government estimates that, for 2016 alone, $2.48 billion is needed (35 per cent for stabilization and 65 per cent for humanitarian programmes). Sector-specific plans require international financial assistance. Job-creation schemes have become more important than ever, given the increase in the size of the labour force. Public works programmes, training or transfers for the unemployed

Figure 3.27 Sectoral allotment of investment, by phase

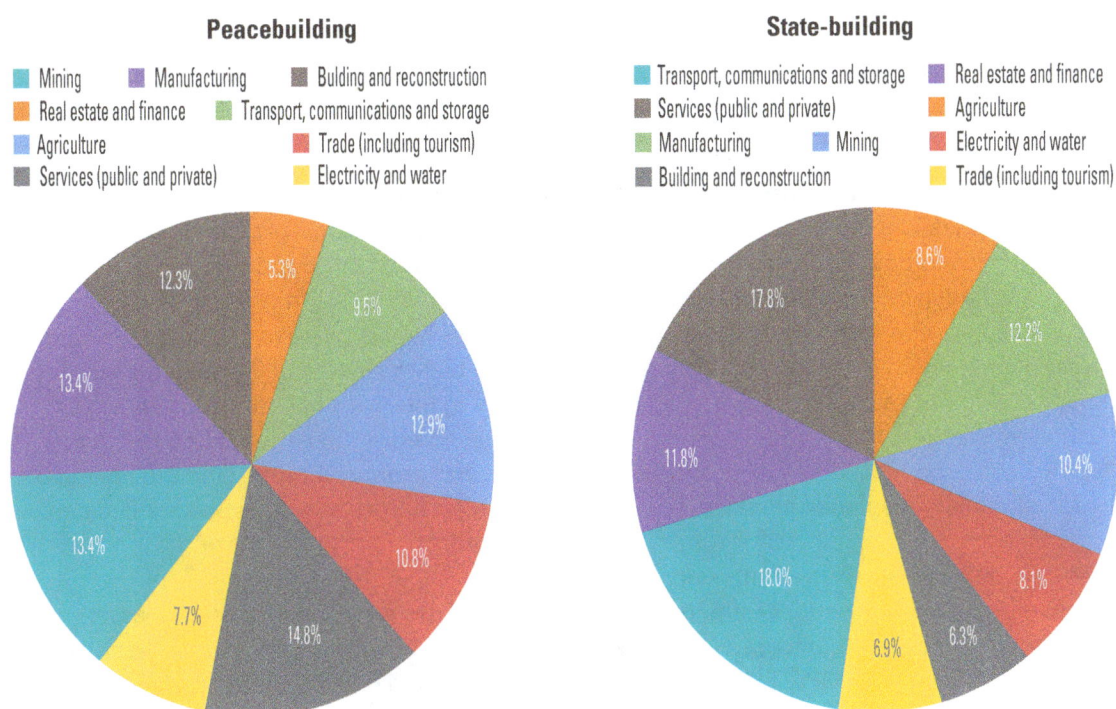

Peacebuilding

- Mining
- Manufacturing
- Bulding and reconstruction
- Real estate and finance
- Transport, communications and storage
- Agriculture
- Trade (including tourism)
- Services (public and private)
- Electricity and water

12.3% 5.3% 9.5% 13.4% 12.9% 13.4% 10.8% 7.7% 14.8%

State-building

- Transport, communications and storage
- Real estate and finance
- Services (public and private)
- Agriculture
- Manufacturing
- Mining
- Electricity and water
- Building and reconstruction
- Trade (including tourism)

8.6% 17.8% 12.2% 11.8% 10.4% 18.0% 8.1% 6.9% 6.3%

Source: NAFS, 2016.

and subsidies for the underpaid could cost between $166 and $242 million per year.

According to the Government, international assistance provided thus far to deal with the influx of refugees amounts to only half of what is required. Moreover, funding for programmes such as those provided by UNRWA and UNHCR is under threat. Greater and more reliable external assistance is needed to deal with impact of the Syrian war on Lebanon, now and after an eventual cessation in hostilities.

4. Tunisia – more international assistance and coordination with the future Libyan Government

With the first glimmers of political stabilization in Libya and the potential for economic recovery in Tunisia, the two countries need to seize the opportunity and prepare logistically and institutionally. For example, they could strengthen their land, sea and air links.

International assistance to Tunisia, particularly to promote trade and regional integration and to help meet increasing security expenditure, should be boosted considerably. In the five years to 2014, aid to Tunisia did not exceed $700 million over five years, while Egypt received more than $15 billion and Jordan nearly $3 billion in the same period.

5. Economic integration for conflict mitigation and prevention

Regional economic integration can help to prevent potential conflict. The Arab countries should implement GAFTA and conduct meaningful negotiations on the ACU. The resulting economic and trade ties will increase the opportunity cost of conflict. Deeper regional trade, more regional industries and stronger value chains will dissuade countries from engaging in disputes with one another, and give them more reason for preventing internal instability.

The economic benefits of integration must reach the broad population through equal economic opportunities.

Deepening trade agreements can create opportunities for job-creating sectors and industries, such as agriculture and manufacturing. Facilitating their growth will also require investment and cross-border sharing of technology. That in turn would help to lift the region's productivity growth rate, which between 1991 and 2010 was the lowest of any region in the world,[83] decrease dependence on primary commodities, and promote more diversified production.

6. Assistance for displaced persons

Given the political interests of outsiders in the Arab region, more international support should be forthcoming to help to integrate refugees in host countries, assist IDPs, and promote improvements in regional migration policies.[84]

Displacement is seldom temporary and often leads to long-term dependency among future generations. Policies are needed to address the lost property rights, and the occupation or destruction of homes by other IDPs.

The reintegration of opposition groups and former fighters is usually insufficient in post-conflict societies, increasing the likelihood of renewed strife.[85] Immediate humanitarian relief for displaced persons must therefore be coupled with longer-term strategies to integrate populations in new locations or reintegrate them upon return, with sufficient employment, education and other opportunities.

More financial support should be allocated to Arab States that are spending more to mitigate the effects of crises. To be successful, peacebuilding requires better long-term economic prospects.

Host countries can benefit from the diversity of skills and talent that refugees and other displaced populations often bring with them, if at the same time they promote diversification and skills development policies.

7. Post-conflict policies and social programmes

Governments must prioritize post-crisis and post-conflict social programmes. Based on the experiences of Egypt and Tunisia since 2011, ESCWA has highlighted a range of strategies for policymakers.[86] Constitutions should be amended and legislation passed reflecting international principles on issues such as non-discrimination, human rights, social and economic rights, and the obligations of the State. Such laws must be applied and enforced.

Programmes are needed to tackle past grievances. In Tunisia, for instance, that means addressing regional disparities and marginalized populations in terms of socioeconomic development. Genuine attempts to combat corruption and promote equal economic opportunities, however tricky politically in such contexts, can help to restore trust in the State. Temporary special measures such as quota systems can be used to promote the rights of marginalized groups and include sunset provisions for eventually phasing them out.

With regard to women, implementation of Security Council resolution 1325 (2000) is key. The region itself provides examples on how to move forward. In Egypt, civil society organizations and human rights activists are creating protection movements, networks and information-sharing channels to combat sexual harassment and assault against girls and women, such as that seen with growing intensity in demonstrations, and prosecute the perpetrators. Governments should embrace and scale up such initiatives.

Countries emerging from conflict typically have a history of poor economic policies. Post-conflict policies need to tackle specific issues that, if left unaddressed, could lead to a return of instability and conflict.[87] Political reform and the expansion of opportunities for participation in political life must ensue immediately after the end of conflict. Aside from rebuilding infrastructure, economic policy should concentrate on managing capital flight and repatriation, and controlling post-conflict commodity and construction booms.

The needs of growing populations must be balanced with those of people directly affected by the recent crises in social and urban planning. Policymakers need detailed risk assessments to model the impact of root causes of conflict on their countries' capacity to achieve SDG targets and plan accordingly.[88]

8. National and regional reforms and conflict-prevention mechanisms

The wars and crises that have shaken the region since 2011 stem from a failure of regional and global diplomacy and should spur countries to create a regional mechanism aimed at preventing conflict in the future. There are models. The African Union suspends members temporarily for coups or other undemocratic changes of power, and provides for the rapid despatch of peacekeeping forces to member countries in crisis. More attention needs to be paid to the role of external actors in contributing to regional instability. Political will, institutional capacity and meaningful engagement with civil society are needed to implement policies, reforms and measures aimed at preventing conflict.

Endnotes

Chapter 1
1. United States Department of Commerce Bureau of Economic Analysis, 2016
2. European Commission, 2016.
3. ILO, 2016a, p. 12.
4. UNHCR, 2016a, p. 2 and pp. 62-66, Annex Table 2.
5. OPEC, 2016, p. 85, tables 10.1 and 10.2.
6. Ibid.
7. Ibid. p.87, table 10.3
8. Lecarpentier, 2015.
9. IMF, 2016.
10. Heffer and Prud'homme, 2015.
11. World Bank, 2016a.

Chapter 2
1. For details of the continuing negative impact of the occupation, see United Nations, 2016.
2. World Bank, 2016b.
3. Yemen, Ministry of Planning and International Cooperation, 2016, p. 4.
4. Federal Republic of Somalia, 2016, p.8.
5. ESCWA staff estimates based on World Bank, 2016c.
6. The GII sheds light on the gender gap in key areas of human development in 155 countries. It is a composite score, ranging from 0 to 1, of a country's loss of achievement due to gender inequality based on three dimensions: reproductive health; empowerment; and labour market participation. The higher GII values indicate greater inequality. See UNDP, 2010a, p.84-94, and UNDP, 2015a, for methodological details.
7. IPU, 2016a.
8. United Nations Statistics Division (UNSD), 2016.
9. The index is used to evaluate countries based on outcomes rather than inputs and ranks them according to proximity to gender equality rather than women's empowerment. It includes four subindices: economic participation and opportunity (unemployment and remuneration for equal work levels), political empowerment (ministerial, senior legislative and managerial posts, share of seats in parliament), education (completion of primary, secondary and tertiary education), health and survival ("missing women" phenomenon and life expectancy). See WEF, 2015, pp. 3-7, for methodological details.

10. Average GGI score of the region is 0.597 equivalent to closing of around 60 per cent of gender gap, based on ESCWA staff calculations of regional average scores weighted by population.
11. Rayman, Izen and Parker, 2016.
12. IPU, 2016b.
13. Ibid.
14. World Bank, 2015b.
15. ESCWA, 2013.
16. ESCWA, 2016a.
17. Ibid.
18. Ibid.
19. ESCWA, 2012.
20. ILO, 2016b.
21. UNDP, 2015b.
22. ESCWA, 2015b.
23. Qatar General Secretariat for Development Planning, 2011.
24. Council for European Palestinian Relations, 2012.
25. Barsoum, Ramadan and Mostafa, 2014, p. 3.
26. ILO, 2016c, Table 15.a.
27. ILO, 2004.
28. ESCWA staff calculations based on Sri Lanka Bureau of Foreign Employment, 2013.
29. Sabban, 2002.
30. ESCWA and IOM, 2015.
31. ILO, 2013a.
32. Female employment to population ratio is the proportion of a country's female working-age population (over 15 years of age) that is employed.
33. Sabban, 2002.
34. Ahmad, 2010.
35. ESCWA and IOM, 2015.
36. Ibid., p.178
37. Ibid., p. 88
38. Ibid., p. 88, box 1.
39. Human Rights Watch, 2016.
40. Afghanistan, Bangladesh, China, India, Indonesia, Nepal, Pakistan, the Philippines, Sri Lanka, Thailand and Viet Nam.
41. IOM, 2016.
42. World Bank, 2015b.
43. Except the Sudan and Somalia.
44. Resolution 1325 (2002) was reinforced by others: 1820 (2008); 1888 (2009); 1889 (2009); 1960 (2010); 2106 (2013); and 2122 (2013).
45. The legislation provides for heavy penalties for acts of domestic violence and harassment of women in the streets, and refers specifically to spouses.

Chapter 3
1. Rodrick and Wacziarg, 2005; Papaioannou and Siourounis, 2008; and Persson and Tabellini, 2006.
2. Collier and others, 2003.
3. Gates and others, 2010.
4. Collier, 1999.
5. ESCWA, 2015b.
6. Collier and others, 2003.
7. Davies, 1962.
8. Jakobsen, 2013.
9. ESCWA, 2015b.
10. Murdoch and Sandler, 2004.
11. Roaf and others, 2014.
12. De Melo, Denizer and Gelb, 1996.
13. ESCWA, 2015b.
14. Including Iraq, Palestine and the Sudan.
15. Including Libya, the Syrian Arab Republic and Yemen.
16. Including Egypt, Jordan, Lebanon and Tunisia.
17. ESCWA, 2015d.
18. ESCWA, 2015a.
19. UNWTO, 2014 and 2015.
20. Abdelfattah, 2011 and ESCWA, 2015a.
21. UNHCR, 2016a.
22. Ibid., p. 65
23. Ibid., p. 2.
24. Ibid.
25. UNHCR, 2016b.
26. Clayton, 2015.
27. ESCWA and IOM, 2015.
28. Ibid.
29. Ibid.
30. Ibid.
31. ESCWA, 2015d.
32. Sarangi and others, 2015.
33. ESCWA, 2015e.
34. Regional Refugee and Resilience Plan 2016-2017 in response to the Syria Crisis, 2016.
35. Gates and others, 2010.
36. OCHA, 2015a.
37. O'Brien, 2016.
38. Gates and others, 2010.
39. Ibid.
40. Chene, 2012.
41. Zaum, 2013.
42. Bamidele and Academy, 2013.
43. Daragahi, 2015.
44. Lund, 2014.
45. Agence France Presse, 2015.
46. Dbwan, 2014.
47. Syrian Centre for Policy Research, 2015.

48. Ibid.
49. Ibid.
50. Ibid.
51. Ibid.
52. World Bank, 2015a.
53. ESCWA and University of St. Andrews, 2016.
54. The Economist, 2016b.
55. Government of Lebanon and United Nations, 2015.
56. United Nations and World Bank, 2013.
57. Cali et al., 2015.
58. Government of Lebanon, 2016.
59. Government of Lebanon and United Nations, 2015.
60. Cali and others, 2015; and United Nations and World Bank, 2013.
61. Bank Audi, 2014.
62. United Nations and World Bank, 2013.
63. Government of Lebanon and United Nations, 2015.
64. Ibid.
65. FAO, 2014.
66. Cali and others, 2015.

67. For full survey results, see ESCWA and World Bank (forthcoming).
68. Based on an annual survey of the business climate and competitiveness conducted by the Tunisian Institute of Competitiveness and Quantitative Studies (ITCEQ). The 2015 field survey involved interviews with 883 companies.
69. ESCWA and World Bank (forthcoming).
70. OCHA, 2015b.
71. PCBS, 2016b.
72. Ibid.
73. Ibid.
74. PCBS, 2016a.
75. Ibid.
76. Constitutes more than 61 per cent of the West Bank.
77. OCHA, 2015b.
78. PCBS, 2015.
79. The estimation is made by rearranging the national income identity so that a sum of net private domestic savings and net government fiscal surplus equals

current account surplus. The total for Arab countries over the period from 2000 to 2015 is used to estimate the amounts.
80. UNDP, 2008; and Valters, Rabinowitz and Denney, 2014.
81. Al Dardari and Bchir, 2014.
82. United Nations and World Bank, 2013.
83. ESCWA and UNEP, 2015.
84. ESCWA and IOM, 2015.
85. ESCWA, 2015b.
86. ESCWA, 2015c.
87. Collier, 2007.
88. ESCWA, 2015d.

Bibliography

Abdelfattah, Dina (2011). Impact of Arab revolts on migration. CARIM analytic and synthetic notes, No. 2011/68. Robert Schuman Centre for Advanced Studies. European University Institute. Available from http://cadmus.eui.eu/handle/1814/19874.

African Development Bank (2011). Rwanda – bank group country strategy paper 2012-2016. Regional Department East A (OREA). Tunis. October.

Agence France Presse (2015). Syria pursuing corruption cases against officials, re-printed in *The Daily Star*, 28 August. Available from www.dailystar.com.lb/News/Middle-East/2015/Aug-28/313080-syria-pursuing-corruption-cases-against-officials.ashx.

Ahmad, Attiya (2010). Migrant domestic workers in Kuwait: The role of State institutions. The Washington D.C.: Middle East Institute. Available from www.mei.edu/content/migrant-workers-kuwait-role-state-institutions.

Al Dardari, Abdallah, and Hedi Bchir (2014). *The Reconstruction of the Syrian Economy: A First Proposal*. Beirut: Economic and Social Commission for Western Asia (ESCWA).

Bamidele, Oluwaseun, and Faith Academy (2013). Corruption, Conflict and Sustainable Development in African States. *The African Symposium*, Volume 13, No. 1, June.

Bank Audi (2014). Lebanon economic report 2014, 3rd Quarter. Beirut. Available from www.bankaudi.com.lb/GroupWebsite/openAudiFile.aspx?id=2418.

Barsoum, Ghada, Mohamed Ramadan, Mona Mostafa (2014*)*. Labour market transitions of young women and men in Egypt. Work4Youth publication series, No. 16. Geneva: ILO. Available from www.ilo.org/employment/areas/youth-employment/work-for-youth/publications/national-reports/WCMS_247596/lang--en/index.htm.

Bernanke, Ben (2005). The global saving glut and the US current account deficit. Sandridge Lecture, Virginia Association of Economists. Richmond, Virginia, 10 March. Available from www.federalreserve.gov/boardDocs/Speeches/2005/200503102/default.htm.

Cali, Massimiliano, and others (2015). *The Impact of the Syrian Conflict on Lebanese Trade*. Washington D.C.: World Bank. April.

Chene, Marie (2012). *Lessons Learned in Fighting Corruption in Post-conflict Countries*. U4 Anti-Corruption Resource Centre.

Clayton, Jonathan (2015). Numbers of internally displaced in Libya double since September, UNHCR, 30 June. Available from www.unhcr.org/5592a8286.html.

Collier, Paul (1999). On the economic consequences of civil war. *Oxford Economic Papers,* vol. 51. Centre for the Study of African Economies. Oxford: Oxford University.

_____ (2007). *Post-Conflict Recovery: How Should Policies be Distinctive?* Centre for the Study of African Economies, Department of Economics. Oxford: Oxford University.

Collier, Paul, and others (2003). *Breaking the Conflict Trap: Civil War and Development Policy*. Washington D.C., World Bank; Oxford, Oxford University Press.

Council for European Palestinian Relations (2012). *Agriculture in Palestine: a Post-Oslo Analysis*. CEPR MEMO. Available from http://thecepr.org/images/stories/pdf/memo%20agriculture.pdf.

Daragahi, Borzou (2015). Corruption and incompetence allegations dog Libya's governments. *Financial Times,* 12 April.

Davies, James (1962). Toward a theory of revolution. *American Sociological Review*, vol. 27, No. 1, February.

Dbwan, Abdulmoez (2014). Fighting the culture of corruption in Yemen. *The World Bank Blogs*, 4 December 2014. Available from http://blogs.worldbank.org/arabvoices/fighting-culture-corruption-yemen.

Del Carpio, Ximena Vanessa, and Mathis Christoph Wagner (2015). The impact of Syrian refugees on the Turkish labor market. Policy research working paper. Washington D.C.: World Bank.

De Melo, M., C. Denizer, and A. Gelb (1996). From plan to market. Policy research working paper 1564. Washington D.C.: World Bank.

The Economist (2016a). A hilly dilemma: should Paul Kagame be backed for providing stability and prosperity or condemned for stifling democracy?,12 March.

_____ (2016b). Peace, bread and work – jobs for Syrian refugees help them and their hosts, and slow their exodus, 7 May.

European Commission (2016). European economic forecast – Spring 2016, institutional paper 025. Luxembourg: European Union. Available from http://ec.europa.eu/economy_finance/publications/eeip/pdf/ip025_en.pdf.

Food and Agricultural Organization (2014). *The Impact of the Syria Crisis on Agriculture, Food Security and Livelihoods in Lebanon*. Cairo. Available from http://fscluster.org/lebanon/document/impact-syria-crisis-agriculture-food.

Gates, Scott, and others (2010). Consequences of armed conflict in the Middle East and North Africa region. Background paper. 23 November 2010. Available from http://folk.uio.no/haavarmn/MENA_Cons_Conflict.pdf.

Gruber, Joseph W., and Steven B. Kamin (2015). The corporate saving glut in the aftermath of the global financial crisis. International finance discussion papers 1150. October. Available from http://dx.doi.org/10.17016/IFDP.2015.1150.

Heffer, Patrick, and Michel Prud'homme (2015). Short-term fertilizer outlook 2015-2016. Paris: International Fertilizer Industry Association (IFA). November. Available from www.fertilizer.org/en/images/Library_Downloads/2015_ifa_paris_summary.pdf.

Hill, Ginny, and others (2013). *Yemen: Corruption, Capital Flight and Global Drivers of Conflict*. Chatham House Report. London: Chatham House. September. Available from http://www.hlrn.org/img/documents/0913r_yemen.pdf.

Human Rights Watch (2016). Kuwait: progress on domestic workers rights, 2 February. Available from https://www.hrw.org/news/2016/02/02/kuwait-progress-domestic-workers-rights.

International Labour Organization (ILO, 2004). *Gender and Migration in Arab States: the Case of Domestic Workers*. Geneva. Available from www.ilo.org/beirut/publications/WCMS_204013/lang--en/index.htm.

_____ (2013a). *Domestic Workers Across the World: Global and Regional Statistics and the Extent of Legal Protection*. Geneva: International Labour Office. Available from www.ilo.org/travail/Whatsnew/WCMS_173363/lang--en/index.htm.

_____ (2013b). *Global Employment Trends: Recovering from a Second Jobs Dip*. Geneva: International Labour Office. Available from www.ilo.org/wcmsp5/groups/public/---dgreports/---dcomm/---publ/documents/publication/wcms_202326.pdf.

_____ (2016a). *World Employment and Social Outlook: Trends 2016*. Geneva: International Labour Office. Available from www.ilo.org/global/research/global-reports/weso/2016/WCMS_443480/lang--en/index.htm.

_____ (2016b). *Women in Business & Management, Gaining Momentum in the Middle East and North Africa*. Geneva: International Labour Office. www.ilo.org/beirut/publications/WCMS_446101/lang--en/index.htm.

_____ (2016c). Key indicators of the labour market (KILM). Eighth edition. Available from http://www.ilo.org/global/statistics-and-databases/research-and-databases/kilm/lang--en/index.htm. Accessed 30 March 2016.

International Monetary Fund (2016). IMF primary commodity prices. Available from www.imf.org/external/np/res/commod/index.aspx. Accessed 30 March 2016.

International Organization for Migration (2016). Abu Dhabi Dialogue. Available from https://www.iom.int/abu-dhabi-dialogue.

Inter-Parliamentary Union (2016a). Women in national parliaments. Available from www.ipu.org/wmn-e/arc/classif010516.htm. Accessed on 10 May 2016.

_____ (2016b). Women in parliament, the year in review 2015. Available from www.ipu.org/pdf/publications/WIP2015-e.pdf.

IRIN (2010). West Bank health and economy up a bit, Gaza down, 18 May. Available from www.irinnews.org/news/2010/05/18/west-bank-health-and-economy-bit-gaza-down.

Jakobsen, Tor G. (2013). The J-curve – James C. Davies' Theory of Revolutions. *Popular Social Science*, 17 April 2013. Available from www.popularsocialscience.com/2013/04/17/james-c-davies-j-curve-theory-of-revolutions.

Kilian, Lutz (2009). Not all oil price shocks are alike: disentangling demand and supply shocks in the crude oil market. *American Economic Review*, vol. 99, No. 3, pp. 1053-69. Available from https://www.aeaweb.org/articles?id=10.1257/aer.99.3.1053.

Kisirwani, Maroun (1997). The rehabilitation and reconstruction of Lebanon, *Remaking the Middle East*. Beirut: American University of Beirut. Available from http://ddc.aub.edu.lb/projects/pspa/kisirwani.html.

Lebanon (2016). London Conference Lebanon statement of intent. Available from www.businessnews.com.lb/download/LondonConferenceLebanonStatementOfIntent4Feb2016.pdf.

Lebanon, and United Nations (2015). *Lebanon Crisis Response Plan 2015-16: Year Two*. Available from http://www.3rpsyriacrisis.org/wp-content/uploads/2016/01/20151223_LCRP_ENG_22Dec2015-full-versionoptimized.pdf.

Lecarpentier, Armelle (2015). Current trends and prospects for natural gas. 4 December. Rueeil-Malmaison, France: International Association for Natural Gas (Cedigaz). Available from www.cedigaz.org/documents/2015/PresAB2015.pdf.

Lund, Aron (2014). Drought, corruption, and war: Syria's agricultural crisis, Carnegie Endowment for International Peace, 18 April 2014. Available from http://carnegieendowment.org/syriaincrisis/?fa=55376.

Murdoch, James C., and Todd Sandler (2004). Civil wars and economic growth: spatial dispersion. *American Journal of Political Science*, vol. 48, pp. 138-151. Available from http://onlinelibrary.wiley.com/doi/10.1111/j.0092-5853.2004.00061.x/full.

National Agenda for the Future of Syria (NAFS, 2016). Post-conflict challenges for the macroeconomic policies for Syria. Beirut: ESCWA.

O'Brien, Stephen (2016). Under-Secretary-General for Humanitarian Affairs and Emergency Relief Coordinator, statement to the Security Council on Yemen. New York, 16 February 2016. Available from http://reliefweb.int/report/yemen/under-secretary-general-humanitarian-affairs-and-emergency-relief-coordinator-stephen-4.

Office for the Coordination of Humanitarian Affairs (OCHA, 2012). Country fact sheet: Jordan, August 2012. Available at http://reliefweb.int/sites/reliefweb.int/files/resources/Jordan.pdf.

_____ (2015a). Fragmented lives – humanitarian overview 2014. East Jerusalem: OCHA – Occupied Palestinian Territory. March 2015. Available from https://www.ochaopt.org/documents/annual_humanitarian_overview_2014_english_final.pdf.

_____ (2015b). Humanitarian needs overview 2016 – occupied Palestinian territory. November 2015. Available from https://www.ochaopt.org/documents/hno_december29_final.pdf.

Office of the United Nations High Commissioner for Refugees (2015a). World at war - global trends: forced displacements in 2014. Geneva. Available from www.unhcr.org/556725e69.pdf.

_____ (2015b). Mid-year trends 2015. Geneva. Available from www.unhcr.ch/fileadmin/user_upload/dokumente/06_service/zahlen_und_statistik/Mid-Year_Trends_2015.pdf.

_____ (2016a). Global trends: forced displacement in 2015. Geneva. Available from www.unhcr.org/statistics/country/576408cd7/unhcr-global-trends-2015.html.

_____ (2016b). Syria Regional Refugee Response Portal. Available from http://data.unhcr.org/syrianrefugees/regional.php (accessed 29 March 2016).

Organization of Petroleum Exporting Countries (2016). OPEC monthly oil market report. Vienna. 14 March. Available from www.opec.org/opec_web/en/publications/338.htm.

Palestinian Central Bureau of Statistics (2015). On the eve of the International Child Day; Palestinian children remain victims of ongoing Israeli violence. 18 November 2015. Available from www.pcbs.gov.ps/portals/_pcbs/PressRelease/Press_En_IntChildDy2015E.pdf.

_____ (2016a). Press report on the labour force survey results. Labour force survey (January-March 2016) Round (Q1/2016). Available from www.pcbs.gov.ps/portals/_pcbs/PressRelease/Press_En_LFSQ12016E.pdf.

_____ (2016b). Press report: preliminary estimates of quarterly national accounts (first quarter 2016). Available from www.pcbs.gov.ps/portals/_pcbs/PressRelease/Press_En_QNAQ12016E.pdf.

Papaioannou, Elias, and Gregorios Siourounis (2008). Economic and social factors driving the third wave of democratization. *The Journal of Comparative Economics*, vol. 36 (2008), pp. 365-387. Available from http://ac.els-cdn.com/S0147596708000218/1-s2.0-S0147596708000218-main.pdf?_tid=4e19766c-6dc9-11e6-84b6-00000aab0f6b&acdnat=1472462384_7d5053f251efc775e30b99e857c4df58.

Persson, Torsten, and Guido Tabellini (2006). Democracy and development: the devil in the details. Working paper No. 11,993. Cambridge, MA: National Bureau of Economic Research (NBER). January. Available from http://www.nber.org/papers/w11993.pdf.

Qatar, General Secretariat for Development Planning (2011). *Qatar National Development Strategy 2011-2016*. Available from www.mdps.gov.qa/en/nds/Documents/Qatar_NDS_reprint_complete_lowres_16May.pdf.

Rayman, Paula, Seth Izen, and Emily Parker (2016). UNSCR 1325 in the Middle East and North Africa: women and security. Special report 388. Washington D.C.: United States Institute of Peace. Available from https://www.usip.org/sites/default/files/SR388-UNSCR-1325-in-the-Middle-East-and-North-Africa-Women-and-Security.pdf.

Regional Refugee and Resilience Plan 2016-2017 in Response to the Syria Crisis (2016). Mid-year report, June 2016. Available from www.3rpsyriacrisis.org/wp-content/uploads/2016/07/3RP-Mid-year-Report.pdf.

Roaf, James, and others (2014). 25 years of transition – post-communist Europe and the IMF. Regional Economic Issues Special Report. October 2014. Available from https://www.imf.org/external/pubs/ft/reo/2014/eur/eng/pdf/erei_sr_102414.pdf.

Rodrik, Dani, and Romain Wacziarg (2005). Do democratic transitions produce bad economic outcomes? *American Economic Review*, vol. 95, No. 2, pp. 50-55. Available from https://www.aeaweb.org/articles?id=10.1257/000282805774670059.

Sabban, Rima (2002). United Arab Emirates: migrant women in the United Arab Emirates, the case of female domestic workers. Gender Promotion Programme (GENPROM) working paper No. 10. Geneva: ILO. Available from www.ilo.org/employment/Whatwedo/ Publications/WCMS_117955/lang--en/index. htm.

Sarangi, Niranjan, and others (2015). Towards better measurement of poverty and inequality in Arab countries: a proposed pan-Arab multipurpose survey. E/ESCWA/SD/2014/WP.1. Available from https://www.unescwa.org/ sites/www.unescwa.org/files/publications/ files/e_escwa_sd_14_wp-1_e.pdf.

Sherry, Hassan (2014). Post-war Lebanon and the influence of international financial institutions: a "Merchant Republic", Civil Society Knowledge Centre, Lebanon Support, August. Available from http://cskc.daleel-madani.org/paper/post-war-lebanon-and-influence-international-financial-institutions.

Somalia (2016). Appropriation Act for 2016 Budget. Act No. 8. Available from http://mof. gov.so/wp-content/uploads/2016/05/Budget-Appropriation-2016-Web.pdf.

Sri Lanka, Bureau of Foreign Employment (2013) Annual statistical report of foreign employment 2013. Available from www.slbfe.lk/page. php?LID=1&MID=54.

Stave, Svein Erik, and Solveig Hillesund (2015). Impact of Syrian refugees on the Jordanian labour market. Beirut: ILO Regional Office for the Arab States and Fafo Institute for Applied International Studies. Available from www. ilo.org/wcmsp5/groups/public/---arabstates/---ro-beirut/documents/publication/ wcms_364162.pdf.

Sustainable Development Solutions Network (2016). Indicators and a monitoring framework: Goal 05. Achieve gender equality and empower all women and girls. Available from http:// indicators.report/goals/goal-5/.

Syrian Centre for Policy Research (2015). Confronting fragmentation – impact of Syrian crisis report. Available from http://scpr-syria. org/publications/policy-reports/confronting-fragmentation/.

Trabelsi, Meriem (2015). Implementation of the UNSCR 1325 on Women, Peace and Security in the Arab States, International Knowledge Network of Women in Politics, 10 December 2015. Available from http://iknowpolitics.org/en/ discuss/e-discussions/implementation-unscr-1325-women-peace-and-security-arab-states.

United Nations, General Assembly (2015). Transforming our world: the 2030 Agenda for Sustainable Development. A/RES/70/1. Available from www.un.org/ga/search/view_ doc.asp?symbol=A/RES/70/1&Lang=E.

_____ (2016). Economic and social repercussions of the Israeli occupation on the living conditions of the Palestinian people in the Occupied Palestinian territory, including East Jerusalem, and the Arab population in the occupied Syrian Golan: Note by the Secretary-General. A/71/86- E/2016/13.

United Nations Development Programme (2008). Post-conflict economic recovery – enabling local ingenuity - crisis prevention and recovery report 2008. New York: Bureau for Crisis Prevention and Recovery. Available from www. undp.org/content/dam/undp/library/crisis%20 prevention/undp-cpr-post-conflict-economic-recovery-enable-local-ingenuity-report-2008. pdf.

_____ (2010a). Human Development Report 2010; The Real Wealth of Nations: Pathways to Human Development. New York. Available from http://hdr.undp.org/sites/default/ files/reports/270/hdr_2010_en_complete_ reprint.pdf.

_____ (2010b). Fighting Corruption in Post-Conflict and Recovery Situations: Learning from the Past. New York. Available from http://www.undp.org/content/undp/en/home/ librarypage/democratic-governance/anti-corruption/fighting-corruption-in-post-conflict---recovery-situations.html.

_____ (2015a). Gender Inequality Index (GII). Available from http://hdr.undp.org/en/ content/gender-inequality-index-gii.

_____ (2015b). Human Development Report 2015: Work for Human Development. New York. Available from http://hdr.undp.org/ en/2015-report.

United Nations, Economic Commission for Africa (2015). Economic Report on Africa 2015 – Industrializing through Trade. Addis Ababa: ECA. Sales No. E.15.II.K.2. Available from www. uneca.org/publications/economic-report-africa-2015.

_____ (2016). Social Cohesion in Eastern Africa. Subregional Office for East Africa. Addis Ababa: ECA. Available from www.uneca. org/publications/social-cohesion-eastern-africa.

United Nations, Economic and Social Commission for Western Asia (ESCWA, 2012). Labour market data: Structures and challenges in the ESCWA region. E/ESCWA/SDD/2011/ Technical Paper.7. Available from https://www. unescwa.org/sites/www.unescwa.org/files/ publications/files/e_escwa_sdd_11_tp-7_e.pdf.

_____ (2013). Policy brief, women and political representation in the Arab region. E/ ESCWA/ECW/2013/Technical Paper.6.

_____ (2014a). Status of Arab Women Report: Access to Justice for Women and Girls in the Arab Region: From Ratification to Implementation if International Instruments. E/ESCWA/ECW/2015/1. Available from https:// www.unescwa.org/sites/www.unescwa.org/ files/publications/files/access-justice-women-arab-region-2015.pdf.

_____ (2014b). SDG priority conceptual issues: towards an Arab approach for the Sustainable Development Goals. E/ESCWA/ SDPD/2013/Technical Paper.8. Available

from https://www.unescwa.org/sites/www. unescwa.org/files/publications/files/e_escwa_ sdpd_13_tp-8_e.pdf.

_____ (2015a). Assessing Arab Economic Integration: Towards the Arab Customs Union. E/ESCWA/EDID/2015/4. Available from https:// www.unescwa.org/sites/www.unescwa. org/files/publications/files/assessing-arab-economic-integration.pdf.

_____ (2015b). Protracted Conflict and Development in the Arab Region. Trends and Impacts Issue No. 4. E/ESCWA/ECRI/2015/2. Available from https://www.unescwa.org/sites/ www.unescwa.org/files/publications/files/ trends-impacts-issue4-protracted-conflict-development-arab-region-english.pdf.

_____ (2015c). What is Left of the Arab Spring: The Long Road to Social Justice in the Arab Region. Case Study on Egypt, Tunisia and Morocco. E/ESDWA/SDD/2015/3.

_____ (2015d). Global and regional issues: The impact of conflict and instability on development in the Arab region. E/ ESCWA/2015/EC.2/4(Part VII). Available from http://css.escwa.org.lb/OES/3799/1500476.pdf.

_____ (2015e). Arab Development Outlook: Vision 2030. E/ESCWA/EDID/2015/3.

_____ (2016a). Against Wind and Tides: A Review of the Status of Women and Gender Equality in the Arab Region, 20 Years after the Adoption of the Beijing Declaration and Platform for Action. E/ESCWA/ECW/2015/3. Available from https://www.unescwa.org/sites/ www.unescwa.org/files/publications/files/ women-gender-equality-arab-region.pdf.

_____ (2016b). A People in Danger: Effects on Health of the 2014 Israeli Offensive on the Gaza Strip. E/ESCWA/ECRI/2015/WP.5. Available from https://www.unescwa.org/sites/ www.unescwa.org/files/publications/files/ people-danger-effects-health.pdf.

United Nations, Economic and Social Commission for Western Asia, and International Organization for Migration (2015). 2015 Situation Report on International Migration: Migration, Displacement and Development in a Changing Arab Region. E/ ESCWA/SDD/2015/1. Available from https:// www.unescwa.org/sites/www.unescwa.org/ files/publications/files/l1500271_0.pdf.

United Nations, Economic and Social Commission for Western Asia, and United Nations Environment Programme (2015). Arab Sustainable Development Report. First Edition, 2015. E/ESCWA/SDPD/2015/3. Available from https://www.unescwa.org/sites/www. unescwa.org/files/publications/files/arab-sustainable-development-report-1st.pdf.

United Nations, Economic and Social Commission for Western Asia, and University of St. Andrews (2016). Syria at War – Five Years On. Available from https://www.unescwa.org/

sites/www.unescwa.org/files/publications/files/syria-war-five-years.pdf.

United Nations, Economic and Social Commission for Western Asia, and the World Bank (forthcoming). Impact of Internal Conflicts on Neighbouring Countries: Case of the Libyan Crisis and the Tunisian Economy.

United Nations Relief and Works Agency for Palestine Refugees in the Near East (2014). Where we work. Available from www.unrwa.org/where-we-work/gaza-strip.

United Nations Statistics Division (2016). Millennium Development Goals Indicators. Available from http://mdgs.un.org/unsd/mdg/. Accessed 15 February.

UN Women (2013). Regional consultation for the proposed general recommendation on women's human rights in situations of conflict and post-conflict contexts. Prepared for Arab States and the Committee on the Elimination of Discrimination Against Women. Amman, Jordan. Available from http://www2.unwomen.org/~/media/field%20office%20arab%20states/attachments/publications/2015/regionalconsultationammanjan2013%20cedaw.pdf?v=1&d=20150624T114528.

_____ (2016). SDG 5: Achieve gender equality and empower all women and girls. Available from www.unwomen.org/en/news/in-focus/women-and-the-sdgs/sdg-5-gender-equality.

United Nations, World Tourism Organization (2015). UNWTO tourism highlights 2015 edition. Madrid. Available from http://www.e-unwto.org/doi/pdf/10.18111/9789284416899.

_____ (2014). UNWTO tourism highlights, 2014 edition. Madrid. Available from http://www.e-unwto.org/doi/pdf/10.18111/9789284416226.

United States, Department of Commerce, Bureau of Economic Analysis (2016). Gross domestic product: fourth quarter and annual 2015 (third estimate); corporate profits: fourth quarter and annual 2015. 25 March 2016. Available from www.bea.gov/newsreleases/national/gdp/2016/gdp4q15_3rd.htm.

Valters, Craig, Gideon Rabinowitz, and Lisa Denney (2014). Security in post-conflict contexts: what counts as progress and what drives it? Working paper 04. London: Overseas Development Institute. Available from https://www.odi.org/sites/odi.org.uk/files/odi-assets/publications-opinion-files/8915.pdf.

World Bank (2015a). *Syria – Overview*. Available from www.worldbank.org/en/country/syria/overview.

_____ (2015b). Women, business and the law 2016: getting to equal. Washington D.C. Available from http://wbl.worldbank.org/~/media/WBG/WBL/Documents/Reports/2016/Women-Business-and-the-Law-2016.pdf?la=en.

_____ (2016a). Commodity markets. Washington D.C. Available from www.worldbank.org/en/research/commodity-markets. Accessed 30 March 2016.

_____ (2016b). Reconstructing Gaza — donor pledges. Washington D.C. 14 April. Available from www.worldbank.org/en/programs/rebuilding-gaza-donor-pledges.

_____ (2016c). World development indicators 2016. Washington D.C. Available from http://data.worldbank.org/products/wdi. Accessed 30 March 2016.

_____ (2016d). Doing business 2016: measuring regulatory quality and efficiency. Washington, D.C. Available from www.doingbusiness.org/reports/global-reports/doing-business-2016.

World Bank, and United Nations (2013). Lebanon: economic and social impact assessment of the Syrian conflict. Report No. 81098-LB. Washington D.C. Available from http://documents.worldbank.org/curated/en/925271468089385165/pdf/810980LB0box379831B00P14754500PUBLIC0.pdf.

World Economic Forum (2015). The Global Gender Gap report 2015. Geneva. Available from http://reports.weforum.org/global-gender-gap-report-2015.

Yemen, Ministry of Planning & International Cooperation (2016). Yemen socio-economic update No. 12. 1 March. Available from http://reliefweb.int/report/yemen/yemen-socio-economic-update-no-12-mar-2016-enar.

Zaum, Dominik (2013). Political economies of corruption in fragile and conflict-affected states: nuancing the picture. U4 anti-corruption resource centre brief. Chr. Michelsen Institute. Available from www.cmi.no/publications/4901-political-economies-of-corruption-in-fragile-and.

Appendix: Sources of National Statistical Data

1. Algeria

Gross oil export revenues (table 1.4)
Bank of Algeria
Bulletin Statistique Trimestriel No. 32 – December 2015
www.bank-of-algeria.dz/pdf/Bulletin_32f.pdf

GDP growth rate (table 2.1)
Office National des Statistiques
Les comptes nationaux trimestriels au 3ème trimestre 2015
www.ons.dz/IMG/pdf/cptnat3t15.pdf

Consumer price inflation rate (table 2.1)
Office National des Statistiques
Indice des prix à la consommation
www.ons.dz/-Prix-a-la-consommation-.html

Trade and current account balances (figure 2.10)
Bank of Algeria
Bulletin Statistique Trimestriel No. 32 – December 2015
www.bank-of-algeria.dz/pdf/Bulletin_32f.pdf

Fiscal positions (figure 2.12)
Ministère des Finances
Note de présentation du projet de la loi de finances pour 2015
www.dgpp-mf.gov.dz/images/stories/PDF/RPLF/RPLF2015.pdf

Secretariat du Gouvernement
Loi n° 15-18 du 18 Rabie El Aouel 1437 correspondant au 30 décembre 2015
portant loi de finances pour 2016, Journal Officiel de la Republique Algérienne No. 72
www.fce.dz/wp-content/uploads/2016/04/lf2016.pdf

Unemployment and labour participation rates (figure 2.23)
Office National des Statistiques
Activité, emploi et chômage en septembre 2015
www.ons.dz/IMG/pdf/DSEmploi0915.pdf

2. Bahrain

Gross oil export revenues (table 1.4)
Central Bank of Bahrain

Statistical Bulletin June 2015
www.cbb.gov.bh/assets/MSB/MSB-Jun%202015.pdf

GDP growth rate (table 2.1)
Central Bank of Bahrain
Economic Indicators September 2015
www.cbb.gov.bh/assets/E%20I/EI%20Sep2015.pdf

Consumer price inflation rate (table 2.1)
Bahrain Open Data Portal
www.data.gov.bh/en/ResourceCenter

Trade and current account balances (figure 2.2)
Central Bank of Bahrain
Statistical Bulletin June 2015
www.cbb.gov.bh/assets/MSB/MSB-Jun%202015.pdf

Fiscal positions (figure 2.4)
Central Bank of Bahrain
Economic Indicators September 2015
www.cbb.gov.bh/assets/E%20I/EI%20Sep2015.pdf

Ministry of Finance, Final Accounts
www.mof.gov.bh/Categorylist.asp?cType=faccount

Ministry of Finance, State Budget
www.mof.gov.bh/Categorylist.asp?cType=budget

3. Comoros

GDP growth rate (table 2.1)
Banque Centrale des Comores
Rapport Annuel 2014
www.banque-comores.km/DOCUMENTS/Rapport_annuel_2014.pdf

Evolution de la situation économique, financière et monétaire des Comores au cours
du 1er semestre de l'année 2015
www.banque-comores.km/DOCUMENTS/Note_de_conjoncture_1er_Semestre_2015.pdf

Consumer price inflation rate (table 2.1)
Banque Centrale des Comores
Rapport Annuel 2014
www.banque-comores.km/DOCUMENTS/Rapport_annuel_2014.pdf

Evolution de la situation économique, financière et monétaire des Comores au cours
du 1er semestre de l'année 2015
www.banque-comores.km/DOCUMENTS/Note_de_conjoncture_1er_Semestre_2015.pdf

Trade and current account balances (figure 2.14)
    Banque Centrale des Comores
    Rapport Annuel 2014
    www.banque-comores.km/DOCUMENTS/Rapport_annuel_2014.pdf

    Evolution de la situation économique, financière et monétaire des Comores au cours
    du 1er semestre de l'année 2015
    www.banque-comores.km/DOCUMENTS/Note_de_conjoncture_1er_Semestre_2015.pdf

Fiscal positions (figure 2.16)
    Banque Centrale des Comores
    Rapport Annuel 2014
    www.banque-comores.km/DOCUMENTS/Rapport_annuel_2014.pdf

    Evolution de la situation économique, financière et monétaire des Comores au cours
    du 1er semestre de l'année 2015
    www.banque-comores.km/DOCUMENTS/Note_de_conjoncture_1er_Semestre_2015.pdf

4. Djibouti

GDP growth (table 2.1)
    Banque Centrale de Djibouti
    Rapport Annuel 2014
    www.banque-centrale.dj/rubriques/27

Consumer price inflation rate (table 2.1)
    Banque Centrale de Djibouti
    Rapport Annuel 2014
    www.banque-centrale.dj/rubriques/27

Trade and current account balances (figure 2.14)
    Banque Centrale de Djibouti
    Rapport Annuel 2014
    www.banque-centrale.dj/rubriques/27
    www.banque-centrale.dj/rubriques/23

Fiscal positions (figure 2.16)
    Banque Centrale de Djibouti
    Rapport Annuel 2014
    www.banque-centrale.dj/rubriques/27

5. Egypt

Gross oil export revenues (table 1.4)
    Central Bank of Egypt
    Monthly Statistical Bulletin 228, March 2016
    www.cbe.org.eg/en/EconomicResearch/Publications/Pages/MonthlyStatisticaclBulletin.aspx

GDP growth (table 2.1)
    Central Bank of Egypt
    Monthly Statistical Bulletin 228, March 2016
    www.cbe.org.eg/en/EconomicResearch/Publications/Pages/MonthlyStatisticaclBulletin.aspx

Consumer price inflation rate (table 2.1)
    Central Bank of Egypt
    Monthly Statistical Bulletin 228, March 2016
    www.cbe.org.eg/en/EconomicResearch/Publications/Pages/MonthlyStatisticaclBulletin.aspx

Trade and current account balances (figure 2.6)
    Central Bank of Egypt
    Monthly Statistical Bulletin 228, March 2016
    www.cbe.org.eg/en/EconomicResearch/Publications/Pages/MonthlyStatisticaclBulletin.aspx

Fiscal positions (figure 2.8)
    Central Bank of Egypt
    Monthly Statistical Bulletin 228, March 2016
    www.cbe.org.eg/en/EconomicResearch/Publications/Pages/MonthlyStatisticaclBulletin.aspx

Unemployment and labour participation rates (figure 2.23)
    Central Agency for Public Mobilization and Statistics
    Economic Activity Rate
    www.capmas.gov.eg/Pages/IndicatorsPage.aspx?page_id=6149&ind_id=1116

    Central Agency for Public Mobilization and Statistics
    Annual Workforce Bulletin
    www.capmas.gov.eg/Pages/Publications.aspx?page_id=5104&YearID=19686

6. Iraq

Gross oil export revenues (table 1.4)
    Central Bank of Iraq
    Annual Statistical Bulletin, 2012, 2013, 2014,
    www.cbi.iq/documents/Annual_2014.pdf
    www.cbi.iq/documents/Annual_2013.pdf
    www.cbi.iq/documents/Annual_2012.pdf

GDP growth (table 2.1)
    Central Statistical Organization
    National Income
    http://cosit.gov.iq/en/national-accounts-statistics/national-income-reports

Consumer price inflation rate (table 2.1)
    Central Bank of Iraq
    Key Financial Indicators
    www.cbi.iq/index.php?pid=Statistics

Trade and current account balances (figure 2.6)
    Central Bank of Iraq
    Annual Statistical Bulletin, 2012, 2013, 2014,
    www.cbi.iq/documents/Annual_2014.pdf
    www.cbi.iq/documents/Annual_2013.pdf
    www.cbi.iq/documents/Annual_2012.pdf

Fiscal positions (figure 2.8)
    Annual Statistical Bulletin, 2012, 2013, 2014,
    www.cbi.iq/documents/Annual_2014.pdf
    www.cbi.iq/documents/Annual_2013.pdf
    www.cbi.iq/documents/Annual_2012.pdf

7. Jordan

GDP growth (fable 2-1)
    Department of Statistics, Jordan
    http://web.dos.gov.jo/sectors/national-account/?lang=en
    http://dos.gov.jo/dos_home_e/main/economic/nat_account/sel2/nat6.htm

Consumer price inflation rate (fable 2-1)
    Department of Statistics, Jordan
    Monthly Consumer Price Index
    www.dos.gov.jo/dos_home_e/main/economic/price_num/index.htm

Trace and current account balances (figure 2.6)
    Central Bank of Jordan
    Monthly Statistical Bulletin – External Sector
    www.cbj.gov.jo

Fiscal positions (figure 2.8)
    Ministry of Finance, Jordan
    General Government Finance Bulletin
    www.mof.gov.jo/Portals/0/MOF_Content_EN/MOF_EN/MOF_EN/General%20Government%20Financial%20
    Bulletins/2015/english%20PDF%20November%202015.pdf

Unemployment and labour participation rates (figure 2.23)
    Department of Statistics, Labor Force Survey
    www.dos.gov.jo/dos_home_e/main/linked-html/Emp&Un.htm

    Department of Statistics, Statistical Yearbook 2013
    http://dos.gov.jo/dos_home_e/main/yearbook_2013.pdf

8. Kuwait

Gross oil export revenues (table 1.4)
    Central Bank of Kuwait

Quarterly Statistical Bulletin October-December 2015
www.cbk.gov.kw/en/statistics-and-publication/statistical-releases/quarterly.jsp

GDP growth (table 2.1)
Central Statistical Bureau
Revised and Provisional Estimates – National Accounts
www.csb.gov.kw/Socan_Statistic_EN.aspx?ID=23

Consumer price inflation rate (table 2.1)
Central Statistical Bureau
Consumer Price Index Numbers
www.csb.gov.kw/Socan_Statistic_EN.aspx?ID=34

Trade and current account balances (figure 2.2)
Central Bank of Kuwait
Quarterly Statistical Bulletin October-December 2015
www.cbk.gov.kw/en/statistics-and-publication/statistical-releases/quarterly.jsp

Fiscal positions (figure 2.4)
Central Bank of Kuwait
Quarterly Statistical Bulletin October-December 2015
www.cbk.gov.kw/en/statistics-and-publication/statistical-releases/quarterly.jsp

9. Lebanon

GDP growth (table 2.1)
Central Administration of Statistics
www.cas.gov.lb/index.php/national-accounts-en

Consumer price inflation rate (table 2.1)
Central Administration of Statistics
www.cas.gov.lb/index.php/economic-statistics-en/cpi-en#cpiresults

Trace and current account balances (figure 2.6)
Banque du Liban
Statistics and Research – Main series – External Sector and Balance of Payments
www.bdl.gov.lb/webroot/statistics/

Fiscal positions (figure 2.8)
Ministry of Finance
Fiscal Performance Reports
www.finance.gov.lb/EN-US/FINANCE/ECONOMICDATASTATISTICS/Pages/FiscalPerformence.aspx

10. Libya

Gross oil export revenues (table 1.4)
Central Bank of Libya

Economic Bulletin, vol. 55, Second Quarter 2015
https://cbl.gov.ly/en/wp-content/uploads/sites/2/2016/03/Q22015.pdf

GDP growth (table 2.1)
Central Bank of Libya
Economic Bulletin, vol. 55, Second Quarter 2015
https://cbl.gov.ly/en/wp-content/uploads/sites/2/2016/03/Q22015.pdf

Consumer price inflation rate (table 2.1)
Bureau of Statistics and Census Libya
Consumer Price Indices 2015
http://bsc.ly

Central Bank of Libya
Economic Bulletin, vol. 55, second quarter 2015
https://cbl.gov.ly/en/wp-content/uploads/sites/2/2016/03/Q22015.pdf

Trace and current account balances (figure 2.10)
Central Bank of Libya
Economic Bulletin, vol. 55, second quarter 2015
https://cbl.gov.ly/en/wp-content/uploads/sites/2/2016/03/Q22015.pdf

Fiscal positions (figure 2.12)
Central Bank of Libya
Economic Bulletin, vol. 55, second quarter 2015
https://cbl.gov.ly/en/wp-content/uploads/sites/2/2016/03/Q22015.pdf

11. Mauritania

Gross oil export revenues (table 1.4)
Banque Centrale de Mauritanie
Bulletin Trimestriel des Statistiques, quatrième trimestre 2015
www.bcm.mr/Etudes%20et%20Recherches%20Economiques/Bulletins%20trimestriels%20des%20
statistiques/Documents/Bulletin%20trimestriel%20des%20statistiques%20du%204em%20trimestre%20
2015.pdf

GDP growth (table 2.1)
Banque Centrale de Mauritanie
Bulletin Trimestriel des Statistiques, quatrième trimestre 2015
www.bcm.mr/Etudes%20et%20Recherches%20Economiques/Bulletins%20trimestriels%20des%20
statistiques/Documents/Bulletin%20trimestriel%20des%20statistiques%20du%204em%20trimestre%20
2015.pdf

Consumer price inflation rate (table 2.1)
Banque Centrale de Mauritanie
Bulletin Trimestriel des Statistiques, quatrième trimestre 2015
www.bcm.mr/Etudes%20et%20Recherches%20Economiques/Bulletins%20trimestriels%20des%20

statistiques/Documents/Bulletin%20trimestriel%20des%20statistiques%20du%204em%20trimestre%20
2015.pdf

Office National de la Statistique
www.ons.mr/index.php/publications/conjonctures/13-indice-national-des-prix-a-consommation-inpc

Trade and current account balances (figure 2.14)
Banque Centrale de Mauritanie
Bulletin Trimestriel des Statistiques, quatrième trimestre 2015
www.bcm.mr/Etudes%20et%20Recherches%20Economiques/Bulletins%20trimestriels%20des%20
statistiques/Documents/Bulletin%20trimestriel%20des%20statistiques%20du%204em%20trimestre%20
2015.pdf

Fiscal positions (figure 2.16)
Banque Centrale de Mauritanie
Bulletin Trimestriel des Statistiques, quatrième trimestre 2015
www.bcm.mr/Etudes%20et%20Recherches%20Economiques/Bulletins%20trimestriels%20des%20statistiques/
Documents/Bulletin%20trimestriel%20des%20statistiques%20du%204em%20trimestre%202015.pdf

12. Morocco

Gross oil export revenues (table 1.4)
Bank Al-Maghrib
Bulletin Trimestriel December 2015
www.bkam.ma

GDP growth (table 2.1)
Haut-Commissariat au Plan
Comptes nationaux
www.hcp.ma/Comptes-nationaux_r126.html

Les comptes nationaux Base 2007
www.hcp.ma/file/168779

Consumer price inflation rate (table 2.1)
Haut-Commissariat au Plan
www.hcp.ma/downloads/IPC-Indice-des-prix-a-la-consommation_t12173.html

Bank Al-Maghrib
Bulletin Trimestriel December 2015
www.bkam.ma

Trace and current account balances (figure 2.10)
Bank Al-Maghrib
Bulletin Trimestriel December 2015
www.bkam.ma

Fiscal positions (figure 2.12)

Bank Al-Maghrib
Bulletin Trimestriel December 2015
www.bkam.ma

Ministry of Finance
Budget 2016
www.finances.gov.ma/fr/Pages/plf2016.aspx?m=Loi%20de%20finances%20et%20Budget

Unemployment and labour participation rates (figure 2.23)

Haut-Commissariat au Plan
Activité, emploi et chômage année 2014
www.hcp.ma/region-drda/Activite-emploi-et-chomage-Annee-2014_a92.html

Haut-Commissariat au Plan
La situation du marché du travail en 2015
www.hcp.ma/La-Situation-du-marche-du-travail-en-2015_a1663.html

Haut-Commissariat au Plan
Taux d'activité selon le sexe
www.hcp.ma/Taux-d-activite-selon-le-sexe_a360.html

Haut-Commissariat au Plan
Taux de chômage selon le sexe
www.hcp.ma/Taux-de-Chomage-selon-le-sexe_a256.html

13. Oman

Gross oil export revenues (table 1.4)

Central Bank of Oman
Quarterly Statistical Bulletin December 2015
www.cbo-oman.org

GDP growth (table 2.1)

National Centre for Statistics and Information
Monthly Statistical Bulletin
https://www.ncsi.gov.om/Elibrary/LibraryContentDoc/bar_Monthly_Bulletin_Jan2016_e51e00ab-0f61-45f1-96a6-107ea3b7a01f.pdf

Statistical Yearbook 2015 (Issue 43)
https://www.ncsi.gov.om/Elibrary/LibraryContentDoc/ben_Statistical_Year_Book_2015_740d0da1-01d2-4f42-a159-6102a49ecf59.pdf

Consumer price inflation rate (table 2.1)

National Centre for Statistics and Information
Monthly Statistical Bulletin – Various issues
https://www.ncsi.gov.om/Elibrary/LibraryContentDoc/bar_MSB%20February%202016%20_7f0d3e53-433e-4826-b19c-5530d15b5f0c.pdf

National Centre for Statistics and Information
Statistical Yearbook 2015 Issue 43
https://www.ncsi.gov.om/Elibrary/LibraryContentDoc/ben_Statistical_Year_Book_2015_740d0da1-01d2-4f42-a159-6102a49ecf59.pdf

Trade and current account balances (figure 2.2)
Central Bank of Oman
Quarterly Statistical Bulletin December 2015
www.cbo-oman.org

Fiscal positions (figure 2.4)
Central Bank of Oman
Quarterly Statistical Bulletin December 2015
www.cbo-oman.org

National Centre for Statistics and Information
Monthly Statistical Bulletin
https://www.ncsi.gov.om/Elibrary/LibraryContentDoc/bar_Monthly_Bulletin_Jan2016_e51e00ab-0f61-45f1-96a6-107ea3b7a01f.pdf

National Centre for Statistics and Information
Statistical Yearbook 2015 Issue 43
https://www.ncsi.gov.om/Elibrary/LibraryContentDoc/ben_Statistical_Year_Book_2015_740d0da1-01d2-4f42-a159-6102a49ecf59.pdf

14. Qatar

Gross oil export revenues (table 1.4)
Ministry of Development Planning and Statistics
Quarterly Bulletin on Foreign Merchandise Trade Statistics – Quarter 2 September 2015
www.mdps.gov.qa/en/knowledge/Publications/Economic/Qatar%20Foreign%20Merchandise%20Trade%20Statistics%20Quarterly%20Bulletin_Q22015.pdf

Quarterly Bulletin on Foreign Merchandise Trade Statistics – Quarter 4 (February 2016)
www.mdps.gov.qa/en/knowledge/Publications/Economic/FT-Q4-2015-En-MDPS.pdf

Qatar Information Exchange - Foreign Trade
www.qix.gov.qa/portal/page/portal/qix/subject_area?subject_area=190

GDP growth (table 2.1)
Ministry of Development Planning and Statistics
National Accounts Bulletin 2015
www.mdps.gov.qa/en/knowledge/Publications/Economic/National-Accounts-Bulletin-2015.pdf

Consumer price inflation rate (table 2.1)
Qatar Central Bank
Quarterly Statistical Bulletin December 2015
www.qcb.gov.qa/English/Publications/Statistics/Pages/Statisticalbulletins.aspx

Trade and current account balances (figure 2.2)
Qatar Central Bank
Quarterly Statistical Bulletin December 2015
www.qcb.gov.qa/English/Publications/Statistics/Pages/Statisticalbulletins.aspx

Balance of Payments, Q4, 2015
www.qcb.gov.qa/English/Publications/Statistics/BalanceofPayments/Pages/default.aspx

Fiscal positions (figure 2.4)
Qatar Central Bank
Quarterly Statistical Bulletin December 2015
www.qcb.gov.qa/English/Publications/Statistics/Pages/Statisticalbulletins.aspx

Unemployment and labour participation rates (figure 2.23)
Ministry of Development Planning and Statistics
Bulletin of Labor Force Statistics 2014, Table 3A, 18A
www.mdps.gov.qa/en/knowledge/Publications/Social/Bulletin_labor_force_2014.pdf

15. Saudi Arabia

Gross oil export revenues (table 1.4)
Saudi Arabian Monetary Agency
Yearly Statistics
www.sama.gov.sa/en-US/EconomicReports/Pages/YearlyStatistics.aspx

GDP growth (table 2.1)
Central Department of Statistics and Information
National Accounts Indicator 2015
www.stats.gov.sa/sites/default/files/gdp2015-indx.pdf#viewer.action=download

Saudi Arabian Monetary Agency
Yearly Statistics
www.sama.gov.sa/en-US/EconomicReports/Pages/YearlyStatistics.aspx

Consumer price inflation rate (table 2.1)
Saudi Arabian Monetary Agency
Yearly Statistics
www.sama.gov.sa/en-US/EconomicReports/Pages/YearlyStatistics.aspx

Saudi Arabian Monetary Agency
Monthly Statistical Bulletin
www.sama.gov.sa/en-US/EconomicReports/Pages/MonthlyStatistics.aspx

Trade and current account balances (figure 2.2)
Saudi Arabian Monetary Agency
Yearly Statistics
www.sama.gov.sa/en-US/EconomicReports/Pages/YearlyStatistics.aspx

Fiscal positions (figure 2.4)
Saudi Arabian Monetary Agency
Yearly Statistics
www.sama.gov.sa/en-US/EconomicReports/Pages/YearlyStatistics.aspx

Ministry of Finance
Recent Economic Developments and Highlights of Fiscal Years 1436/1437 (2015) & 1437/1438 (2016) Press
Release, 28 December 2015
https://www.mof.gov.sa/en/docslibrary/Documents/Budget%20Data/Ministry's%20of%20Finance%20
statment%20about%20the%20national%20budget%20for%202016.pdf

Unemployment and labour force participation rates (figure 2.23)
General Authority for Statistics
Economic Revised Activity Rates 1999 – 2015
www.stats.gov.sa/en/1446

General Authority for Statistics
Unemployment Rates 1999 – 2015
www.stats.gov.sa/en/node/4932

16. State of Palestine

GDP growth (table 2.1)
Palestine Monetary Authority
Statistics Time Series Data – National Accounts
www.pma.ps/Default.aspx?tabid=202&language=en-US

Palestinian Central Bureau of Statistics
National Accounts
www.pcbs.gov.ps/site/lang__en/741/default.aspx

Consumer price inflation rate (table 2.1)
Palestinian Central Bureau of Statistics
Consumer Price Index
www.pcbs.gov.ps/site/lang__en/695/default.aspx
http://pcbs.gov.ps/Portals/_Rainbow/Documents/e-cpi-ave-2015-baseyear-2010.htm

Palestine Monetary Authority
Statistics Time Series Data – Price Indices: Consumer Price Index
www.pma.ps/Default.aspx?tabid=202&language=en-US

Trade and current account balances (figure 2.6)
Palestine Monetary Authority
Statistics Time Series Data – External Sector: Palestine Balance of Payments
www.pma.ps/Default.aspx?tabid=202&language=en-US

Fiscal positions (figure 2.8)
Palestine Monetary Authority

Statistics Time Series Data – Public Finance: Revenues, expenditures and financing sources of PNA fiscal
operations (cash basis)
www.pma.ps/Default.aspx?tabid=202&language=en-US

Unemployment and labour participation rates (figure 2.23)
Palestinian Central Bureau of Statistics
Labour Force Participation Rate of Persons Aged 15 Years and Above in Palestine by Sex and Governorate,
2000-2015
www.pcbs.gov.ps/Portals/_Rainbow/Documents/labour%20force-2015-01e.htm

Palestinian Central Bureau of Statistics
Unemployment Rate Among labour Force Participants of Persons Aged 15 Years and Above in Palestine by
Sex and Governorate, 2000-2015
www.pcbs.gov.ps/Portals/_Rainbow/Documents/unemployment-2015-01e.htm

17. Sudan

Gross oil export revenues (table 1.4)
Central Bank of Sudan
Economic and Financial Statistics Review
www.cbos.gov.sd/node/7927
July – September 2015
www.cbos.gov.sd/sites/default/files/q03_2015.pdf
September – December 2014
www.cbos.gov.sd/sites/default/files/q04_14.pdf

GDP growth (table 2.1)
Central Bank of Sudan
Annual Report 2013
www.cbos.gov.sd/sites/default/files/annual_report_e_2013.pdf

Central Bank of Sudan
Economic and Financial Statistics Review
www.cbos.gov.sd/node/7927
July – September 2015
www.cbos.gov.sd/sites/default/files/q03_2015.pdf
September – December 2014
www.cbos.gov.sd/sites/default/files/q04_14.pdf

Consumer price inflation rate (table 2.1)
Central Bank of Sudan
Economic and Financial Statistics Review
www.cbos.gov.sd/node/7927

July – September 2015
www.cbos.gov.sd/sites/default/files/q03_2015.pdf
September – December 2014
www.cbos.gov.sd/sites/default/files/q04_14.pdf

Trade and current account balances (figure 2.14)
Central Bank of Sudan
Economic and Financial Statistics Review
www.cbos.gov.sd/node/7927

July – September 2015
www.cbos.gov.sd/sites/default/files/q03_2015.pdf
September – December 2014
www.cbos.gov.sd/sites/default/files/q04_14.pdf

Fiscal positions (figure 2.16)
Central Bank of Sudan
Annual Report 2013
www.cbos.gov.sd/sites/default/files/annual_report_e_2013.pdf

Central Bank of Sudan
Economic and Financial Statistics Review
www.cbos.gov.sd/node/7927
July – September 2015
www.cbos.gov.sd/sites/default/files/q03_2015.pdf
September – December 2014
www.cbos.gov.sd/sites/default/files/q04_14.pdf

18. Syrian Arab Republic

Consumer price inflation (table 2.1)
Central Bureau of Statistics
www.cbssyr.sy/index-EN.htm

19. Tunisia

Gross oil export revenues (table 1.4)
National Institute of Statistics
Evolution des valeurs d'exportations; Echanges par groupement sectoriel d'activité; Principaux produits exportés par groupement sectoriel d'activité
Energie et lubrifiants
www.ins.tn/fr/themes/commerce-ext%C3%A9rieur

GDP growth (table 2.1)
National Institute of Statistics
National accounts: quarterly national accounts; economic growth (YoY at prices of the previous year)
www.ins.tn/sites/default/files/taux_croissance_EN.xlsx

Consumer price inflation (table 2.1)
National Institute of Statistics
Price: household price index; household consumer price index per monthly level - CPI (2010 = 100)
www.ins.tn/sites/default/files/IPC_EN_0.xlsx

Trade and current account balances (figure 2.10)

Central Bank of Tunisia

Evolution des principaux flux et soldes des paiements extérieurs

www.bct.gov.tn/bct/siteprod/tab_trimestriel.jsp?params=PL120010,PL120020,PL120030&cal=t&page=
P120&tab=040&pos=3

Fiscal positions (figure 2.12)

Central Bank of Tunisia

Les comptes de la nation (finances publiques)

www.bct.gov.tn/bct/siteprod/tableau_n.jsp?params=PL150010,PL150020,PL150030,PL150040

Ministry of Finance and Economy

Synthèse des résultats des finances publiques (budget de l'Etat)

www.finances.gov.tn/index.php?option=com_content&view=article&id=134&Itemid=304&lang=fr

Unemployment and labour force participation rates (figure 2.23)

National Institute of Statistics

National survey on population and employment

www.ins.tn/fr/page-de-base/micro-données

National Institute of Statistics

Unemployment rate by gender 2006-2015 (%). http://dataportal.ins.tn/en/
DataAnalysis?DVKpE7Ze3EyjaHo1uKNw

20. United Arab Emirates

Gross oil export revenues (table 1.4)

Central Bank of United Arab Emirates

Annual Report 2015

www.centralbank.ae/en/pdf/reports/CBUAEAnnualReport-2015_En_2.pdf

Annual Report 2014

www.centralbank.ae/en/pdf/reports/CBUAEAnnualReport2014_en_new.pdf

Annual Report 2013

www.centralbank.ae/en/pdf/reports/CBUAEAnnualReport2013_English3.pdf

GDP growth (table 2.1)

Federal Competitiveness and Statistical Authority

National Accounts Estimates 2001-2014

http://fcsa.gov.ae/EnglishHome/ReportsByDepartmentEnglish/tabid/104/Default.aspx?MenuId=1&NDId=516

Consumer price inflation rate (table 2.1)

Federal Competitiveness and Statistical Authority

Consumer price indices

http://fcsa.gov.ae/EnglishHome/ReportsByDepartmentEnglish/tabid/104/Default.aspx?MenuId=1&NDId=372

Trace and current account balances (figure 2.2)

Central Bank of United Arab Emirates

Annual Report 2015

www.centralbank.ae/en/pdf/reports/CBUAEAnnualReport-2015_En_2.pdf
Annual Report 2014
www.centralbank.ae/en/pdf/reports/CBUAEAnnualReport2014_en_new.pdf
Annual Report 2013
www.centralbank.ae/en/pdf/reports/CBUAEAnnualReport2013_English3.pdf

Fiscal positions (figure 2.4)
Central Bank of United Arab Emirates
Annual Report 2015
www.centralbank.ae/en/pdf/reports/CBUAEAnnualReport-2015_En_2.pdf
Annual Report 2014
www.centralbank.ae/en/pdf/reports/CBUAEAnnualReport2014_en_new.pdf
Annual Report 2013
www.centralbank.ae/en/pdf/reports/CBUAEAnnualReport2013_English3.pdf

Federal Competitiveness and Statistical Authority

National Accounts Estimates 2001-2014 (Public Finance)
http://fcsa.gov.ae/EnglishHome/ReportsByDepartmentEnglish/tabid/104/Default.aspx?MenuId=1&NDId=516

21. Yemen

Gross oil export revenues (table 1.4)
Money and Banking Development January 2015
www.centralbank.gov.ye/App_Upload/Jan2015.pdf

GDP growth (table 2.1)
Central Statistical Organization
Statistical Yearbook 2013

Consumer price inflation (table 2.1)
Central Bank of Yemen
Money and Banking Development January 2015
www.centralbank.gov.ye/App_Upload/Jan2015.pdf

Trade and current account balances (figure 2.14)
Central Bank of Yemen
Money and Banking Development January 2015
www.centralbank.gov.ye/App_Upload/Jan2015.pdf

Fiscal positions (figure 2.16)
Central Statistical Organization
Statistical Yearbook 2013

www.ingramcontent.com/pod-product-compliance
Lightning Source LLC
Chambersburg PA
CBHW080426270326
41929CB00018B/3178